This book is due for return on or before the last date shown above but it may be renewed by personal application, post, or telephone, quoting this date and the book number.

HERTFORDSHIRE COUNTY LIBRARY

THE WOOL TRADE
IN TUDOR AND STUART ENGLAND

THE WOOL TRADE
IN TUDOR AND STUART
ENGLAND

BY

PETER J. BOWDEN

LECTURER IN ECONOMIC HISTORY IN THE
UNIVERSITY OF SHEFFIELD

LONDON
MACMILLAN & CO LTD
NEW YORK · ST MARTIN'S PRESS
1962

MACMILLAN AND COMPANY LIMITED
St Martin's Street London WC 2
also Bombay Calcutta Madras Melbourne

THE MACMILLAN COMPANY OF CANADA LIMITED
Toronto

ST MARTIN'S PRESS INC
New York

PRINTED IN GREAT BRITAIN

To the Memory of
my Father

FOREWORD

In her classic study of *The Wool Trade in Medieval English History* the late Eileen Power described an English economy whose prosperity rested largely on sacks of wool. When Dr. Bowden's story begins, the English economy had become even more dependent on wool, no longer exported mainly raw but now made up into cloth; the cloth was increasing in its local variety and it was becoming more and more a cottage industry scattered over a score of English counties. Until the middle of the sixteenth century only the worsted industry of Norfolk suffered from serious foreign competition: for the other clothing counties there seemed no limit to the capacity of the home and foreign markets to soak up whatever cloth was produced, and the main task of the traders in wool was to match the variegation of local demand with the variety of supplies which different local breeds and pastures could produce. The increase in total supply was brought about by absorbing most of the wools that had previously been exported raw, and by a steady rise in price which tempted farmers to consider whether wool was not a more profitable crop than corn, and shepherds more attractive a labour force than husbandmen. Only the Company of the Staple shivered in the wind, shorn. Its members still had the monopoly of raw wool exports that Eileen Power described, but there were hardly any wool exports.

After the mid-sixteenth century the situation was different in one fundamental aspect. Stagnating woollen cloth exports created unemployment at home and faced the government with adjustments to contraction, and the whole industry (from Northamptonshire sheep pastures to the activities of Baltic traders) became a prey for anatomists and diagnosticians, and the dispossessed husbandman was not the only voice crying that sheep had eaten up too much of England. When the historian and traveller William Camden came to Halifax he rejoiced to see somewhere in England at last where the human population was growing faster than the sheep population.

In this spate of self-examination and recrimination the historian must rejoice at the publicity given to private matters. With so lucrative a trade as wool it is not surprising that the proposals to regulate the wool trade were the occasion of much special pleading by different sectors of the wool-textile industry, and Dr. Bowden is able to show that much of the Tudor and Stuart legislation and official regulation which used the language of public welfare was in fact the cover for private interest. Among the themes which emerge, the new role coveted by the under-employed Staplers and the hostility between the capitalistic and non-capitalistic sections of the clothmakers are perhaps the most important. Unpublished material now explored enables Dr. Bowden to show government regulation and the administration of monopolistic privileges in their sordid — and not very efficient — reality.

Another consequence of a contracted trade and of new government regulations from which an historian can profit is the litigation which follows: the clothier seeks to evade a bargain made with a wool dealer in fatter years; creditors seek to recover losses from reluctant debtors; the unlucky, the foolish and the rogues jostle each other in the records of the Court of Requests and the Chancery; while in the Exchequer the common informers were pursuing those who had offended against the regulating statutes. Dr. Bowden has broken much new ground in analysing this type of record, and from it he has been able to draw a more realistic picture of the role of the wool trader, the much discussed middleman or *brogger*, who was the scapegoat for many sins. He is seen to be the inevitable and useful servant of an industry which was developing more and more local specialization and needing the wools of a wider and wider area; his sorting function grew to be of great importance and as an importer he showed the growing dependence of the industry on the wools of Ireland and Spain.

Dr. Bowden's final service is to suggest an answer to a crucial question: why did our woollen cloth fall in the esteem of foreigners? an answer which does not depend on any change in the ration of original sin, deceptiveness or skill possessed by the ordinary English weaver. His suggestion — which I will not reveal here — takes us back to where the wool trade had always begun, to the pastures of rural England: and it serves to explain the rapid development of one transformed section of the cloth industry in the seventeenth century, the worsted cloths.

Finally, it is appropriate to record that Dr. Bowden's work was first made possible by the generous donation which Mr. W. H. Dean made to this Department soon after the War in order to stimulate academic research into the woollen industry. As befitted a graduate of a Department whose first Head had been J. H. Clapham, Mr. Dean made the funds available both for economists and economic historians; and from them arose Dr. Bowden's study as well as those of Dr. K. J. Allison on wool and cloth in East Anglia and Dr. E. M. Sigsworth's *Black Dyke Mills*.

M. W. BERESFORD
Professor of Economic History

Department of Economics
The University, Leeds
August 1961

PREFACE

This book originated in my interest in that picturesque figure,
the Halifax wool driver. What started as a local study of limited
scope took on more substantial proportions when I discovered
that a mass of largely unexplored manuscript material existed
which threw light on national developments in the wool trade
hitherto unsuspected or imperfectly understood. My results
were submitted as a thesis for the degree of Ph.D. at Leeds in
1952. Since then, the interest kindly shown by fellow economic
historians and others has encouraged me to pursue my research
further and to produce the present study.

The author of even a short book must owe many debts. It is a
pleasant duty to record my gratitude to the University of Leeds
for the award of a Dean Research Scholarship in 1949, which
made it possible for my thesis to be written. I am likewise
grateful to the University of Sheffield for financial assistance
from the Knoop Research Fund, which has enabled me to
examine additional source material, and so to strengthen or
modify certain of the conclusions previously reached.

Like most historical research workers, I owe much to the
knowledge and enthusiasm of archivists and librarians in many
places. In this connexion I am especially indebted to officials of
the Public Record Office, British Museum, Brotherton Library
in the University of Leeds, Henry E. Huntington Library,
Institute of Historical Research, National Register of Archives,
National Library of Scotland, Newcastle Central Reference
Library, and the County Record Offices of Essex, Kent,
Lancashire, Lincolnshire and Oxfordshire. My thanks are also
due to the Society of Antiquaries and the Yorkshire Archae-
ological Society for permission to use their libraries, and the
Earl of Scarbrough, Mr. T. Cottrell-Dormer, Mrs. E. Dunlop,
Mrs. A. Heneage, Mr. M. Kirkby and Miss M. Simpson for
allowing me to examine manuscripts in their private possession.
I am grateful also to the editors of the *Yorkshire Bulletin of
Economic and Social Research* and of *Wool Knowledge* for authority to
reproduce material published in these two journals.

For advice, help and criticism, I am indebted to a wide circle of teachers, colleagues and friends. But I should particularly like to thank for their interest and encouragement Professor A. J. Brown, Professor R. H. Tawney and Mr. Lawrence Stone; for the preparation of maps, Miss M. Thom and Mr. H. Walkland; and for the task of typing the manuscript from my handwriting, Miss P. Beardmore and Miss P. Rudiforth. My greatest debt, however, is to Professor M. W. Beresford, who first aroused my interest in economic history and has since been both guide and mentor in the labyrinth of historical research.

P.J.B.

CONTENTS

LIST OF MAPS

INTRODUCTION

'FIRST IT WAS LAID AS A GROUND THAT WHEN WOOLLS WERE DEAREST THEN WAS THIS KINGDOM THE RICHEST.'
Parliamentary Committee on the Bill 'for the free liberty of buying and selling of wool', 1621.[1]

Until the era of the Industrial Revolution wool was, without question, the most important raw material in the English economic system. The staple article of the country's export trade in the Middle Ages, it remained until the nineteenth century the indispensable basis of her greatest industry. Every class in the community, whether landlord, farmer, merchant, industrial capitalist or artisan, had an interest in wool, and it was the subject of endless economic controversy.

In the agricultural sphere, sheep predominated in most pastoral areas besides playing a fundamental part in arable cultivation. Sheep farming made the fortunes of more than one great landed family, and the price of wool determined the welfare of many smaller cultivators.

To Englishmen in the thirteenth and fourteenth centuries the export trade was synonymous with wool, and the continental textile industries relied heavily upon England for their supplies of finer raw material. It was in connection with the export of wool that the first English trading company of any kind — the Fellowship of the Merchants of the Staple — was organized. Wool likewise provided the home cloth industry with its raw material; and increasingly, as the Middle Ages drew to a close, English wool was exported as cloth instead of being shipped raw.

As early as 1454 Parliament declared that 'the making of cloth within all parts of the realm is the greatest occupation and living of the poor commons of this land';[2] while an Act of Parliament after the Revolution praised the woollen manufacture as 'the greatest and most profitable commodity of this kingdom on which the value of lands and the trade of the nation do chiefly depend'.[3] A petition of the Commons to the King at

---

[1] *Commons Debates, 1621*, ed. W. Notestein, F. H. Relf and H. Simpson (New Haven, 1935), v, 468.
[2] *Rotuli Parliamentorum*, v, 274.
[3] *Statutes of the Realm*, 10 William III, c. 16.

the Restoration referred to the wool-textile industry as 'the principal foundation upon which the foreign commerce of this kingdom moveth';[1] and though that importance declined somewhat in the decades that followed, wool and wool textiles had prior to 1660 accounted for more than three-quarters (and in some years more than nine-tenths) of the export trade of Tudor and Stuart England.

The government's interest in wool was understandably great, as well as being many-sided. In the Middle Ages and early Tudor period export duties on wool provided the Crown with a major part of its revenue, while both then and later the royal finances were augmented by fines and fees arising from the enforcement or dispensation of the law as it related to the shipment or purchase of wool. The production and export of cloth were also taxed.

As the basis of the country's external trade the shipment of wool, raw or manufactured, was the main means of securing a favourable balance of payments and a net influx of bullion. An export surplus was further desired in order to maintain domestic employment. There can be little doubt that employment opportunities during the sixteenth and seventeenth centuries were growing less rapidly than population; and the lack of demand for labour was a matter which gave Tudor and Stuart statesmen cause for some concern. In the sixteenth century unemployment was thought of mainly as an agrarian problem brought about by the displacement of labour through the spread of sheep farming; while in the seventeenth century it was discussed largely in terms of a decline in overseas demand for industrial products. In either case the cloth industry was regarded as mainly responsible: in the Tudor age because it was too prosperous; in the Stuart period because it was too depressed.

Such, indeed, was the importance of wool during the sixteenth and seventeenth centuries that no issue of general economic significance can be adequately discussed without reference to it. Such, also, was the influence of the established wool-merchanting and clothing interests that the government was at times prepared to sacrifice any class in the community in order to meet their demands. These demands did not remain constant, but varied with the different stages of economic development.

[1] *H. of C. Journals*, viii, 149.

During the period covered by this study three main economic phases may be distinguished. In the early sixteenth century England was in the midst of a transition from a wool-exporting to a cloth-exporting nation. The export trade in the raw material, though declining, was still considerable; the home manufacture of woollen cloth was rapidly expanding; and the production of worsted was, by comparison, negligible. Wool prices were rising and sheep farmers were experiencing a period of remarkable prosperity. The internal wool-middleman trade was largely in the hands of the growing class of 'wool broggers'. Apart from some transitory legislation against these dealers, and an Act forbidding some of the sharper practices used in the winding of wool, the government did not greatly concern itself directly with the wool trade, but reserved its main energies for dealing with the encloser and depopulator. This phase lasted until the mid-sixteenth century. It was brought to an end by the violent contraction in the export market.

The succeeding phase embraced Elizabeth I's reign and the early, comparatively prosperous, years of James I's reign. During this second period the wool-export trade passed away; woollen-cloth exports remained for the most part sluggish; and the production of worsted fabrics considerably increased. Wool prices continued their upward trend, but except for several relatively short periods, the incentive to convert arable land into sheep pasture was less strong than hitherto. The government now became more actively concerned with the wool trade; and with the backing of the wealthier clothiers and, at first, the Company of the Staple it endeavoured to keep down the price of wool by making the activities of common wool dealers illegal: a policy which was against the interests of the small manufacturers, the wool growers and, of course, the middlemen themselves. This policy was not resolutely pursued. The story of the dispensations which were granted to particular places and individuals is a long one which need not be entered into here. Partly because of these exemptions, and partly in spite of the government's endeavours, the wool middlemen's activities continued. Indeed, this was the hey-day of the small unspecialized wool dealer, and a period in which men with larger amounts of capital appeared on the scene.

With the industrial depression in the reign of James I there

B

began a new phase which continued throughout the remainder of the seventeenth century. During this third period increasing quantities of wool were imported from Ireland and Spain; the woollen-cloth industry was, for the most part, chronically depressed; and the worsted manufacture rapidly expanded. Wool prices showed, on the whole, a downward trend, and native wool growers did not experience the best of times. In the belief that the continental textile industry found British wool indispensable, numerous measures were passed to prevent its export from England in the hope of eliminating foreign competition, and the trade in Irish wool was strictly regulated. Though wool dealing continued to attract men from many walks of life, it became more and more a business for the specialist; and in spite of outbursts against the wool middlemen, their trade was not restrained.

The changes which have been mentioned here and which will be traced in greater detail later on did not form a simple process, but in them two central influences may be seen at work. The first, is the price of wool; the second, the change in the nature of the English wool supply. The rise in the price of wool in the sixteenth century was in no small measure responsible for the enclosures for sheep farming, for the decline of the wool-export trade, and for the government's anti-middleman policy; while the low price of wool in the seventeenth century was both a cause and a consequence of the prohibition placed on its export. The change in the character of the wool supply had important consequences in a number of directions. First, it made the wool middleman's trade more necessary and, at the same time, more specialized. Secondly, it led to changes in the geographical distribution of English wool and to an increase in the import of wool from Spain. Finally, and most important, it exerted a profound influence on the development of the English wool-textile industry. The influence of the wool supply on industrial development was to continue long after the end of the seventeenth century; but that is a story which will have to be told elsewhere.

Chapter 1

SHEEP FARMING AND WOOL PRODUCTION

I

One has only to look at a sample of sixteenth- and seventeenth-century wills and inventories to realize the important part which sheep farming played in the life of Tudor and Stuart England. In agricultural areas, even in those regions where tillage predominated, large numbers of farmers owned some sheep. Nor was sheep farming practised only by men who gained their sole means of livelihood from agriculture. Quite often sheep were owned by men whose main interests and vocations lay in other fields — in industry or in trade, in politics or in law.

In the sixteenth and seventeenth centuries, as at the present day, sheep farming was an industry of great diversity. It was practised in a wide variety of environments and varied enormously in the scale of enterprise. The environment might be the relatively densely settled and largely unenclosed parts of the midland plain, or the thinly populated, more barren areas of the north; the reclaimed Lincolnshire fens or the Sussex downs. At one end of the scale of enterprise came the two or three sheep which an open-field peasant might own, though the average figure in some areas was probably 20 to 30[1]. At the other extreme were the 15,500 sheep distributed among 20 flocks, belonging to Sir Henry Fermor of East Barsham, co. Norfolk, in 1521.[2] Sheep ownership was affected to some extent by the Act passed in 1533 which made it an offence to keep flocks of more than

[1] W. G. Hoskins, *The Midland Peasant. The Economic and Social History of a Leicestershire Village* (1957), p. 158. See also Joan Thirsk, *English Peasant Farming. The Agrarian History of Lincolnshire from Tudor to Recent Times* (1957), p. 118, where mention is made of three wealthy villagers of Bolingbroke (co. Lincs.) having 2,700 sheep between them and the rest of the villagers having another 7,000 — apparently in the early seventeenth century.

[2] K. J. Allison, 'Flock Management in the Sixteenth and Seventeenth Centuries', *Economic History Review*, 2nd series, xi (1958), 100.

2,400 sheep, except under certain circumstances.[1] A further statute passed in 1555 sought to ensure that large-scale sheep farming did not lead to the neglect of dairy farming. For every 60 sheep that he owned, a sheep farmer was ordered to keep one milch cow, and for every 120 sheep, one calf.[2]

Little definite is known about sheep ownership in Tudor and Stuart times, but such evidence as is available suggests that, while the flocks of the great sheep masters reached a peak under the early Tudors, the sixteenth and seventeenth centuries as a whole were marked by a progressive decline in the relative importance of the small producer. Sheep ownership was becoming concentrated in fewer hands, while the proportion of men owning no sheep at all was tending to rise.[3]

This trend in favour of the large and medium-sized producer was bound up with developments, such as the enclosure-movement, which affected the balance of land distribution, but in part it simply reflected the economies of large-scale production. When it came to sheep grazing the lord and country gentleman had many advantages over the peasant. Their flocks were more likely to be self-supporting, and their costs of purchase and management proportionately less. The existence of many separate closes, by enabling constant changes of pasturage, benefited a flock, so that productivity both in respect of wool and lambs was likely to be greater. On the sales side, it is likely that more advantageous contracts could be made with buyers. A great grazier, such as Spencer of Althorp, in Northamptonshire, with a reputation for his flocks and in a position to provide credit, was likely to obtain a higher price for his wool than the small farmer of limited means; and he could probably secure a better price for his sheep, because he was able to deal direct with distant butchers, and in great quantities.[4] But even among

---

[1] *Statutes of the Realm*, 25 Henry VIII, c. 13. The excepting clauses allowed that (i) lambs under one year old might be excluded; (ii) more than 2,400 might be kept for private consumption; (iii) temporal persons might keep any number on inherited lands, but then no others on rented lands; (iv) spiritual persons might keep their customary number.

[2] Ibid., 2 & 3 Philip and Mary, c. 3. Also, one cow was to be kept for every 10 oxen and one calf for every two milch cows.

[3] W. G. Hoskins, *Essays in Leicestershire History* (1950), pp. 174–5; K. J. Allison, *The Wool Supply and the Worsted Cloth Industry in Norfolk in the Sixteenth and Seventeenth Centuries* (Leeds University Ph.D. thesis, 1955), pp. 113–22. See also J. Thirsk, op. cit., pp. 128–9, 152–4, 173–5, 187–9.

[4] M. E. Finch, *The Wealth of Five Northamptonshire Families, 1540–1640* (Northants Rec. Soc. XIX, Oxford, 1956), p. 44.

flocks belonging to the same owner, the larger units tended to give a higher rate of profit per sheep than the smaller ones.[1]

The number of sheep which any single farmer might own was dependent upon a variety of factors. With stock to be bought, normal running expenses to be met and, in the case of tenant farmers, rent payments to be made, an obvious limit was imposed by the farmer's financial resources. Sometimes, however, a man could add to his flocks by hiring sheep instead of by purchasing them.[2] At other times, he could extend his business by renting additional pastures and sharing their overhead expenses in partnership.[3]

There were, of course, other reasons why even wealthy farmers did not always possess large flocks of sheep. Such reasons are perhaps best summed up in the term 'profit motive'. Land could be used for purposes other than the grazing of sheep. It could be used, for instance, to grow wheat or raise cattle. Only when the capital invested in sheep farming yielded a higher return than when laid out in alternative uses was a farmer likely to specialize in sheep grazing. The incentive to do this varied considerably from time to time and from place to place. Much depended upon the nature of the soil and the locality of the farm in question. But where land could be adapted equally well to pasture or tillage the relative market prices of wool and grain often determined what the farmer produced.

II

In general, the sheep farmer in Tudor and Stuart times valued his flocks primarily in terms of the wool which they grew. The importance of the sheep's wool-bearing capacity, in comparison with its other productive functions, may be illustrated by the fact that towards the end of Elizabeth's reign — midway through the period under consideration — the wool clip of the wether sheep[4] was worth between one-third and one-quarter of its value on the hoof. Today, the corresponding figure, in the case of an average short-wool breed, is approximately one-sixth, the difference largely reflecting the greater

[1] K. J. Allison, *thesis*, p. 259.   [2] Infra, p. 12.
[3] P.R.O. Req. 2/114/46.   [4] i.e. the gelded male sheep.

emphasis placed nowadays upon the production of mutton.[1] Throughout the Tudor period, and to some extent under the Stuarts, the price of wool was a major factor in the determination of the price of sheep, and both tended to move up and down together. Again, the quality of the wool produced by the sixteenth-century sheep had an important bearing on its market price, a fine-woolled animal costing more than a sheep of the coarse-woolled variety. For many, if not all, specialist sheep farmers, the largest single market transaction in the year was the sale of the summer wool clip; while even among graziers who supplied the mutton market in bulk, receipts from the sale of wool often exceeded those from the disposal of stock. Thus, in the year ending 31st October, 1631, fleece wool sold from the Earl of Middlesex's estates in Warwickshire, Gloucestershire and Worcestershire brought in £1506 14s. 6d. as against £1002 13s. 3d. from the sale of sheep, sheep skins and locks.[2] Wool being such a profitable commodity, it is hardly surprising that, in the early sixteenth century at least, the sheep which could be shorn was normally given field room until such time as it had to be culled by reason of its age, poor condition or disease.

It was the profitability of wool growing as against corn production that was largely responsible for the spread of sheep farming, especially in central England, between the mid-fifteenth and mid-sixteenth centuries. Since early in the Middle Ages, consolidation and enclosure of open-field holdings and common land — sometimes for more efficient tillage, sometimes for use as pasture — had been very gradually changing the appearance of the countryside. In the middle years of the fifteenth century the movement towards enclosure for pasture farming accelerated in response to the rising demand for wool and the low price of grain. After more than a hundred years of population stagnation and decline, the pressure on land which had characterized the pre-Black Death era had disappeared. Resources were now relatively plentiful and foodstuffs cheap. Low corn prices were further encouraged by the government's

[1] R. Trow-Smith, *A History of British Livestock Husbandry to 1700* (1957), p. 170.
[2] Kent Archives Office, U.269/A.423. Locks were often sold in small quantities to villagers, but if tarry and inferior were sometimes given away. See K.A.O. U.269/ A.418/1; U.269/A.418/5, fol. 7; *Rural Economy in Yorkshire in 1641, being the Farming and Account Books of Henry Best of Elmswell, in the East Riding of the County of York* (Surtees Soc. XXXIII, Durham, 1857), ed. C. B. Robinson, pp. 21–2.

'policy of provision' which led to a partial restraint being imposed upon the exportation of grain[1] in an attempt to safeguard the Englishman's necessities of life. Encouraged by a high level of real wages at home and abroad and by a gradually increasing population at last beginning to recover from the ravages of a century of plague, the English cloth industry emerged from the doldrums to become set on an upward phase of production that was destined to continue almost uninterruptedly until the 1550's.

As the output and export of cloth increased, wool prices rose. Taking the decade 1451–60 as base, the price of home-grown wool had approximately doubled by 1541–50.[2] Grain prices remained comparatively stable during the late fifteenth century and showed no marked tendency to rise until after 1520, when prices in general moved upward. On land which had been marginal to corn in 1450 there was therefore a strong price incentive to go over to pasture. Factors on the cost side probably exercised a less decisive influence, but in the conditions of the mid-fifteenth century, with dear labour and cheap land, these also favoured the production of wool rather than grain. By enclosing his arable land and converting it to pasture, a farmer was able to cut down his labour costs by changing from a crop using a comparatively large amount of labour to one using little; and the fact that land was plentiful meant that there was little need to economize in its use. Possibly more important than these considerations, however, were the relative incremental yields of wool and corn resulting from enclosure — a subject which as yet has received scant attention from economic historians. Admittedly, enclosure increased the products of husbandry, but there seems reason to believe that it worked even more favourably on the output of wool.[3] Not only did enclosure make

[1] In 1437 the export of corn was allowed when it did not exceed a certain price (in the case of wheat 6s. 8d. the quarter); above that price an export licence was necessary (see *Statutes of the Realm*, 15 Henry VI, c. 2, made perpetual by 23 Henry VI, c. 5). In 1491 the export of grain except with a special licence was forbidden. Mary in 1555 reverted to the Act of 1437. This was followed under Elizabeth by an enactment which raised the limit within which corn might be exported to 10s. the quarter in the case of wheat. In 1463 an Act was passed which forbade the importation of wheat except when the price reached 6s. 8d. (ibid., 3 Edward IV, c. 2) — a limit which the advance in prices made inoperative.

[2] See p. 219.

[3] Infra, p. 27; B.M. Lansd. MS. 152, fol. 229; P. J. Bowden, 'Movements in Wool Prices, 1490–1610', *Yorkshire Bulletin of Economic and Social Research*, iv (1952), 109–24.

possible an increase in fleece weights, but it also enabled more sheep to be kept per acre. Thus Hooker, writing at the end of the sixteenth century, alleged that the small enclosed fields of Devon carried more sheep than any other county in England.[1]

By the mid-sixteenth century, however, the urge to switch from grain to wool was weakening. Land was becoming scarcer and labour more abundant. Corn prices, which had been rising since the 1520's, doubled in the 1540's, when the general price level moved sharply upwards. Then, in 1551, the foreign market for English cloth collapsed and wool prices tumbled. The failure of cloth exports to make any substantial recovery in the second half of the sixteenth century depressed the price of wool, and twenty-five years passed before it again reached its 1550 level. Hence, while wool prices doubled between 1541–50 and 1601–10, wheat prices trebled. Though some land continued to be laid down to pasture (the reduced profitability of wool being compensated to some extent by the rising demand for mutton, beef and dairy products), the great drive against arable in the Midlands was halted and even reversed. In Norfolk, home of the foldcourse system[2] and large-scale sheep farming, several of the big flock masters subsided into *rentiers* after 1560; others reduced their flocks below the top capacity of the foldcourses, or moved over from sheep farming to cattle grazing.[3]

The rise in corn and other food prices continued almost without interruption until the middle decades of the seventeenth century. Wool prices, on the other hand, reached a high point in the exceptional prosperity of the first few years of the century, but thereafter were usually stationary or declining. By 1610 there had been a substantial fall from the peak reached in 1603, and though the next few years witnessed a complete recovery, the cloth industry became depressed after 1618 and prices again began to decline. 1622 marked the bottom of the most severe trade depression experienced yet and the lowest

[1] B.M. Harl. MS. 5827, fol. 10.
[2] This system was the basis of the Norfolk sheep-corn husbandry. Each flock was confined to a foldcourse, this being a strictly defined area providing various kinds of pasture — open-field arable land, when unsown, heathland, and sometimes arable and pasture closes. See K. J. Allison, 'The Sheep-Corn Husbandry of Norfolk in the Sixteenth and Seventeenth Centuries', *Agric. Hist. Rev.* V (1957), 12–30.
[3] A. Simpson, 'The East Anglian Foldcourse: Some Queries', *Agric. Hist. Rev.* VI (1958), 92.

wool prices for many years. In Lincolnshire, wool was sold at 10s. per stone, as against 14s. per stone in 1618 and 12s. in 1595. During the next twenty years, Lincolnshire wool fluctuated in price between 10s. 6d. and 13s. 8d.[1]

The great rise in wool prices was over, and despite a growing demand for mutton, the third and fourth decades of the century saw some farmers reducing their flocks or giving up sheep altogether. In Northamptonshire, the Fitzwilliams found tenants for their pastures at the end of the 1620's, and by 1639 the Spencer sheep farm had been reduced to about one-third of its former size of 10,000 sheep plus lambs.[2] To the north, in Lincolnshire, Sir George Heneage of Hainton sold the bulk of his sheep in 1628 for £400 and let out some of his best grazing land.[3] To the south, in Buckinghamshire, Sir Thomas Temple of Stowe sold his flocks in 1623 and 1624, and established a system of leaseholds on his pastures.[4] Further west, on the midland estates of the Earl of Middlesex, receipts from the sale of wool and sheep declined from 62 per cent. of total gross income in the year ending 1st November, 1630, to 34 per cent. five years later. During the same period, receipts from rent increased from 33 per cent. to 49 per cent.[5]

For those farmers who decided to continue with sheep, the middle decades of the century brought rather better wool prices, but the post-Restoration period saw the fortunes of wool growers at a very low ebb. Improved farming techniques and increased wool imports helped to swell the supply of the raw material, while on the demand side the woollen industry, never very prosperous, became chronically depressed. As a result of these various influences the price of wool fell in some years to well under half of what it had been at the beginning of the century. In Lincolnshire, Sir Drayner Massingberd could obtain only 6s. 8d. per stone for wool sold in 1677,[6] while John Newton, Esq., visiting London in the summer of 1686, received

---

[1] Lincolnshire Archives Office, And. 1, fol. 17; H.97/22/1, 2; Account Book of Sir George Heneage 1613–1642 (formerly in the possession of Mrs. A. Heneage of Hainton Hall, and now at the Lincolnshire Archives Office, reference HEN.3/2).
[2] Finch, op. cit., pp. 46, 48, 166.
[3] L.A.O. HEN.3/2.
[4] E. F. Gay, 'The Temples of Stowe and their Debts', *Huntington Library Quarterly*, ii (1938–9), 430.
[5] K.A.O. U.269/A.423.
[6] L.A.O. MM. VI/5/4.

word from his agent that wool was 'like to be a very great dragg'.[1] In 1690, best Lincolnshire wool was still selling at only 8s. od. per stone and 'small wool' at 6s. od.;[2] but by 1696 a very marked improvement had taken place,[3] and the last years of the century were a period of comparative prosperity for the wool grower.

III

The production of wool was, of course, only one of the sheep's useful functions: it was also a source of meat, dung, pelts and milk. Many farmers kept some sheep partly, if not mainly, for domestic consumption, and in large households and institutions the number of animals killed for the table was often considerable. For example, in the year ending Michaelmas, 1616, the estates of Lord Dormer supplied his kitchens with more than 760 sheep and 120 lambs, not to mention 50 beasts and other provisions.[4] At the same time, the part played by mutton in the sheep farmer's commercial calculations varied greatly, depending upon such factors as the size of his undertaking, when he farmed, and where.

In the sixteenth and seventeenth centuries the production of meat was probably never a major reason for the small sheep breeder's activities, and even among larger graziers few appear to have paid much attention to the mutton market before the early Stuart period. In the first half of the sixteenth century, the sheep farmer's profit was very largely determined by the price of wool,[5] and the role of the sheep as a meat-producing animal was almost completely ignored: it was kept for its wool and dung, and became a carcase only when its useful working life was over. Among both large and small flock masters alike, the production of mutton was incidental to the more rewarding business of growing wool. In the second half of the century the meat market continued to be supplied mainly with old, weak and inferior stock, but even before the opening years of Elizabeth's reign the demand for prime mutton had begun to make itself felt and was being met by large producers well located to do so. Thus from

---

[1] L.A.O. M.7/12/56.   [2] L.A.O. M.7/12/70.   [3] L.A.O. M.7/12/89.
[4] Lord Dormer's Papers, 1600–30 (in the possession of T. Cottrell-Dormer, Esq., of Rousham Hall, Oxfordshire).
[5] K. J. Allison, *Econ. Hist. Rev.* 2nd ser. xi (1958), 110–12.

Norfolk in the 1540's and 50's, Sir Roger Townshend of East Rainham and Coke of Holkham were selling prime sheep and hoggs[1] to Suffolk and Cambridgeshire men, while Sir Henry Bedingfeld of Oxborough was despatching fat wethers — as well as crones and pucks[2] — to fairs in Norfolk, Suffolk and Essex.[3]

In the late sixteenth and seventeenth centuries the continued growth of population, together with the uncertain fortunes of the English woollen industry, helped to bring into greater prominence the sheep's virtues as a source of meat. During Elizabeth's reign the Spencers of Althorp produced great quantities of mutton for the market. In the year ending October, 1577, for instance, 3,071 lambs and 2,765 sheep (including 1,800 wethers) were sold. It is clear from the family sheep accounts that some of these sheep were purchased during the year in order to be fattened for the butcher.[4] The Spencers were the outstanding flock masters of their age, and it would be a mistake to regard them as representative of either sheep farmers in general or large graziers in particular. Thus in the late 1590's, a substantial gentleman farmer like Thomas Grantham, Esq., of Lincoln, who owned between 1,500 and 2,000 sheep, was selling more ewes than wethers and was relatively much less affected than Spencer by the market for food.[5] On the other hand, Dormer, who had estates in Oxfordshire and Buckingham, was buying hundreds of wethers in Wiltshire and elsewhere in 1600, for fattening and despatch to London.[6] Much obviously depended upon the extent of the market for mutton, and whether the sheep farmer was well situated geographically to take advantage of it.

The depressed condition of the cloth industry in the 1620's and 30's was doubtless partly instrumental in persuading some wool growers to take a more active interest in mutton production. Unlike wool prices, mutton prices in the seventeenth century tended, if anything, to rise. Among larger farmers the greater emphasis placed upon meat, was reflected by a change

[1] i.e. young sheep between about 3 and 15 months.
[2] i.e. old ewes and poor quality lambs.
[3] Ibid., pp. 108–9.
[4] Finch, op. cit., p. 42.
[5] L.A.O. And. 1.
[6] Lord Dormer's Papers, 1600–30.

in the composition of flocks. In Lincolnshire, the number of wethers kept by Sir George Heneage increased, while the proportion of ewes among his sheep declined from 53 per cent. in 1618–20 to 23 per cent. in 1633–5.[1] At West Harling, in Norfolk, the main aim of Framlingham Gawdy between 1650 and 1666 was the production of wether lambs for sale; and a flock of 180 wethers 'fit for the butcher' was kept by Coke at Holkham in 1634.[2] Further north, at about the same time, farmers like Henry Best, one of the minor gentry of the East Riding, were keeping a business-like eye on the market in order to take advantage of any shortages which might develop. Best and his fellow north countrymen normally took at least four years to finish a wether for the butcher. Anything younger than this would 'neaver feede kindly', but at this age wethers could be made ready for the Easter trade by keeping them in a sheltered close in winter and removing them to good pasture in early spring.[3] At the end of the century mutton production was already associated with new crops and methods of husbandry: Sir Robert Walpole's hoggs, for example, were purchased in the autumn, wintered at Houghton on turnips, sometimes finished on early grass in the spring, and sold at Cambridge or to Norwich and King's Lynn butchers.[4]

The increase in the demand for mutton which took place in Tudor and Stuart England was not limited to any particular part of the country, but by far the greatest single influence on the meat market at this time was exercised by London — 'the most populous, the most rapidly growing, the wealthiest and the most compact' of all the various centres of consumption.[5] We should be careful, however, not to exaggerate the importance of metropolitan demand. Apart from the Northamptonshire Spencers and an enterprising handful of men from the home counties, East Anglia and south Midlands, probably few sheep farmers made fortunes in the sixteenth century by supplying the capital with its meat. At the very end of the century London was said still to be fed 'principallie . . . from some fewe shires near

[1] L.A.O. HEN.3/2.
[2] Allison, *Econ. Hist. Rev.* 2nd ser. xi (1958), 109.
[3] *Rural Economy in Yorkshire in 1641*, p. 10.
[4] J. H. Plumb, 'Sir Robert Walpole and Norfolk Husbandry', *Econ. Hist. Rev.* 2nd ser. v (1952), 86–9.
[5] F. J. Fisher, 'The Development of the London Food Market, 1540–1640', *Econ. Hist. Rev.* v (1935), 46.

adioyninge'. But in the years that followed the city's tentacles spread over the provinces until by the middle of the seventeenth century they reached much farther afield.[1] As early as 1600, Oxfordshire and Wiltshire sheep were being fattened for the London market,[2] and in 1622 Cotswold sheep were being sold at Smithfield.[3] In Lincolnshire, the Hatchers of Careby had apparently been untouched by metropolitan demand in the 1630's.[4] But in the 1670's and 80's Sir Drayner Massingberd, who owned land at South Ormsby in the uplands and rented grazing land at Ingoldmells in the nearby marsh, was sending fat wethers with a drover to London.[5] At this time the Lincolnshire fenland was specializing more and more on the fattening of sheep bred on the neighbouring hill country and finally destined for sale at Smithfield.[6] Welsh mutton was sweet, and for this reason sheep from Wales were driven to London and there slaughtered to feed the city's growing population.[7] The capital also drew upon other distant parts of Britain for its supplies of mutton.

Not all the sheep intended for the London meat market reached the capital, however, and not all the remainder were slaughtered on arrival. Sometimes animals were sold en route to farmers wishing to replace or to increase their flocks. In the late seventeenth and eighteenth centuries, Lincolnshire and Leicestershire sheep were purchased at Smithfield in September or October by graziers of Essex and other nearby counties, to be sold a few months later for mutton at enhanced prices.[8] West-country wethers were purchased at Weyhill fair by the farmers of the south and east Midlands and the home counties, and then fattened for killing.[9] The Dorset or Wiltshire sheep farmer was placed in a very advantageous position for supplying the London early fat lamb market, for, according to writers of the early

---

[1] Ibid., pp. 47–8.
[2] Lord Dormer's Papers, 1600–30.
[3] A. J. and R. H. Tawney, 'An Occupational Census of the Seventeenth Century', *Econ. Hist. Rev.* v (1934), 27, n. 2.
[4] L.A.O. H.97/22/1,2.
[5] L.A.O. MM. VI/5/9, 31.
[6] Thirsk op. cit., pp. 138, 177.
[7] R. E. Prothero (Lord Ernle), *English Farming Past and Present* (1912), p. 139. In the 1660's and 70's the Petre family of Ingatestone, in Essex, was buying and selling 'Welch ewes and contry sheep' (Essex Record Office, D/DP. A.47).
[8] D. Defoe, *Tour Through Great Britain* (edn. 1927), i. 9.
[9] Ibid., i, 289–90.

eighteenth century, his ewes often possessed the peculiar ability to lamb twice a year. By early spring the Dorset or Wiltshire lamb, dropped in September or October, could be driven on the hoof to Smithfield, fattening in the pastures of the home counties, and still beat its competitors by many weeks. The metropolitan demand for Dorset and Wiltshire fat lambs grew rapidly at the end of the seventeenth century, while the ewes found a ready sale to breeders more conveniently placed than the west countrymen for the London trade.[1]

Apart from providing mutton and wool, sheep had other productive uses. Of these, their ability to enrich the land they ran on was by far the most important. Even in the Middle Ages, sheep dung had been highly prized by the arable farmer, and rising corn prices added to its value. Hence, in the mixed farming areas of Wiltshire and Norfolk, where soils were chalky or otherwise light, sheep came to be kept as much for their fertility as for their wool. On the thin chalk-land of Berkshire it was possible for a substantial yeoman farmer, such as Robert Loder, to think of his flock, in 1611, primarily in terms of their wool and dung and to ignore their meat-producing potentialities.[2] In an age when there were no artificial fertilizers, sheep were essential to tillage if the best possible corn yield was to be obtained. For this reason, arable farmers with no large flocks of their own sometimes found it necessary to borrow or to lease sheep in order that something of the richness which constant cropping took out of their soil, should be replaced. Sheep were frequently leased for a period of one year or longer, often upon the condition that one-half of their yearly yield of wool and lambs should be allowed to the owner. At other times the terms might be one-third or the whole of the wool and the lambs produced, or, in some cases, a specified amount of wool.[3]

Among the sheep farmer's minor sources of income were receipts from the sale of skins belonging to animals which had been killed for domestic consumption or which had otherwise perished. In the case of large undertakings the number of fells

---

[1] Ibid., i, 210–11, 290; Trow-Smith, op. cit., p. 178.

[2] *Robert Loder's Farm Accounts, 1610–1620* (Camden Soc. 3rd ser., liii, 1936), ed. G. E. Fussell, pp. 40–1.

[3] P.R.O. C.1/803/6; C.1/879/38; C.1/1243/56; C.1/1472/58; C.3/10/88; C.3/18/92; M. Campbell, *The English Yeoman under Elizabeth and the Early Stuarts* (Yale, 1942), p. 199.

sold might be substantial. Thus in 1536, Norwich Cathedral Priory, whose flocks had increased from about 2,500 to 8,000 over the period 1470 to 1520, sold 516 sheep skins, for which £4 6s. od. was received, as against £46 os. 6d. from the sale of wool.[1] Nearly a century later, in the year ending Michaelmas, 1616, Lord Dormer sold 884 fells for £62 12s. od., while debts outstanding on wool sold the previous year brought in £773.[2] The value of a pelt depended to a large extent upon the amount of wool that covered it. This point is well illustrated by an entry in John Hatcher's account book, dated June, 1629, to the effect that two sheep skins 'in wooll' were sold for 2s. 1od. each, while four skins 'clipt' brought in only 1od. apiece.[3] Butchers as well as farmers had pelts for sale, and customers were found among the glovers and fellmongers who lived in most towns. The sheep's skin was made into leather or parchment, while the fell wool, having been plucked from the pelt, was used in the manufacture of blankets and bayes.

As regards the sheep's other productive function — that of a supplier of milk — not a great deal need be said. The practice of milking ewes was certainly widespread in the Middle Ages, and we have Camden's picturesque account of the Essex milking flocks at the end of the Tudor period.[4] But enlightened opinion appears to have been against the practice, and throughout the early modern period the cow was gradually establishing itself as the unrivalled source of milk supply.

IV

The sheep farmer in Tudor and Stuart times had many problems, and for the small man life was often difficult. Not least of the small man's problems was lack of capital. With sheep to be bought, day-to-day expenses to be met, and, in many cases, rent payments to be made, the financial resources of the husbandman or small breeder were frequently stretched to the utmost. Sheep were often purchased on credit and paid for after the summer wool clip had been sold. Likewise, the payment of rent frequently waited upon the sale of wool.[5]

[1] K. J. Allison, *thesis*, pp. 241, xliii.
[2] Lord Dormer's Papers, 1600–30.
[3] L.A.O. H.97/22/2, fol. 24.
[4] W. Camden, *Britannia* (edn. 1789), p. 407.
[5] *Infra*, p. 96; P.R.O. S.P. 16/515/139; Req. 2/171/24.

Shortage of capital was a problem which scarcely affected the large flock masters, some of whom were men of great substance. Unlike the ordinary husbandman, who was often in urgent need of cash, the large grazier frequently dispensed credit. It was not unusual for a big flock master, such as the Earl of Middlesex, to allow one year's credit or more to the less wealthy farmers, dealers and butchers who purchased his sheep.[1] In order to benefit from the seasonal rise in price, he was often willing to wait until late in the wool-growing year before selling his wool.[2] A man of means, he gave credit to wool middlemen and manufacturers, instead of receiving it, and in this way obtained a correspondingly higher price for his produce.[3]

Probably the greatest single problem which all sixteenth and seventeenth century livestock farmers had to solve was that of feed. This problem, being closely associated with the available supply of grazing land, tended to be most acutely felt in densely settled districts. In many open-field villages in the Midlands and in the vale lands of northern England, waste was turned into arable at the expense of common grazing as population increased. The introduction of stints on the commons, or the reduction of old stints, was a frequent expedient for sharing the land more equitably.[4]

Rights of common were of vital importance to the sheep farmer who possessed no enclosed pasture of his own, and the details concerning them were usually carefully reproduced in leases and deeds of land conveyance. The normal arrangement was that the number of sheep kept on the common should be in proportion to the sheep owner's holdings on the manor. For instance, in some places the regulation was that the holder of every tenement should be given pasture for six sheep on the common, and then for as many additional sheep as there were acres in his holdings. This might lead, as on a Wiltshire manor, to every copyholder having from 80 to 200 sheep on the common.[5] In such cases it is hardly surprising that complaints were made about the commons being overstocked and the sheep

[1] K.A.O. U.269/A.418/1, 6; U.269/A.419/4; U.269/A.421.
[2] Infra, p. 87.
[3] Infra, p. 101.
[4] Joan Thirsk, *Tudor Enclosures* (Historical Association Pamphlet, General Series: G.41), p. 8.
[5] Campbell, op. cit., pp. 199, 204.

underfed. And the position was made worse by the abuse, the invasion and the sale of rights of common which not infrequently took place.[1] One aspect of this pressure on grazing land was the growing practice of agistment, or taking another man's stock in to graze for a money payment or a share in the progeny of that stock.

Roots and artificial grasses — together with enclosure — were to provide the eventual solution to the problem of how to carry livestock through the winter in good condition. But these crops were almost unknown in England before the Restoration, and it was only during the eighteenth century that they became generally adopted.[2] In the meantime, the grazier or dairyman, whether his beasts were grazed upon open fields or enclosed pastures, could keep alive throughout the winter months only so many animals as his supply of grass, hay, straw and other fodder crops, such as peas, beans and oats, permitted. A balance had to be drawn in allocating land for tillage and for pasture; grasslands and winter feed had to be apportioned among the different kinds of livestock; and a maximum use had to be made of corn stubble after the harvest was over. 'Convertible husbandry', whereby lands were used for a year or longer for tillage and pasture alternately, was becoming increasingly popular throughout the period. This practice, commonly referred to nowadays as 'ley farming', is a means of increasing the yield of both arable and pasture, since by taking the plough all round the farm, the pasture benefits from being cropped, while the arable is greatly improved by a period of rest under grass.[3]

Even though an adequate supply of food might be assured, the Tudor or Stuart sheep farmer's troubles were far from ended. Sheep were liable to suffer from many ailments and diseases. Of these, a condition of the liver known as the rot and a disease of the skin known as the scab, were the most serious. The rot — nowadays referred to as the 'liver fluke' — was par-

[1] E. C. K. Gonner, *Common Land and Inclosure* (1912), pp. 337–8. For further examples of the stinting of common rights and the position of common rights in the sixteenth century, see the *Report of the Royal Commission on Common Land, 1955–1958*, Cmd. 462 (1958), pp. 155–7.

[2] E. Lipson, *The Economic History of England* (edn. 1947), ii, 373–4. But as early as 1677 it was claimed that there had been a great increase of sheep in England due to the improvement of lands by cinquefoil and other seed and through the draining of the fens (*Cal. S.P. Dom. 1677–8*, p. 37).

[3] Thirsk, *Tudor Enclosures*, pp. 17–18; G. E. Fussell, 'Farming Methods in the early Stuart Period', *Journal of Modern History*, vii (1935), 129–32.

c

ticularly apt to attack animals which were fed upon moist and
marshy grounds. It was believed that sheep kept on marshland
should be given salt. Coastal marshes naturally possessed this
antidote, but shepherds were chary of inland marshes and wet
commons.[1] After wet seasons the mortality rate among sheep as
a result of the rot was sometimes extremely high. The year
ending November, 1628, must have been an unusually rainy
period on Tyneside, for during this time the sheep of Sir Ralph
Delaval 'rotted and decayed', and his stock was reduced from 12
or 13 hundred to 860.[2] The incidence of the disease was apt to
be particularly high among the large flocks of open-field sheep.
The small flocks, kept on enclosed pasture and given periodic
changes of grazing, normally enjoyed a much higher survival
rate. Wrote Houghton in February, 1693, 'I hear that sheep are
so rotten that there remains scarce two in twenty in the Fallow;
and those in the inclosures begin to fail.'[3] Once rot was suspected, farmers took immediate steps to dispose of their sheep
before it was too late. Thus a Northamptonshire gentleman in
1592, 'havinge intelligence by his servantes that had the chardge
of his said sheepe that some of them were perished and the
residue in daunger to be loste by means of the rotte,' decided to
make 'speedye sale of the same sheepe', despite the fact that by
so doing he placed himself open to proceedings upon a bond of
£250 for non-delivery of wool.[4] This practice of selling sheep
which were known to be suffering from the rot, made it all the
more necessary for buyers to be on their guard when making
their purchases. In spite of their watchfulness, however, they
could often count on buying a few rotten sheep. In 1586, one
Berkshire yeoman bought 100 sheep for £20, only to have them
all die from the rot within a month of their purchase.[5] The scab,
if not as deadly as the rot, stood foremost among the diseases
of the skin 'in frequency of occurrence and mischief to the wool,
the flesh and the general constitution of the animal'.[6] It was a

[1] L. Mascall, *The Countreyman's Jewel: Or the Governmente of Cattell* (1587), pp. 213,
339–40; Fitzherbert, *The Book of Husbandry, 1534* (ed. W. W. Skeat, 1882), pp.
50–2.
[2] Newcastle Central Reference Library, Delaval Papers, Box 17/A, fol. 22.
[3] J. Houghton, *A Collection for the Improvement of Husbandry and Trade* (edn. 1728),
p. 81.
[4] P.R.O. Req. 2/212/72.
[5] Campbell, op. cit., p. 201. See also *Robert Loder's Farm Accounts, 1610–1620*, p. 40.
[6] W. Youatt, *Sheep, Their Breeds, Management and Diseases* (edn. 1890), p. 536.

contagious disease and could cause considerable loss to farmers once it broke out among their flocks.

Sheep ailments were dealt with in detail by many contemporary medical and household books. One of the most popular preventative measures was probably that used by Henry Best, who treated his lambs and young sheep all over their bodies with a mixture of melted tallow and tar in the belief that this would keep the animals 'free from both scabbe and fith', make them more resistant to bad weather, and increase the weight of their fleeces.[1] Various other treatments were also tried. Among the commodities purchased by Sir Drayner Massingberd for sheep salve in 1657 and 1658 were small quantities of white mercury, tobacco and alum, as well as grease and tar.[2] Severe winters and accidents, as well as diseases, could make sheep farming a hazardous business; and if the profits that were made were sometimes large, at other times there might be heavy losses.

v

When a farmer desired to buy sheep, either to stock his lands for the first time or to add to his flocks, he usually visited one or more of the nearby markets or fairs. Markets were frequently held. Sheep fairs were rarer and more important occasions. Held usually in the spring, late summer or early autumn, they gave the farmer every opportunity to sell off unwanted stock and a wide selection from which he could buy in new.

The size of individual transactions naturally varied. Sometimes a substantial yeoman or a well-to-do gentleman might buy as many as 1,000 sheep at a single purchase,[3] but such cases were probably exceptional. Yeomen were numerous among the buyers of sheep; but their purchases at the sales in certain Leicestershire markets from 1612 to 1624 were seldom in excess of 200 sheep and lambs at one time, and more frequently were between four or five to twenty or thirty animals apiece.[4]

Middlemen were also active among the buyers and sellers of sheep, and some at least of their business was done with farmers who could not afford the expense or time involved in visiting

[1] *Rural Economy in Yorkshire in 1641*, p. 29.
[2] L.A.O. MM. VI/1/3.
[3] P.R.O. Req. 2/32/73; Req. 2/198/32.
[4] Campbell, op. cit., p. 204.

the fairs. The activities of these dealers were restricted, however, by a statute passed in 1551–2,[1] which required that sheep should not be resold within five weeks of purchase.

Sheep dealers and farmers alike incurred charges and toll payments, both at the fairs and markets and on the roads to and from them. Drivers and other helpers had to be paid, and both they and the sheep which they herded required overnight accommodation and food if on the roads for more than one day. The total expense involved in despatching or collecting sheep varied considerably, the main factor being the distance between the points of departure and destination. Thus the cost to Lord Dormer of sending sheep from Oxfordshire to London in the summer of 1600 amounted to between one and two per cent. of the value of the animals involved,[2] while the corresponding figure in the case of sheep purchased locally for the Earl of Middlesex's estates in the Midlands in 1628 averaged only one half per cent.[3]

Once a farmer had accepted delivery of sheep, responsibility for their safe-keeping rested mainly with the shepherd and his dog. In open-field villages a common shepherd was engaged by the tenantry to tend sheep and guard them against thieves and wool pluckers. In the large specialized undertakings shepherds were quite often the only permanent employees, though the wealthiest graziers usually appointed a sheep reeve to exercise supervision over the shepherds of the various flocks, and in the mid-sixteenth century, Sir Richard Southwell of Wood Rising, in Norfolk, found it necessary to employ a 'Supervisor of all the flocks' as well.[4] Of the fourteen flocks, totalling almost 10,000 sheep, which Southwell possessed at this time, seven consisted of ewes, four of wethers, two were mixed and one was composed of hoggs. Southwell's sheep farm was entirely self-supporting. After selling his poor quality lambs to butchers, he either transferred his store lambs directly to other flocks or sent them to the hogg reserve.[5] Also largely self-supporting, but on a much less ambitious scale, were the three flocks — of ewes, wethers,

---

[1] *Statutes of the Realm*, 5 Edward VI, c. 14. This Act was not intended to hamper the trade of the common drovers, who moved animals considerable distances before reselling them.
[2] Lord Dormer's Papers, 1600–30.
[3] K.A.O. U.269/A.418/2.
[4] Allison, *Econ. Hist. Rev.* 2nd ser. xi (1958), 110.
[5] Ibid., p. 101.

and hoggs and shearlings[1] — owned by Thomas Grantham, Esq., in the 1590's and in charge of his three shepherds, Edward Lamming, William Brinkell and Richard Brinkell respectively.[2]

Shepherds were usually hired annually, at Midsummer, Michaelmas or Martinmas (11th November). Their wages varied considerably from employer to employer and from flock to flock, and were normally paid annually, biannually or quarterly. A substantial part of the shepherd's wage often took the form of allowances. These might include permission to keep a specified number of sheep with the master's flock, gifts of lambs and fleeces, the provision of house or land rent-free, an allowance of grain or clothes, and the opportunity to purchase old hurdles for firewood.[3] For instance, in the year commencing Martinmas, 1624, Henry Best hired Simon Hewson as shepherd to his flock of 250 sheep, allowing him '4^{li} in money 6 sheep wintered his howse rent and two bush[els] of oats besides 1^s godspenny'.[4] The total value of these items contrasted favourably with the payment which Best's other agricultural workers received. Apart from shepherd's wages the substantial sheep farmer also incurred other labour charges. Additional workers were required for a variety of purposes during the year. For example, assistance might be required with the greasing of hoggs or the gelding of lambs. At shearing time a whole host of extra workers had to be taken on; but even on less hectic occasions there was much to be done.

Whenever a farmer purchased any sheep, he or his employees marked them with his sign at the first favourable opportunity. He similarly marked the lambs from his own flock, usually within about a month of their birth, and his sheep as soon as they had been sheared. Some such form of identification was necessary as a safeguard against animals being lost or stolen; and more especially so when they were grazed on the commons or the moors together with those of other owners. Even when they were marked, sheep were sometimes stolen and their symbol altered so as to resemble that of someone else. Under such circumstances it is hardly surprising that farmers endeavoured

---

[1] i.e. sheep between about 15 and 27 months.
[2] L.A.O. And. 1, fols. 26–7, 35–6, 42–3, 50–1.
[3] Allison, *Econ. Hist. Rev.* 2nd ser. xi (1958), 110.
[4] Account Book of Henry Best, 1617–44, fol. 27 (in the possession of Mr. M. Kirkby of York).

to make their identity marks as clear and as indelible as possible. Accordingly they chose a fair and dry day for the task in order to avoid marking wet wool which did not retain the sign.[1] Sheep bought by Adam Eyre at Tidesell fair were later marked with an H for Haverhead, the name of his farmstead. Like many other farmers, Eyre used fresh ruddle for the marking.[2] A mixture of tar and pitch, which was extremely difficult to remove from the fleece, was also used for marking purposes. Its employment was viewed with great disfavour by cloth manufacturers and wool middlemen, who never tired of pointing out that the wool which they purchased was often spoilt by irremovable pitch marks.[3] Badly tarred wool was accordingly sometimes put on one side to be sold at a substantial discount.[4]

Scientific breeding was impracticable under the open-field system of agriculture. When the sheep and cattle of all owners were herded together, even ordinary care in management was made difficult. Farmers with enclosed pastures were better placed to improve their stock; but even with them, there was little that could be called 'scientific' in the methods employed. If a farmer wanted and could afford a superior breed of sheep, he simply bought animals of the type which he fancied and stocked his grounds with them, or crossed them with the inferior breed which he wished to improve. As the leading flock masters in the country, the Northamptonshire Spencers were sometimes asked for their assistance in the matter. Thus in 1602 Sir Robert Spencer received a letter from Thomas, Lord Burghley, asking if he might buy '60 yowes and fower Tuppes[5] oute of yor choysest' in order to stock certain grounds with 'suche as are of good breede'.[6] This was a favour which farmers poorer or less influential than Burghley would probably neither ask for nor could afford;[7] and for them the problem of obtaining a suitable

---

[1] Campbell, op. cit., pp. 200–1; *Rural Economy in Yorkshire in 1641*, pp. 22, 71, 83.

[2] Campbell, op. cit., p. 200; *V.C.H. Dorset*, ii, 325.

[3] *B.M. Pamphlets, 712. g. 16 (3)*, p. 1; Youatt, op. cit., p. 556; *Rural Economy in Yorkshire in 1641*, pp. 22, 27.

[4] L.A.O. HEN.3/2; K.A.O. U.269/A.418/5, fol. 7b; U.269/A.418/6, fol. 5; U.269/A.419/2, fol. 1; U.269/A.419/3; U.269/A.424; Lumley MS. 2305 (in the possession of the Earl of Scarbrough).

[5] i.e. rams.

[6] B.M. Add. MS. 25079, fol. 55.

[7] Writing in 1662, Fuller noted that good Buckinghamshire breeding rams were selling at more than £10 apiece (T. Fuller, *The History of the Worthies of England* (edn. 1840), i. 193).

breed was usually solved by a visit to a fair or market, or by a purchase from a grazier of lesser repute than the Spencers.

Though there was still much to be learnt about breeding, enlightened farmers were well aware of the most fundamental of all principles in improving flock management. 'The most judicious sheep men,' stated Henry Best, 'endeavour by all meanes possible to provide goode tuppes for their ewes; for they say "a bad ewe may bringe a bad lambe yet she spoyles but one, butt an ill tuppe is likely to spoyle many".'[1] The ratio of rams to ewes varied considerably from flock to flock and, within the same flock, from year to year. On the estates of the Heneage family, an average of one tup to every 16 ewes was allowed during the years 1619–32, the ratio ranging from 1 : 7 (in 1622) to 1 : 31 (in 1619).[2] At Careby in the 1630's the Hatchers kept an average of 20 ewes for every ram.[3] At Spindleston Farm, near Bamburgh, Northumberland, Sir Francis Radcliffe was allowing one tup to every 39 ewes in 1676, and one to 29 in 1681.[4] The latter ratio came near to that of one to 30 advocated by Best forty years earlier. Best used a ram between two and five shear (that is, between about 27 months and six years old). The female was also restrained from breeding until after it had been shorn twice.[5] Best disposed of his ewes before they reached the age of eight but many men, he stated, found it profitable to keep them for several years longer.[6] In fixing the tupping period, Tudor and Stuart farmers paid due regard to the time of growth and the quality of the succeeding spring pasture. The earlier and better the spring keep the earlier was lambing practicable. Early lambing had a number of advantages, not least of which was the fact that it made possible the finishing of some forward lambs by May, when they were still scarce and selling well. Best ensured that his ewes should be well stocked with milk at lambing time by putting them into a good pasture, or on peas or oats. He favoured a long suckling period, for he found that lambs weaned early proved 'short runtish sheep'.[7]

[1] *Rural Economy in Yorkshire in 1641*, p. 4.
[2] L.A.O. HEN.3/2.
[3] L.A.O. H.97/22/1, fol. 48.
[4] Spindleston Farm Accounts, 1676–95 (in the possession of Miss M. Simpson of Wooler, Northumberland).
[5] *Rural Economy in Yorkshire in 1641*, pp. 2, 4.
[6] Ibid., pp. 1–2.
[7] Ibid., pp. 3, 12; Fitzherbert, op. cit., pp. 42–3; Trow-Smith, op. cit., pp. 243–4.

Nowadays, lambing rates in Britain seldom fall below 1·0 and sometimes rise to 2·0 lambs per ewe per annum. In Tudor and Stuart England lambing rates sometimes fell to 0·3, and though in a good flock they occasionally reached 0·95 — as at Spindleston in 1676[1] — an average of 1·0 was (with the possible exception of Dorset and Wiltshire ewes)[2] rarely, if ever, achieved. Rates varied a great deal from flock to flock and from year to year. Inferior feed and management doubtless contributed much to the ewes' infertility, while bad winters brought down the lambing average quite sharply. A slight long-term improvement can be discerned over the sixteenth and seventeenth centuries as a whole, this probably being due to better feeding together with improved knowledge and methods.[3]

After lambing time — usually late February or March — it was not long before preparations began to be made for the summer clipping. Sheep shearing involved three major operations: washing, clipping and winding. Sheep were usually sheared between the beginning and middle of June. Experienced farmers were not to be hurried into clipping their sheep. They preferred to wait until the wool had become loose and well risen from the skin. This facilitated both clipping and winding, and was a guarantee that the sheep would be left with a good undergrowth whereby they would be the better protected against a storm.[4]

The purpose of washing sheep was to remove, so far as was possible, such impurities as dirt, sand and grease which had collected in the fleece. Impurities added to the weight of the fleece, and wool not properly washed was subjected to severe criticism by those who bought it. For the same reason, damp wool was also censured.[5] The washing of sheep was carried out either by the farmer himself, or, if he owned a substantial number of sheep, by hired workmen who were known as washers. According to Henry Best, a man proficient at the task could wash more than 100 sheep in a day. At the time Best wrote, in 1641, a washer was usually paid 3d. for every score of sheep which

[1] Spindleston Farm Accounts, 1676–95.
[2] See supra, pp. 11–12.
[3] Allison, *Econ. Hist. Rev.* xi (1958), 103–4; Allison, *thesis*, pp. 320–1; L.A.O. HEN.3/2.
[4] *Rural Economy in Yorkshire in 1641*, pp. 17–20.
[5] Ibid., p. 27; P.R.O. C.1/705/20; C.1/841/45; C.1/1111/60; Req. 2/118/37.

passed through his hands. Some farmers had additional payments to make:

> ... such as are forced to goe to other townes for wante of water att hoame, pay oftentimes 2d. a score for gatelaw, and 2d. a score towards the maintaining of the sheep-dyke, besides that they pay to the washers.[1]

The shearing of sheep was undertaken from one day to a fortnight after they were washed, depending on the length of time it took the wool to rise and the promise of continuing fine weather.[2] When a great flock master's sheep were sheared, the scene was one of great activity. Sir Moyle Finch, who had four flocks shorn at the same time, employed 49 clippers at the task, besides numerous other helpers.[3] At Spindleston the 1,560 sheep which required rounding up and shearing in 1676, kept 12 clippers and 3 'takers' busy for three days. Almost a month later — in early July — 8 clippers and 2 'takers' were employed to shear the flock's 770 lambs.[4] This practice of clipping lambs was the custom in some parts of the country, though it was not generally adopted.

It took longer to shear sheep than to wash them. Best alleged that a man proficient at the task could clip 80 or 90 sheep a day, given an early start,[5] but this target seems to have been beyond most workers. At Careby in the 1630's and at Spindleston in the 1670's each clipper averaged only 40–45 sheep daily. Possibly part of the explanation for this difference lies in the system of wage payment used. Both Hatcher and Radcliffe paid their clippers time rates: 1s. and 1s. 2d. per day respectively.[6] The four or five clippers employed by Best, on the other hand, received piece-rates: 4d. for every score of sheep sheared, plus ale, bread and cheese at noon, a dinner at night and an extra 2d. or 3d. for drink.[7] A few years earlier, in 1626, Sir Richard Townshend paid the clippers who dealt with his 1,747 sheep, 3s. for every 100 ewes and hoggs sheared and 3s. 4d. for every 100

[1] *Rural Economy in Yorkshire in 1641*, p. 18.
[2] Ibid., pp. 19–20.
[3] Ibid., pp. 96–7.
[4] Spindleston Farm Accounts, 1676–95.
[5] *Rural Economy in Yorkshire in 1641*, p. 21.
[6] L.A.O. H.97/22/1, 2; Spindleston Farm Accounts, 1676–95.
[7] *Rural Economy in Yorkshire in 1641*, p. 21.

wethers. The clippers were also fed by Townshend, four cheeses costing him 9s. 4d.[1]

An essential pre-requisite at shearing-time was tar, which large sheep farmers bought in considerable quantities.[2] The tar, which was always at hand, was to apply to the skin of sheep if they were pricked during the shearing and to mark them with afterwards.

After clipping, fleeces, were 'wound' (i.e. wrapped or folded up). This work called for care and a certain amount of skill, for it was desirable that kempy or hairy parts of the fleece should not be visible after winding as this tended to detract from the market value. Specialist wool winders travelled about the countryside during the summer months looking for employment. They were not always on hand at shearing time, however, and a farmer might engage part-time workers to fold his fleeces. William Walker and John Short, who wound 4,662 fleeces for the Earl of Middlesex in August and September, 1628, were evidently specialists. They were well paid for their labour, wrapping 3,390 fleeces at Milcote (co. Warwick) at 4d. per score and 1,272 at Sezincote (co. Gloucs.) at 6d.[3]

After wool had been wound it was normally laid out on a boarded and damp-free floor to await tithing and sale. Both wool and lambs were regarded as small tithes; and whether they were paid in kind or whether the incumbent accepted cash payment in lieu, the difference they made to the sheep owner's income was substantial. Farmers naturally disliked paying the tithe, and sometimes used tactics which varied from dishonesty to downright refusal in order to avoid doing so. Not surprisingly, tithe wool was a subject of frequent litigation. Broadly speaking, the law was invoked for one of two reasons: to enforce the payment of unpaid tithes, or else to settle disputes which had arisen as to their rightful ownership. Controversy sometimes arose over the payment of tithe wool due from sheep which had been bought and sold. The usual ruling made the buyer responsible for payment if the sheep were purchased before Candlemas (2nd February) and the seller liable if they were sold after that

---

[1] Allison, *thesis*, pp. 223–4.
[2] For example, in the period 29th May–30th December, 1676, Sir Francis Radcliffe purchased 49½ gallons of tar and 8 lbs. of pitch, at a total cost of £2 9s. 9d. See Spindleston Farm Accounts, 1676–95.
[3] K.A.O. U.269/A.418/2, fol. 23; U.269/A.419/1.

date. At other times there were differences of opinion when
farmers sheared their sheep in one parish and refused to pay
tithes in a neighbouring parish where the sheep had been fed
during the year; and disputes as to which church or chapel
should receive the tithes were also frequent.[1]

VI

The main object of sheep farming in Tudor and Stuart times was
the production of wool, and to a consideration of wool types we
must now turn. The kinds of wool produced in different parts of
the country varied considerably, and although in discussing this
subject we shall indicate the predominant characteristics of a
fleece by referring to its wool as being fine or coarse, short or
long, it should be borne in mind that fleeces were never of a
uniform fineness or length of staple throughout. Long and short
wool, fine and coarse wool, might all grow in the same fleece,
though in different proportions.[2]

Various influences determined the fineness of fibre and the
length of staple. Until Robert Bakewell's time, the type of wool
which a sheep produced depended almost exclusively on its
environment; and even today, when management plays a much
more important role, a breed adapts itself to environment and
the wool very quickly manifests this adaptation. Soil, herbage
and climate have a conclusive effect on fleece weights and wool
types, and it has been remarked that sheep moved, for instance,
from Suffolk to Yorkshire today would show a change in wool
characteristics within a few months.[3]

According to Youatt, who wrote in the nineteenth century,
'the natural tendency to produce wool of a certain fibre being
the same, sheep in a hot climate will yield a comparatively coarse
wool, and those in a cold climate will carry a finer, but at the
same time a closer and a warmer fleece.' Thus if sheep are carried

---

[1] P.R.O. C.1/1067/27; C.1/1170/59; C.1/1222/73–5; C.1/1315/36; C.1/1368/14–7;
C.3/397/6; Req. 2/32/73; St. Ch. 8/190/21; E.134/2 James I. East. 12; *Rural
Economy in Yorkshire in 1641*, pp. 24, 26; Allison, *Econ. Hist. Rev.* 2nd ser. xi (1958),
106.

[2] P.R.O. S.P. 16/515/139; Youatt, op. cit., p. 66. There were other ways in
addition to fineness of fibre and length of staple in which wools could vary from
each other. They could, for instance, differ in the 'trueness' of staple, in strength of
fibres, in softness, in elasticity and in colour (Youatt, pp. 72–8). A consideration of these matters, however, lies outside the scope of this study.

[3] H. Haigh and B. A. Newton, *The Wools of Britain* (1952), pp. 5, 42–3.

from a cold to a warmer climate, their fleece from being fine and thick, tends to become thin and coarse, and at length degenerates into hair. When sheep are starved, however, extreme cold is injurious to the quality of the fleece and it becomes coarse, or loses much in weight, strength and usefulness.[1]

Pasturage — which is itself affected by climate — has a much greater direct influence than temperature upon the fineness of the fleece and the length of its staple. The more nutriment which a sheep receives the larger it becomes. The staple of the wool is no exception and, like every other part of the animal, increases in length and bulk as a result of better feeding.[2] The short-woolled sheep is the native of poor pastures, hills, moors and downs. The long-woolled sheep belongs to rich grasslands, marshes and fens. In the Middle Ages, however, potentially the richest grazing area in England — the great midland clay plain — was largely under the plough, with the open-field sheep finding what grazing they could on the common wastes and the corn-stubble left after harvest. Before the Tudor period the production of long-staple wool in England was negligible; but the enclosures for pasture farming of the mid-fifteenth century onward provided improved grassland feeding for sheep, and the predominantly short and fine medieval wool of the Midlands and Lincolnshire was gradually replaced by a longer and coarser staple.[3] It was in central England that the bulk of the country's fine, short-staple wool had been produced in the Middle Ages. This had enjoyed an unsurpassed reputation for fineness in the markets of medieval Europe. But with the spread of the enclosures for sheep farming and the deterioration in the quality of the English fleece Spanish wool began to be held in greater esteem. Already, in the early sixteenth century, it was

[1] Youatt, op. cit., pp. 68–70; *An Enquiry into the Nature and Qualities of English Wools, By a Gentleman Farmer* (1788), p. 18. In 1480–1, when 2,000 of Sir Roger Townshend's sheep died and a bad winter reduced the increase of lambs, his accountant declared that it was 'an evell yere for wull' and the normal average rate of 10 fleeces per stone was increased to 14 (Allison, *Econ. Hist. Rev.* 2nd ser. xi (1958), 105).

[2] Youatt, op. cit., p. 70.

[3] The findings of Dr. M. L. Ryder, who has examined the follicle remains in some British parchments, support historical records which mention the extreme fineness of medieval wool and provide additional evidence of an increase in the supply of long-staple wool in the sixteenth and seventeenth centuries. See M. L. Ryder, 'Follicle Remains in Some British Parchments', *Nature*, vol. 187, no. 4732 (1960), 130–2.

noticed that English wool was losing its reputation for fineness to Spanish wool,[1] and by the end of the Tudor period the latter was almost certainly superior. After the mid-seventeenth century not even English writers could deny that Spanish wool was the finest in the world.[2]

These developments, however, were not without their compensations for the English sheep farmer, for while the quality of wool went down, the yield per sheep went up.[3] If contemporary estimates are to be trusted, the average weight of the English fleece increased from about 1·4 lbs. in the mid-fourteenth century to 1·9 lbs. in the mid-sixteenth, and to 3·5 lbs. in the mid-eighteenth century.[4] By the latter date new fodder crops and improved farming techniques were helping to provide better feed for livestock, so that in 1741 an estimated 44 per cent. of the raw wool produced in the United Kingdom was of the long-staple variety.[5] It is doubtful whether the corresponding figure for the year 1600 reached 20 per cent.

In Fig. 1 an attempt has been made to plot the geographical distribution of long and short wools in England at the end of the Tudor period. Based mainly upon statements made by contemporaries and on inferences drawn from the uses to which different types of wool were put,[6] due allowance should be made for the possibility of a fairly wide margin of error. There can, however, be no doubt as to the preponderance of short-wool production in England at this time. Even in that central, north-eastern to south-western wedge of counties, where the production of long wool was mainly concentrated, there were very

[1] *Tudor Economic Documents*, ed. R. H. Tawney and E. Power (1924), iii, 102.

[2] See, for example, *England's Glory, by the Benefit of Wool Manufactured therein* (1669), p. 11; Lipson, op. cit., iii, 31.

[3] P. J. Bowden, 'Wool Supply and the Woollen Industry', *Econ. Hist. Rev.* 2nd ser. ix (1956), 44–51.

[4] *Tudor Economic Documents*, iii, 180; P. Deane, 'The Output of the British Woolen Industry in the Eighteenth Century', *Journal of Economic History*, xvii (1957), 211, n. 11.

[5] P. Deane, op. cit., p. 211. The production of long wool was estimated at 114,000 packs out of a total of 262,175 packs.

[6] The division of wool into short and long staple is one of convenience. In actual fact, there were considerable variations in the length of staple. Broadly speaking, very short to medium length wool was used in the production of woollen cloth and medium to long wool used in the manufacture of worsted (see infra, pp. 41–2). The criterion for short wool employed in the compilation of Fig. 1 was suitability for manufacture into woollens; the criterion for long wool was suitability for worsted. Wool of medium length staple has been included with long wool, even though it may have been used in the production of woollen cloth.

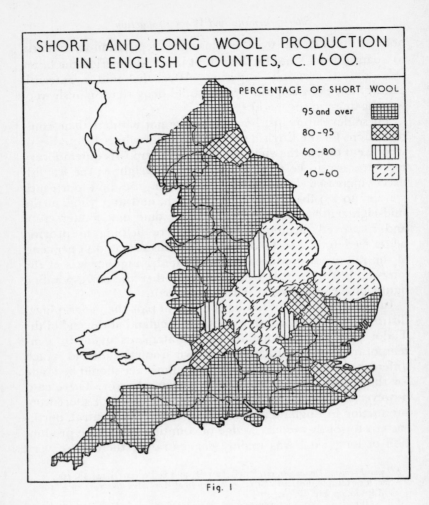

SHORT AND LONG WOOL PRODUCTION IN ENGLISH COUNTIES, C. 1600.

PERCENTAGE OF SHORT WOOL

95 and over

80 - 95

60 - 80

40 - 60

Fig. 1

considerable quantities of short-to-medium length staple grown.

The qualities of wool given in Fig. 2 are essentially averages for a county. The criterion of high quality was fineness of fibre, and the finest wools commanded the highest prices. The main sources of evidence which have been drawn upon in compiling this diagram have therefore been price-lists of different varieties of wool, and the opinions expressed by contemporaries on the subject.

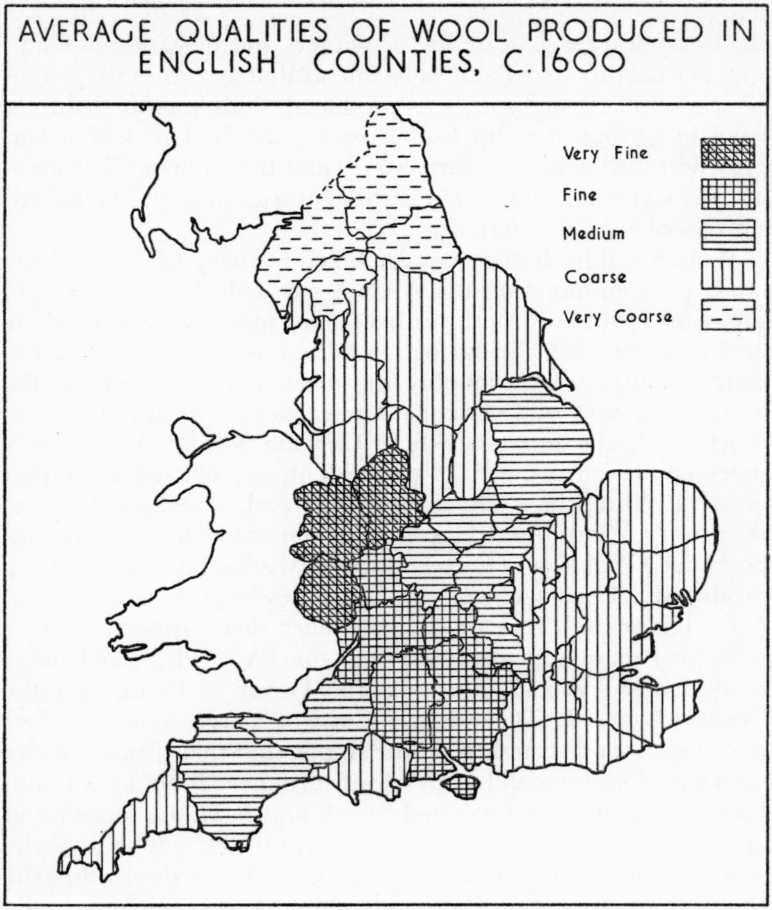

AVERAGE QUALITIES OF WOOL PRODUCED IN
ENGLISH COUNTIES, C.1600

Very Fine
Fine
Medium
Coarse
Very Coarse

Fig. 2

VII

Among English wools 'Lemster Ore' held first place for fineness
from the fifteenth century until long after the end of the seventeenth. Of short staple, and usually weighing not more than
one pound in the fleece,[1] this wool was obtained from the small
Ryeland or Herefordshire breed of sheep: a breed better able

[1] *V.C.H. Hereford*, i, 409. Even in the nineteenth century the weight of the fleece
rarely exceeded 2 lbs. (Youatt, op. cit., p. 258).

than any other to endure severe winters and privation of food.[1] Further north, a wool almost as fine as that grown in the neighbourhood of Leominster, was produced. This was the 'March' wool of Shropshire and Staffordshire, the best of which was grown in the vicinity of Shrewsbury and Bridgnorth.[2] Throughout the sixteenth and seventeenth centuries only the Herefordshire wool was finer than this.

Worcestershire had no county breed of sheep.[3] Possibly Ryelands predominated on the fallows, particularly in the west of the county, with Shropshires becoming more numerous in the north. Cotswolds, being better suited to the hilly pastures further south, were probably the most popular breed on the high lands east of Evesham. These breeds produced a fine, short wool, the finest of which Gervase Markham, an early seventeenth-century writer on agriculture, classed with that grown in Shropshire. On the enclosed and richer grasslands of the county, a 'large boned sheep of deepest staple' had made its appearance.[4] Probably of the transformed Midland breed, this sheep produced a fleece varying from four to seven pounds in weight.[5]

In Tudor and Stuart Gloucestershire there appears to have been two main varieties of sheep: the Ryelands, which were numerically few and inhabited the Forest of Dean, and the Cotswolds breed. The original Cotswolds were heavier, their wool longer and straighter in the staple, and their fleece coarser than was the case with the Herefordshire sheep;[6] but for all that, they were a fine short-woolled breed, and in Gloucestershire at any rate, they largely remained so until after the end of the seventeenth century. There can, however, be no doubt that the characteristics of the Cotswolds sheep were very gradually changing. The deterioration in the quality of their wool and the increase in its length of staple became general in the eighteenth century; and when Rudder wrote in 1779, it was used only for the manufacture of worsteds and coarse cloths.[7]

[1] Ibid.
[2] P.R.O. C.3/200/90.
[3] *V.C.H. Worcester.* ii, 310.
[4] G. Markham, *Cheap and Good Husbandry* (edn. 1676), p. 85; Prothero, op. cit., p. 138.
[5] *Commons Debates, 1621*, ed. W. Notestein, F. H. Relf and H. Simpson (New Haven, 1935), vii, 499.
[6] Prothero, op. cit., p. 138.
[7] *V.C.H. Gloucester*, ii, 163; P. J. Bowden, *Econ. Hist. Rev.* 2nd ser. ix (1956), 50.

The exaggerated praises which Defoe[1] and other writers of the seventeenth and eighteenth centuries bestowed upon the long wools of Lincolnshire and Leicestershire[2] are too well-known to need repetition. It is perhaps unfortunate that the same authors failed to mention that short wools were also grown in the two counties, though in smaller quantities than in earlier years; had they not made this omission, it is doubtful whether economic historians would have been so ready to persuade themselves that all Lincolnshire and Leicestershire wools were long, in spite of evidence suggestive of the contrary. Though an abundance of long wool was grown in these two counties at the end of the seventeenth century, this had not been the case in the Middle Ages nor, indeed, at the beginning of the Tudor period. Until at least the mid-sixteenth century the greater part of the wool produced in Lincolnshire and Leicestershire must have been short or comparatively short in staple — the produce of potentially long-woolled sheep.[3] The output of short and middle[4] wools was still very substantial at the end of the early Stuart period, and in the 1660's and 70's it could still take four, five, six and even seven Lincolnshire fleeces to make a stone.[5] Indeed, short-woolled sheep were yet to be found in the two counties at the beginning of the nineteenth century;[6] not even the efforts of Bakewell and other improvers of the long-woolled breeds had succeeded in totally eradicating them.

The finest Lincolnshire staple came from the Wolds. This wool had been the finest in England in the mid-fourteenth century,[7] and in the mid-fifteenth it was inferior only to the higher qualities of wool produced in Hereford, Shropshire and the Cotswolds. The wools grown in the remainder of the county and in Leicestershire were less fine, but a price-list for the year 1454 shows that their quality was, on the whole, considerably above the average of wools produced elsewhere in

---

[1] Defoe, op. cit., ii, 488.

[2] Including Rutland.

[3] It is possible, though far from certain, that the wools grown in Lincolnshire and Leicestershire had always been, on average, slightly longer than those grown elsewhere in England. Even so, unless their staples were more than about six inches in length, they would count as short, and not as long wools.

[4] i.e. wools of an intermediate length of staple.

[5] L.A.O. MM. VI/5/2, 4, 5, 17, 18, 27, 28; *V.C.H. Lincoln*, ii, 335; P. J. Bowden, *Econ. Hist. Rev.* 2nd ser. ix (1956), 48–51.

[6] Youatt, op. cit., p. 344.

[7] *Foedera*, ed. T. Rymer (1708), v, 369.

D

England.[1] Though much good-quality wool was still being produced in the two counties during the early years of the seventeenth century, it was neither as fine nor as short as formerly.[2] The worst wool came from the salt marshes of Lincolnshire. The sheep kept here were stated to be the largest in England; of them Markham commented, 'their legges and bellies are long and naked, and their staple is coarser than any other.'[3] The fleece of the Lincolnshire breed continued to deteriorate as the seventeenth century progressed. But Mortimer was able to report in 1707 that recent endeavours to improve the quality of the wool had met with encouraging results.[4]

The wools produced in Oxfordshire, Buckinghamshire, Warwickshire and Northamptonshire went through the same stages of development as those grown in Lincolnshire and Leicestershire, and by 1570 the four counties had become recognized as important suppliers of wool for the worsted manufacture.[5] The increase in the production of long wool in these counties is apparent from the remarks and writings of contemporaries. Writing at the end of the sixteenth century Camden noted 'vast numbers of well-fleeced sheep' at Quarrendon, Eythorp and Winchinden in Buckinghamshire.[6] The Eythorp sheep may well have belonged to Lord Dormer, who had large flocks grazing at Eythorp and Wing (co. Bucks.) in 1615.[7] The sheep at Quarrendon were probably the property of the Lee family, who were lords of the manor here and at Ditchley (co. Oxford), and who possessed pastures sufficiently rich and extensive to permit the sale in 1598 of 4,905 fleeces at an average weight of 4·1 lbs. each.[8] In the early decades of the seventeenth century attention was drawn to the increase in the production of heavy fleeces in Oxfordshire and Buckinghamshire,[9] and it was remarked, 'the ordinary sheep about War-

---

[1] *Rotuli Parliamentorum*, v. 275. (Printed in J. E. T. Rogers, *A History of Agriculture and Prices in England* (Oxford, 1886), iii, 704).

[2] The deterioration in the quality of the Lincolnshire and Leicestershire wools after 1454 is apparent from their lower ranking in price-lists of 1536 and 1582. See P.R.O. S.P. 1/102, fols. 1–2; S.P. 12/154/30; Hist. MSS. Comm. *Salisbury MSS.* xiii, 55.

[3] Markham, op. cit., p. 85.

[4] Prothero, op. cit., p. 139.

[5] Infra, p. 132.

[6] Camden, op. cit., pp. 326–31.

[7] Lord Dormer's Papers, 1600–30.

[8] Oxfordshire Archives Office, DIL.III/b/2; *V.C.H. Buckingham*, iv. 101.

[9] *Commons Debates, 1621*, vii, 499.

wicke and those which will prosper there are exceeding coarse.'[1]
According to Markham, parts of Warwickshire and Northamptonshire and all Buckinghamshire produced a 'large-boned
sheep, of the best shape and deepest staple'.[2] Some time later
Fuller was greatly impressed by the Vale of Aylesbury sheep,
which he claimed were 'the best and biggest bodied' in England.[3]
By the third quarter of the seventeenth century, therefore, the
major part of the wool produced in the four counties was being
manufactured into worsted.[4]

While the wools of the Midlands were losing their reputation
for fineness, those grown in the western peninsula were gaining
in estimation. The latter wools had been almost too coarse to be
worth exporting during the later Middle Ages. Somerset wool
had then been the best of these and Cornish wool, which was
contemptuously referred to as 'Cornish hair', the worst.[5] The
wools of Dorset and Devonshire had occupied an intermediate
position.

Throughout the Tudor and Stuart periods the wools of all
four counties apparently improved relatively to those grown
elsewhere in England. Cornish wool, which was mainly used in
the manufacture of coarse cloth during Elizabeth's reign,[6] was
stated in 1582 to be 'verye good and much bettere and plenty
fullere then in tymes past'.[7] It continued to gain in estimation
during the seventeenth century, when it was frequently used in
the production of medium-quality cloth: a use to which most of
the Devonshire wool was put in the sixteenth, as well as in the
seventeenth century.[8] Though a certain amount of good-
quality wool was produced in Dorset at the beginning of the
Stuart period, the larger part of the county's wool was comparatively coarse and of less value than that grown in Devonshire.[9] It appears to have improved in later years, and by the end

[1] *H. of C. Journals*, i. 653.
[2] Markham, op. cit., p. 85.
[3] Fuller, op. cit., i. 193.
[4] *England's Glory, by the Benefit of Wool Manufactured therein* (1669), pp. 11–12;
V.C.H. Northampton, ii. 332.
[5] E. Power, 'The Wool Trade in the Fifteenth Century', *Studies in English Trade in
the Fifteenth Century*, ed. E. Power and M. M. Postan (1933), p. 49.
[6] *Statutes of the Realm*, 27 Elizabeth I, c. 18.
[7] *Tudor Economic Documents*, i, 194.
[8] Infra, pp. 49–50, 60.
[9] P.R.O. E.134/6 James I. East 30. One witness stated: '. . . the best wolle
growen in Devon' is 'better then the dorsetshier wolle by five pence or vj[d] in the
pound'.

of the Stuart period was being classed with that of Somerset.[1] The sheep kept in the four south-western counties were all short-woolled breeds.[2] In spite of what has been said to the contrary,[3] Devonshire does not appear to have produced long combing wool in any quantity until towards the end of the eighteenth century. Even in 1800, most of the Devon sheep and all those kept in Somerset, Dorset and Cornwall were of the short or middle-woolled variety.[4]

Like the wools produced in the south-west of England, those grown in Wiltshire, Hampshire and Sussex had never been highly regarded during medieval times, but, like the south-western wools, they gained in esteem as the Midlands and Lincolnshire fleeces deteriorated in quality. The Wiltshire and Hampshire wools were highly praised, both at an inquiry held in 1638, and also subsequently by various surveyors of the industrial scene,[5] while the wool produced on the South Downs in Sussex seems to have so improved during the seventeenth century that John Haynes, writing in 1706, was able to rank it with 'Lemster Ore' as 'little inferior to the Spanish wool',[6] then the finest in the world. The Wiltshire, Hampshire and Sussex sheep all produced a short-staple fleece, which during the early Stuart period normally weighed between about $1\frac{1}{2}$ and 3 lbs.[7] A short-staple, good quality wool also seems to have been produced by the Berkshire sheep.[8]

In the later Middle Ages the wools grown in eastern England south of the Wash, with the notable exception of the relatively fine Banstead Down wool, had been generally coarse in quality; during the sixteenth and seventeenth centuries they probably became even coarser. Some of the best wool grown in this region during the Tudor period came from the counties of Bedford and Huntingdon, but this was no better than the inferior grades of

---

[1] *England's Glory* . . . , p. 11; *The Clothiers Complaint, or reasons for passing the Bill against the Blackwell Hall Factors* (1692), p. 7; *V.C.H. Dorset*, ii, 361.

[2] P.R.O. S.P. 16/515/139.

[3] See W. G. Hoskins, *Industry, Trade and People in Exeter, 1688–1800* (1935), p. 35; Stephens, op. cit., p. 4; B.M. Harl. MS. 5827, fol. 10.

[4] Youatt, op. cit., p. 344.

[5] P.R.O. E.134/14 Charles I. Mich. 20; *England's Glory* . . . , p. 11; *The Clothiers Complaint* . . . , p. 7; *V.C.H. Hampshire*, v, 426.

[6] J. Haynes, *A View of the Present State of the Clothing Trade in England* (1706), p. 14.

[7] Fielder Farm Accounts, 1630–1733. Bundle 19/1 (in the possession of Mrs. E. Dunlop of Funtington, Sussex); *Commons Debates, 1621*, vii, 499.

[8] P.R.O. S.P. 1/102, fols.1–2; S.P. 12/154/30; Hist. MSS. Comm. *Salisbury MSS.* xiii, 55.

Lincolnshire staple. Though Norden was broadly correct in stating that 'the moste barren and heathye groundes yelde beste woull', the 'verie fine woull' which he recorded as growing on the heaths of Essex in 1594[1] could, in fact, have been no more than medium quality. Though Kentish wool was described as 'thin' and 'hungry', the best of it ranked in 1669 as superior to that produced elsewhere in eastern and south-eastern England, with the exception of the Sussex downs.[2] The wools grown in Norfolk and Suffolk were among the coarsest in the country at the end of the early Stuart period, at about which time the price paid for the Suffolk wool was only one-fifth of that paid for the superior Herefordshire staple.[3]

By far the greatest proportion of the wool produced in eastern England south of the Wash must have been short in staple. But considerable quantities of longer wool were grown in Norfolk, in and around the Fens, and on Romney Marsh.

The bulk of the wool grown in Norfolk during the sixteenth and seventeenth centuries, and probably in the later Middle Ages, seems to have been of a medium-length staple, weighing between 1 and 2 lbs. in the fleece.[4] The coarseness of the wool and its poor felting property made it unsuitable for the manufacture of fine broadcloth and, until at least the beginning of the seventeenth century, it was worked up chiefly into worsted and, to a lesser extent, into coarse woollen cloth.[5] Later, when supplies of the longer and finer wools of Lincolnshire and Leicestershire became more abundant, Norfolk wool seems to have been used only for manufacture into the coarser varieties of woollens.[6]

Many of the sheep kept in Cambridgeshire during the early Stuart period were of the Norfolk and West Country breeds.[7] Though definite evidence is lacking, it seems probable that considerable quantities of long or middle wool were being grown

---

[1] *Norden's Description of Essex* (Camden Soc. 1st ser. ix, 1840), p. 9.
[2] *England's Glory* . . . , p. 11; *The Clothiers Complaint* . . . , p. 7; P.R.O. E.134/5 George I.Trin. 5.
[3] P.R.O. E.134/14 Charles I. Mich. 20; *Reasons Presented to the Parliament for a More Strict Prohibition of the Transportation of Wool, on Behalf of the Traders and Manufacturers in Wool.*
[4] Allison, *Econ. Hist. Rev.* 2nd ser. xi (1958), 104–5.
[5] *Statutes of the Realm*, 33 Henry VIII, c. 16; P.R.O. S.P. 14/80/13; E.134/44–5 Elizabeth I. Mich. 1.
[6] A. Young, *Tour through the East* (edn. 1771), ii, 74.
[7] *The Beauties of England: Cambs.* (1610), p. 19 (quoted *V.C.H. Cambridge*, ii, 75).

here and in the neighbouring county of Huntingdon at the beginning of the seventeenth century, particularly in the marshiest regions. A middle type of wool was certainly being produced in Bedfordshire at this time, to be used in the manufacture of worsted and coarse woollen cloth.[1]

At the beginning of the seventeenth century the fleece of the Romney Marsh sheep, like that of almost every other long-woolled breed, was probably little more than medium in length of staple. It, too, became longer and coarser, and in 1668 was stated to be fit only for combing.[2] Due mainly to the infiltration of the Romney Marsh breed,[3] long wool was also produced in other parts of Kent at this time, though in much smaller quantities than on the Marsh.

Most of the wool grown in England north of the Trent during the sixteenth and seventeenth centuries was both coarse and short. The four most northern counties had always produced very coarse wool.[4] During the early Stuart period attempts may have been made at improving the northern breeds of sheep.[5] If they were made, they seem to have met with little immediate success; for in 1638 the northern wools were still regarded as being among the worst that were grown in England.[6] With the possible exception of the wool produced on the banks of the Tees,[7] these were all short-staple wools, and were manufactured into only the most inferior types of woollen cloth.[8] Little, if at all better, were the wools of Lancashire and Cheshire.

A coarse fleece was also produced by the Yorkshire sheep. In Markham's opinion the breed was 'of reasonable bigge bone, but of a staple rough and hairie'[9]: a view which was subscribed to by Halifax manufacturers in 1638, when they stated that the Yorkshire wool was generally inferior to that grown in Lincoln-

---

[1] P.R.O. E.134/44–5 Elizabeth I. Mich. 1.

[2] P.R.O. S.P. 29/251/95 (i).

[3] Owing to the exposed character of the Marsh, young sheep could not be wintered in it. They were therefore removed inland, and did not return until the late spring of the following year. See Youatt, op. cit., p. 336; *V.C.H. Kent*, i. 464.

[4] Infra, p. 108.

[5] See P.R.O. E.134/14 Charles I. Mich. 20.

[6] P.R.O. E.134/14 Charles I. Mich. 21.

[7] See D. Defoe, *The Complete English Tradesman* (edn. 1738), ii, 279.

[8] B.M. Add. MS. 34324, fol. 15. Fleeces clipped at Spindleston, Northumberland, averaged 2·0 lbs. in 1681 and 1·6 lbs. in 1695 (Spindleston Farm Accounts, 1676–95).

[9] Markham, op. cit., p. 85; Prothero, op. cit., p. 139.

shire and Leicestershire.[1] Some middle or long wool may have been grown in parts of Holderness and on the banks of the Humber and the Tees; but the great bulk of the wool produced in Yorkshire during the seventeenth century — on the Wolds, the Moors and the Pennines — seems to have been of the coarse, short-staple variety,[2] the produce of a fleece of two to three pounds.[3] A similar type of wool was probably grown in most of Derbyshire; in parts of the county, however, a finer wool may have been produced by the small forest sheep.[4] In Nottingham-shire, a good-quality wool was supplied by the small Forest of Sherwood breed. During the early Stuart period this wool seems to have ranked equal for fineness with some of the shorter Lincoln and Leicester wools. A larger sheep, with a longer and coarser fleece, was kept in the remainder of the county;[5] and by the third quarter of the seventeenth century much of the wool produced by this animal was being adapted for the manufacture of worsted.[6]

VIII

It is possible to form a very approximate estimate of the number of sheep kept in England and Wales in the sixteenth century by calculations based on the amount of wool and cloth exported. During the period 1540–7, for example, the annual export of raw wool averaged 5,025 sacks, and the annual export of cloth (including worsted) averaged 124,750 cloths.[7] The latter, on the basis of $4\frac{1}{3}$ cloths to the sack,[8] would be the equivalent of 28,790 sacks of wool. If an addition of fifty per cent.[9] is made for wool used in the manufacture of cloth for the home market, we obtain a figure of 50,723 sacks as the total annual wool production in

[1] P.R.O. E.134/14 Charles I. Mich. 20.
[2] See Youatt, op. cit., p. 344.
[3] This was the average weight of the fleece produced by Henry Best's sheep (*Rural Economy in Yorkshire in 1641*, p. 24).
[4] See S. Glover, *History of Derbyshire* (1829), i, part i, p. 239; Youatt, op. cit., p. 304.
[5] P.R.O. E.134/14 Charles I. Mich. 20; Prothero, op. cit., pp. 138–9; *V.C.H. Nottingham*, ii, 343, 376.
[6] *England's Glory* . . . , pp. 11–12.
[7] These figures have been calculated from the table of export statistics of wool, cloth and worsted given in L. Stone, 'State Control in Sixteenth Century England', *Econ. Hist. Rev.* xvii (1947), 119.
[8] This is the equivalent used by the author of P.R.O. S.P. 10/2/13 (printed in *Tudor Economic Documents*, i, 178–83).
[9] The choice of fifty per cent. here, and ten per cent. below, is purely arbitrary.

the kingdom at this time. Converted into pounds at 364 lbs. to the sack, this amounts to 18,463,172 lbs. of wool. Assuming that the average weight of a sheep's fleece was 1·9 lbs.,[1] this wool was therefore the produce of 9,717,459 sheep. If we again make an addition of ten per cent. in respect of lambs and other sheep not sheared, our estimate of the total sheep population approximates to 10,700,000 sheep and lambs.

Owing, among other things, to deficient export statistics and lack of information about wool imports, it is even more difficult to form a reliable estimate of the number of sheep kept in England during the seventeenth century. An estimate made at the end of the century credited England (including Monmouthshire) with the production of 21,216,000 lbs. of fleece wool.[2] This figure, of course, may be wildly inaccurate, but in the absence of anything better can be used to calculate the number of sheep. Adopting the same procedure as before, except that we allow three pounds as the average weight of each fleece, we obtain a figure of approximately 7,780,000 as the sheep population of England at the end of the seventeenth century. The production of fleece wool in Wales at this time is estimated at 4,800,000 lbs., and in Scotland 6,000,000 lbs. We can calculate from these figures, allowing two pounds as the weight of each fleece,[3] that there were approximately 2,640,000 sheep and lambs in Wales and 3,300,000 in Scotland. In all, therefore, this gives us a total of 13,720,000 sheep and lambs for Great Britain. By way of comparison, Gregory King gave a figure of eleven million as the sheep population of England and Wales in 1688–95,[4] while the anonymous author of *A Short Essay upon Trade* estimated that there were 16,640,000 sheep in Great Britain in 1741.[5]

A contemporary estimate[6] of the amount of wool produced in the different counties of England at the end of the seventeenth

[1] This is equivalent to the estimate of 15 fleeces to the tod (28 lbs.) made in P.R.O. S.P. 10/2/13. Using this estimate and inaccurate export statistics, the author of this document (which is entitled 'Estimates of Exports of wool and cloth and of number of sheep') reckoned that there were 8,407,819 sheep in England in 1546.

[2] B.M. Stowe MS. 354, fol. 158ᵇ. Fleece wool does not, of course, include fell wool.

[3] Long wool was not grown in Wales or Scotland at this time. For further on Welsh and Scottish wools, see infra. pp. 59, 69, 108.

[4] *Two Tracts by Gregory King*, ed. G. E. Barnett (Baltimore; John Hopkins, 1936), p. 38.

[5] P. Deane, op. cit., p. 211, n. 11.

[6] B.M. Stowe MS. 354, fol. 158ᵇ.

century is given in Table I. From this, it would appear that the two largest wool-producing counties were those of Lincoln and Kent. The former county owed its position partly to its production of long, heavy wool; the latter to the great numbers of sheep which were supported on Romney Marsh.[1] The next largest wool-producing counties after Lincoln and Kent are shown to be those of Dorset, Sussex, Northumberland and Northamptonshire. The first three grew only short wool, the fourth considerable quantities of long. An abnormally high number of sheep per square mile must have been kept in Dorset,[2] considering the relatively small size of the county and the type of wool produced there. The remaining counties of England are shown as producing less wool. This may have been due to one or more of three reasons: to the small size of the county; to the rearing of sheep which grew a short and light fleece; and to the utilization of land for purposes other than sheep farming. Rutland, for example, falls into the first category, and Herefordshire into the second. Concerning the third it may be said that in some parts of England, like the dairy sections of Cheshire, parts of Shropshire, eastern Suffolk and south-west Norfolk, cattle raising was more important than sheep raising;[3] while in some counties like Wiltshire and Hampshire, where 'many Thousand acres of Carpet Ground being of late years turned into Arable Land and sowed with wheat',[4] tillage had reasserted itself.

During the eighteenth century the better feeding provided by roots, clovers and new grasses enabled a far larger number of sheep to be kept in the country. It was mainly due to this, to enclosure, and to the popularization of the long-woolled New Leicester sheep, that the wool production of England at the end of the eighteenth century was perhaps between

[1] It was stated in 1677: 'Romney and its neighbouring levels . . . contain about 44,000 acres; each acre one with another in Romney Marsh feeds three sheep (besides other stock) at the least, suppose then we rate the whole level thus; there will be found 132,000 sheep: whereof 300 fleeces will at the least make 4 packs of good wool (240 pound to the pack) so then there are yearly shorne 160 Packs . . .' (*Reasons for a Limited Exportation of Wool* (1677), p. 6).

[2] Defoe was told that 'there were 600 Thousand sheep fed on the Downs, within Six Miles every way of Dorchester' (*Tour*, ii, 210); but this would seem to be an exaggeration.

[3] Campbell, op. cit., p. 204.

[4] Defoe, *Tour*, ii, 282.

TABLE I

Wool Production of English Counties, c. 1700

County	Packs of wool shorn*	Packs per sq. mile†	County	Packs of wool shorn	Packs per sq. mile
Lincoln	6,000	2·30	Oxford	2,000	2·60
Kent	5,500	3·54	Hereford	2,000	2·37
Dorset	4,000	4·10	Cheshire	2,000	2·09
Northampton	4,000	3·98	Gloucester	2,000	1·80
Sussex	4,000	2·73	Lancashire	1,500	0·79
Northumberland	4,000	1·98	Cornwall	1,400	1·01
Leicester	3,000	3·49	Middlesex	1,000	3·58
Derby	3,000	3·42	Bedford	1,000	2·08
Berkshire	3,000	3·35	Monmouth	1,000	1·62
Wiltshire	3,000	2·37	Surrey	1,000	1·47
Shropshire	3,000	2·00	Cambridge	1,000	1·16
Hampshire	3,000	1·83	Warwick	1,000	1·02
Yorkshire	3,000	0·52	Essex	1,000	0·71
Buckingham	2,500	3·93	Cumberland	1,000	0·66
Hertford	2,500	3·59	Norfolk	1,000	0·49
Nottingham	2,500	3·02	Huntingdon	800	2·47
Suffolk	2,500	1·72	Durham	600	0·50
Somerset	2,500	1·50	Stafford	600	0·50
Devon	2,500	0·98	Rutland	500	2·94
Worcester	2,000	2·89	Westmorland	500	0·63
			TOTAL	88,400	1·75

* At 240 lbs. to the pack.
† Based on present-day administrative boundaries.

three and four times as great as it had been a hundred years earlier.[1]

[1] According to Luccock, there were just over 19 million sheep in England in the year 1800. These produced 193,475 packs of short wool and 131,794 packs of long wool (Youatt, op. cit., p. 344).

Chapter II

THE WOOL-TEXTILE INDUSTRY AND
ITS SOURCES OF WOOL SUPPLY

I

In the sixteenth and seventeenth centuries the English wool-textile industry was divided into two main branches: the woollen, or clothing, branch, and the worsted branch. The woollen industry manufactured broadcloth, medley cloth, kersies, dozens, penistones, friezes, cottons and other varieties of cloth, while the main products of the worsted industry were worsted proper and the wide range of fabrics known as the 'new draperies' or 'stuffs'. The latter included bayes, sayes, serges, perpetuanas, rashes, frisadoes, minikins, bombasines, grograines, buffins, russells, sagathies, mockadoes, shalloons and tammies — and the list could be considerably extended. The various types of cloth differed little from each other save in fineness, weight and size; but there were fundamental differences between cloth and worsted fabrics, and between ordinary worsted and the new draperies. These differences lay mainly in the character of the yarn that was used, and this in turn depended partly upon the character of the wool and partly upon the processes through which the wool was passed prior to spinning.

Cloth relied for its strength on the felting property of wool; and it was made from short-staple fibres which, being more curly than long ones, were more easily matted together. The cohesiveness of the wool was accentuated by a process known as carding, in which the fibres were converted into a maze by being worked between two boards covered with wire spikes. Worsted, on the other hand, largely neglected the strength given by felting, and relied to a great extent on the strength of warp and weft. This was particularly so in the case of full worsted: a material made entirely from long-staple wool, which was combed instead of carded. Combing straightened the wool fibres and laid them in a similar parallel direction. In addition, it extracted from the long fibres any short ones which might be present, by causing them (by reason of their greater curl) to twist round the teeth of the comb.[1] When combed, long wool produced roughly a quarter or a sixth of its weight in these short fibres,[2] which were known as noils, pinions or combings. These fibres were carded and spun into yarn for coarse woollens or made into weft for worsted stuffs,[3] but as they were of an inferior quality their use in the manufacture of broadcloth was forbidden by statute.[4] Both the warp and weft of full worsted were made from combed long-staple wool; in the case of the new draperies, however, combed wool was used for the warp and usually carded short-staple wool for the weft. In some parts of the country these light worsted fabrics were manufactured entirely from fleece wool; but in East Anglia the bayes makers used fell wool,[5] and sometimes noils[6] and lambswool,[7] to make their weft. An even more radical departure from the traditional worsted was the production of fabrics in which silk, linen or cotton constituted the weft.[8]

The difference in the treatment of cloth and worsted fabrics continued after weaving. With one or two exceptions all woollen cloths were fulled: a process in which the material was soaped and beaten in a damp state so as to make it warmer, opaque and more durable. During this operation the fibres of warp and weft interlocked still more thoroughly until the woven pattern of the

---

[1] H. Heaton, *Yorkshire Woollen and Worsted Industries* (Oxford, 1920), pp. 260–2.

[2] *The Clothiers Complaint, or reasons for passing the Bill against the Blackwell Hall Factors* (1692), p. 17; J. Haynes, *A View of the Present State of the Clothing Trade in England* (1706), p. 13.

[3] *The Clothiers Complaint*, p. 3; Haynes, op. cit., pp. 13–14, 82; P.R.O. S.P. 14/80/16; S.P. 15/33/71; E.134/44–5 Elizabeth I. Mich. 1. Noils were used chiefly in the manufacture of druggets, kersies, serges, bayes and milled stockings.

[4] *Statutes of the Realm*, 4 James I, c. 2.

[5] P.R.O. E.134/15 James I. Mich. 31; Hist. MSS. Comm. *Buckingham MSS.* p. 49. In the 1570's, bayes manufacturers were using 20–25 lbs. of fell wool in making the weft of their cloth (*The Ordinance Book of the Merchants of the Staple*, ed. E. E. Rich (Cambridge, 1937), p. 68). Fell wool was also used in the manufacture of blankets, druggets, kersies, penistones, long-ells, stockings and hats (J. Haynes, *Great Britain's Glory* (1715), p. 6; J. Haynes, *A View of the Present State of the Clothing Trade in England*, pp. 15–16.

[6] P.R.O. E.134/44–5 Elizabeth I. Mich. 1: S.P. 14/80/16; S.P. 15/33/71.

[7] P.R.O. E.134/15 James I. Mich. 31.

[8] For the different varieties of worsted made with silk or linen weft, see P.R.O. E.134/44–5 Elizabeth I. Mich. 1.

cloth often ceased to be visible.[1] Worsted proper was not fulled, but bayes and stammetts were, at least at first.[2] The practice, however, was much less general with worsted fabrics than with woollen cloth.

Finally, the chief superficial differences between the main categories of wool textile may be mentioned. Both the new draperies and the old-type worsted were lighter than broadcloth, and used much less wool per yard than the latter.[3] Woollen cloth, being warm and heavy, as well as monotonous in design, was best fitted for wear in colder climates. Its principal markets were therefore in northern, central and eastern Europe and, after the early Stuart period, North America. Most worsted fabrics, on the other hand, were light in weight and possessed a wide range of patterns. They were admirably suited for the warm, but non-tropical Mediterranean, Spain and Portugal, though a not unimportant proportion of them were sold in northern Europe.[4]

II

One of the most notable features of the development of the English wool-textile industry during the sixteenth and seventeenth centuries was the contrast between the fortunes of its two main branches. In the early Tudor period the woollen-cloth industry, spread geographically as never before or since, achieved an ouput that was not to be surpassed for many years to come. This was the golden age of the traditional broadcloth manufacture; but by the opening years of Elizabeth's reign the long phase of expansion, starting in the middle decades of the fifteenth century, had come to an end. Cloth exports — upon which the industry's growth had been mainly based — practically trebled in volume during the first half of the sixteenth century, but fell during the third quarter to become stabilized in the last quarter of the century at a level considerably lower than that which had obtained at the height of the 1550–1 boom. During the seventeenth century, once the post-war boom

[1] E. Lipson, *The History of the English Woollen and Worsted Industries* (1921), p. 139; Heaton, op. cit., p. 262.
[2] Evidence was given in a law suit of 1618 that 'the Dutch have alwaies used to thicke their hall bayes at the foote and the blew listes, stamettes and country bayes at the mill' (P.R.O. E.134/15 James I. Mich. 31).
[3] Allison, *thesis*, p. 495.
[4] P. J. Bowden, *Econ. Hist. Rev.* 2nd ser. ix (1956), 53.

which followed the ending of hostilities with Spain in 1604 was over, the volume of cloth exports shrank still further and the fine broadcloth industry thereafter languished in an almost continual state of chronic depression and decay. Although subject to periods of bad trade the coarse woollen industry appears to have fared somewhat better. The output of coarse woollens at the end of the seventeenth century may in fact have been considerably higher than it had been 150 years earlier, but a much larger percentage of the total now came from the expanding industrial region of the West Riding of Yorkshire.[1]

The fortunes experienced by the worsted branch of the textile industry were in outline the reverse of those already described for the woollen manufacture. While the trade in woollen cloth was booming during the early Tudor period, the production of worsted was on the decline. By the second decade of the sixteenth century the annual export of worsted had fallen to 5,000–8,000 pieces, and this was further reduced to 1,000 in the 1540's.[2] This decline seems to have been mainly attributable to the increase in competition from the continental new draperies, which, having greater consumer appeal than the traditional English worsted, successfully invaded the latter's foreign markets. Possibly the new draperies had been made in England during the early sixteenth century, but if so, their production had been quantitatively insignificant. During the opening years of Elizabeth's reign, however, the manufacture of bayes, sayes and other worsted fabrics previously manufactured on the continent became established in England on a considerable scale. The manufacture of these new products substantially increased during the latter half of the sixteenth century, and rapidly expanded after the end of the war with Spain. By 1700 there could be no question that the new fabrics had established a predominance in the nation's wool-textile exports.[3]

The striking difference between the experiences of the two

[1] Ibid., pp. 51–2; F. J. Fisher, 'Commercial Trends and Policy in Sixteenth-Century England', Econ. Hist. Rev. x (1940), 96; B. E. Supple, Commercial Crisis and Change in England, 1600–1642 (Cambridge, 1959), pp. 136–7.

[2] L. Stone, Econ. Hist. Rev. xvii (1947), 119.

[3] F. J. Fisher, 'London's Export Trade in the Early Seventeenth Century', Econ. Hist. Rev. 2nd ser. iii (1950), 151–61; P. J. Bowden, Econ. Hist. Rev. 2nd ser. ix (1956), 52–3; C. Wilson, 'Cloth Production and International Competition in the Seventeenth Century', Econ. Hist. Rev. 2nd ser. xiii (1960), 210–11; Supple, op. cit., p. 153.

branches of the wool-textile industry resulted from the com-
bination of a number of factors, of which the most important
was the changing character of the English wool supply. With
the enclosures for sheep farming, central England, which had
produced the bulk of the country's fine, short-staple wool in
medieval times, became increasingly important as a source of
supply for longer and coarser wool. Fine, short wool was best
suited for the manufacture of high-quality cloth, while long,
coarse wool was better adapted for the production of worsted
fabrics. As the amount of long-staple wool grown abroad was
comparatively small,[1] the English worsted manufacturers were
thus well placed to exploit the growing demand which the
variety and cheapness of the new draperies helped to create,
while the English woollen manufacturers, using a wool supply
which was deteriorating in quality, found their competitive
position increasingly difficult to maintain.[2]

The broad lines along which the English wool-textile industry
developed were reflected in many smaller, local movements. By
the end of the seventeenth century the woollen-cloth manufacture, which had been widespread 150 years earlier, had
disappeared from numerous towns and villages in England,
while the production of worsted, from being localized in and
around Norfolk, had spread to many other areas.

III

The most important industrial region in England during the
sixteenth century was the West Country, the seat of the fine
broadcloth manufacture. The broadcloth industry extended over
large portions of Gloucestershire, Somerset and Wiltshire, and
over smaller parts of the counties of Oxford and Worcester,
the main region stretching roughly from Witney and Painswick
in the north to Shepton Mallet, Warminster and Salisbury in
the south, with principal concentrations along the river valleys
which radiated from the Cotswolds and Mendips. Cheaper and
lighter cloths known as kersies were also made in this region,
particularly in south Wiltshire, along the Wylie valley.[3]

[1] Infra, p. 214.
[2] P. J. Bowden, *Econ. Hist. Rev.* 2nd ser. ix (1956), 45–54.
[3] G. D. Ramsay, *The Wiltshire Woollen Industry in the Sixteenth and Seventeenth Centuries* (Oxford, 1943), p. 1.

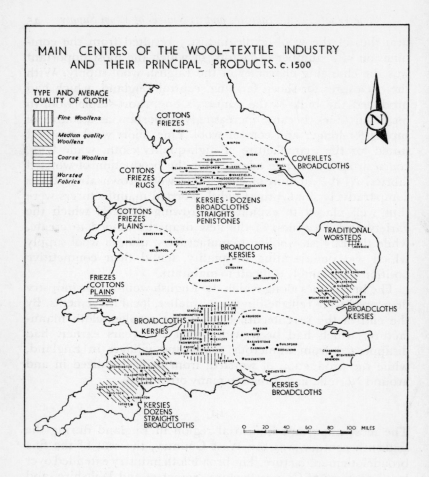

MAIN CENTRES OF THE WOOL–TEXTILE INDUSTRY
AND THEIR PRINCIPAL PRODUCTS. c.1500

TYPE AND AVERAGE
QUALITY OF CLOTH

Fine Woollens

Medium quality
Woollens

Coarse Woollens

Worsted
Fabrics

The growing shortage of fine home-grown wool spelt the eventual doom of the traditional broadcloth industry of the West of England, though the end was a long time in coming. After the depression of the 1620's the shortcomings of the English wool supply led increasing numbers of West Country clothiers, especially along the Somerset-Wiltshire border, to abandon the manufacture of broadcloth in favour of making Spanish, or medley, cloth: a new high-quality product made wholly or in part from fine Spanish wool.[1]

[1] P. J. Bowden, *Econ. Hist. Rev.* 2nd ser. ix (1956), 56–7.

Though Spanish wool had been imported into England at least as early as the twelfth century,[1] its use in the manufacture of English cloth apparently marked a new departure. In earlier times imports of such wool had been negligible, and it was not until the reign of Henry VIII, when the making of felt hats was firmly settled in England,[2] that the trade became established on a regular basis.[3] The new hat manufacture soon proved a formidable rival to the old capping industry, and imports of wool from Spain accordingly increased.[4] By the 1570's the trade had become large enough to attract the attention of would-be patentees; and in 1577 and 1594, grants for the 'only bringing in of Spanish woolles' were in turn made to Dr. Hector Nunez and Sir Michael Stanhope.[5] Buyers of Spanish wool in England during the sixteenth century seem to have been either feltmakers or haberdashers, but never clothiers;[6] and it is noticeable that when the new importation of dyed Spanish wool was disputed by the London merchants in 1607, it was the feltmakers, and not the cloth manufacturers, who were brought forward to testify to the excellence of the raw material.[7] What little evidence there is, in fact, points to the conclusion that it was not until the depressed years of the 1620's that some English woollen manufacturers were led to experiment with Spanish wool in the production of their cloth.

[1] J. Klein, *The Mesta, A Study in Spanish Economic History, 1273–1836* (Cambridge, Mass., 1920), p. 34.

[2] G. Unwin, *Industrial Organization in the Sixteenth and Seventeenth Centuries* (Oxford, 1904), p. 131.

[3] Though the finest felts were made of Spanish wool, the coarsest, which were 'covered with velleytt taffittaes and such like' were often made of 'Estridge' or French wool (B.M. Lansd. MS. 29, fol. 56). English, Welsh and Irish wools were also sometimes used, much to the dismay of the Spanish Eastland merchants and the Company of Haberdashers. See P.R.O. S.P. 14/94/116; *A.P.C. Jan. 1618–June 1619*, pp. 149–50; *July 1619–June 1621*, pp. 18–19.

[4] For figures of Spanish-wool imports between Michaelmas, 1578, and Easter, 1585, see B.M. Lansd. MS. 29, fol. 56; ibid., 48, fol. 152. At first, Spanish and other foreign wools were imported into England only by aliens; but by 1579 wool imports were being made mostly by 'English merchauntes, Aldermen and of the best Comoners of London and other Cittis and townes in the West partes' (ibid., 28, fol. 71). Imports into Exeter in the seventeenth century are given in W. B. Stephens, *Seventeenth-Century Exeter. A Study of Industrial and Commercial Development, 1625–1688* (Exeter, 1958), p. 170.

[5] P.R.O. Signet Office Docquets, IND. 6800, 17 September, 1594; S.P. 38/4/17 September, 1594. Both patents were granted for a term of twenty years; and a customs duty of 4s. 2d. per cwt. was levied on imports. See also B.M. Lansd. MS. 28, fol. 71; ibid., 29, fols. 59–60; Hist. MSS. Comm. *Salisbury* MSS. xviii, 160, 161, 386.

[6] See P.R.O. E.101/457/36; C.3/199/28; Req. 2/41/61; Req. 2/54/39; Req. 2/142/22.

[7] P.R.O. S.P. 15/39/34.

E

Originally made, at least in part, from dyed wool imported from Spain, and later from Spanish wool dyed in England,[1] Spanish cloth proved an immediate success, and by 1630 it had become one of the most sought-after English cloths abroad.[2] Although other factors may have contributed to its success,[3] the popularity of the new fabric may be attributed largely to the superior texture which it obtained through the use of fine Spanish wool. By the 1630's the new industry had become firmly established,[4] and it continued to expand throughout the remainder of the seventeenth century.[5] The main seat of the manufacture lay along the borders of Somerset and Wiltshire from Frome to Bradford: an area formerly given over to the making of fine white broadcloth.[6]

The manufacture of Spanish cloth, though the most important, was not the only, nor the most striking innovation in the western broadcloth region during the seventeenth century. In a number of different localities the manufacture of worsted fabrics gradually began to take root. By the end of the century Wiltshire had a relatively small, but not insignificant, serge industry. Devizes was a chief centre of the manufacture, but serge was also made at Calne, Slaughterford and elsewhere in the county.[7] Similarly, a number of the Gloucestershire clothiers turned their attention to the making of 'stuffs'; and by the beginning of the eighteenth century the manufacture was being carried on at Bristol, Tetbury and several other towns and parishes within the county.[8] In Worcestershire, the old broadcloth industry kept the allegiance of the majority of the clothiers; but the manufacture of 'stuffs' was taken up at Kidderminster

[1] Ramsay, op. cit., p. 103.
[2] Ibid., p. 106.
[3] The export duty on cloth was levied irrespective of value, and this must have favoured the new manufacture; for as Spanish cloths were finer and more costly than broadcloth, the merchants stood to gain by exporting the former rather than the latter (ibid.).
[4] Ibid., p. 103.
[5] Ibid., pp. 112, 114–16; M. Priestley, 'Anglo-French Trade and the Unfavourable Balance Controversy, 1660–1685', *Econ. Hist. Rev.* 2nd ser. iv (1951), 46–7.
[6] Ramsay, op. cit., p. 103. According to Defoe, at the beginning of the eighteenth century fine medley cloths were also made in Dorset, Gloucestershire, Worcestershire, Kent, Surrey and Devonshire (*Tour Through Great Britain*, i, 280–1; *The Complete English Tradesman*, ii, 282).
[7] Ramsay, op. cit., pp. 110–11. The serge manufacture was probably also carried on at Bradford, Trowbridge, Chippenham, Milksam and Castlecombe. See *H. of C. Journals*, xvi, 595.
[8] *H. of C. Journals*, xv, 533; ibid., xvi, 111, 119, 127.

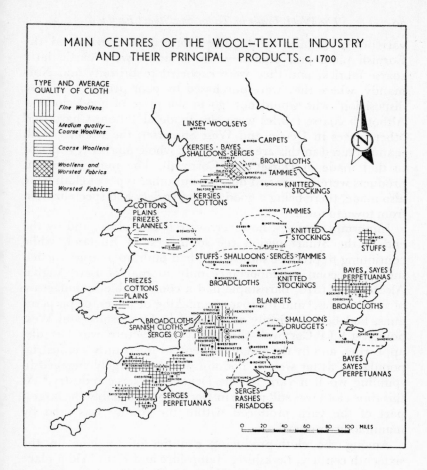

MAIN CENTRES OF THE WOOL–TEXTILE INDUSTRY
AND THEIR PRINCIPAL PRODUCTS. c.1700

and soon became the staple industry of the town.[1] In Somerset, the serge manufacture rapidly expanded west of the River Parret, and by the end of the century had made incursions into the broadcloth region in the north-east of the county.[2]

South and west of the main broadcloth region — in West Somerset, Devon, Dorset and Cornwall — the wool-textile industry in the sixteenth and early seventeenth centuries was largely engaged in the production of kersies and other coarse

[1] *V.C.H. Worcestershire*, ii, 293.
[2] *H. of C. Journals*, xv, 544; ibid., xvi, 575.

varieties of woollen cloth. The Dorsetshire dozens and the Cornish plain and pinned white straights were particularly coarse fabrics; and they were exported to Brittany and Normandy, where they were purchased by poor people 'of a base disposicion' who would not 'go to the price of good clothe'.[1] Although coarse fabrics were also made at Pilton, Chard and other places in Devon and West Somerset, the woollen cloth manufactured in this area was on the whole markedly superior to that made in Dorset and Cornwall. The most important products were kersies and dozens; but other types of cloth were also made, there being a good deal of variety and specialization from town to town.[2]

Important changes, however, were taking place, and by the end of the Stuart period the south-west of England, while continuing to produce some cloth, had built up a large worsted industry second in importance only to that of East Anglia. Already, by 1610, Barnstaple had a considerable manufacture of single bayes,[3] and by 1630 the making of serges, or perpetuanas, had become firmly established in Devonshire and West Somerset.[4] In Cornwall the cloth manufacture was fast disappearing, and by the end of the century the county's industrial population as far west as Bodmin was very largely engaged in spinning woollen yarn for the Devonshire serge industry.[5] At this time cloth was still made in Dorset, but probably the largest part of the yarn produced within the county was used by manufacturers elsewhere.

Among the cloth-producing counties of England in the sixteenth century, Berkshire, Hampshire and Kent held a place of some importance, and together with the adjacent counties of Surrey and Sussex they constituted what may be described as the south-eastern industrial region. The principal types of cloth produced in this area were kersies and broadcloths; and for the most part they were of a somewhat coarse texture. But good-quality fabrics were also made, particularly in Berkshire and Hampshire; and the Reading kersies enjoyed a reputation for

---

[1] P.R.O. E.134/6 James I. East. 30; *Statutes of the Realm*, 27 Elizabeth I, c. 18.

[2] *Statutes of the Realm*, 5 and 6 Edward VI, c. 6; *V.C.H. Somerset*, ii, 414; T. Westcote, *A View of Devonshire in 1630* (edn. 1845), pp. 60–1.

[3] Hist. MSS. Comm. *Downshire MSS.* ii, 336.

[4] Westcote, op. cit., pp. 60–1.

[5] *H. of C. Journals*, xvi, 72–4, 92, 99, 120, 554.

fineness only a little inferior to that of West Country broadcloth.[1] The different kinds of woollen cloth produced in Kent included broadcloth, kersies and 'cottons'. The most important manufacture was that of dyed broadcloth, and the chief centres of the industry were at Cranbrook, Tenterden, Benenden and nearby towns.[2] In Surrey and Sussex only a handful of towns and their neighbouring villages engaged in the cloth manufacture. Of these, Guildford, Godalming and Farnham in Surrey, and Chichester in Sussex, were the most important. These towns were situated at no great distance from the Hampshire border, and may be considered as outlying parts of the Hampshire industrial zone. The bulk of the cloths made in the two counties were, in fact, known as 'Hampshire kersies', and together with the 'Guildford cloths' these accounted for practically the entire output.[3]

The decline of the English woollen industry which occurred during the late sixteenth and seventeenth centuries, was most clearly manifested in these south-eastern parts of the country. As early as 1620 the south-eastern clothing towns were feeling very severely the pinch of Italian and West Riding competition,[4] and by the end of the seventeenth century the woollen cloth manufacture had almost completely disappeared from the region.[5]

As the old cloth industry declined it was replaced to some extent in Kent, Hampshire and Berkshire by the manufacture of the new draperies. In the early years of Elizabeth's reign alien worsted makers settled at Canterbury, Maidstone, Sandwich and Southampton. Later, Englishmen in other parts of Hampshire and in Berkshire took up the worsted manufacture. The aliens who lived in Kent made bayes, sayes, perpetuanas and many other types of fabric.[6] In Southampton, the immigrants manufactured mainly rashes and serges.[7] By the end of the reign

---

[1] The cloths manufactured at Newbury, Wallingford and Cookingham were similar to those made in Reading (P.R.O. E.134/41 Elizabeth I. East. 1).

[2] *V.C.H. Kent*, iii, 404–6.

[3] *V.C.H. Surrey*, ii, 243–5, 342–5; *V.C.H. Sussex*, ii, 256–7.

[4] B.M. Lansd. MS. 152, fol. 229; P.R.O. S.P. 14/111/69.

[5] Hist. MSS. Comm. *Portland MSS*. iii, 548; *V.C.H. Berkshire*, i, 392–4; *V.C.H. Hampshire*, vi, 485–6; *V.C.H. Surrey*, ii, 347–8; Defoe, *Tour*, i, 115.

[6] F. W. Cross, *History of Walloon and Huguenot Church, Canterbury* (Huguenot Soc. xv), pp. 183–4, 191; *V.C.H. Kent*, iii, 350, 405–7; P.R.O. E.134/15 James I. Mich. 31.

[7] P.R.O. S.P. 12/250/47; *A.P.C. 1601–4*, pp. 347–8; *V.C.H. Hampshire*, v, 451.

of James I, the worsted industry had spread to other places in Hampshire. There was a small serge manufacture at Winchester and in parts of the New Forest;[1] while serges, rashes and frisadoes were made at Christchurch and Romsey.[2] By the close of the seventeenth century Southampton had lost much of its importance as a centre of the worsted manufacture and, possibly owing to competition from the south-western industry, the manufacture of serges had largely given way to the production of other types of fabric. Alton, Andover, Basingstoke and Romsey had become the chief centres of the worsted industry in the county: the first three towns producing shalloons and druggets, and the fourth making coarse, broad rashes.[3] In Berkshire, the worsted manufacture does not appear to have been taken up until the second half of the seventeenth century. When Defoe wrote in 1724 the inhabitants of Newbury were 'generally imployed in making Shalloons',[4] and there was a smaller manufacture of druggets at Reading.[5]

East Anglia is usually associated with the worsted industry, but until at least the last quarter of the sixteenth century it was the manufacture of woollens, and not of worsted, that was the main industrial activity in the region. In the late fifteenth century Suffolk had been the largest cloth-producing county in England, and Essex had also possessed a considerable woollen industry. Norfolk, of course, was largely devoted to the worsted manufacture, though here, too, some woollen cloth was produced.[6]

The products made in Suffolk ranged from good-quality broadcloth, on the one hand, to very inferior fabrics known as 'sett clothes', on the other.[7] But the cloth industry in Suffolk, like that in the south-eastern counties, began to decline in the late sixteenth century, and by 1693 it could be stated that the manufacture of woollens had almost disappeared from the county.[8] In Essex the woollen industry appears to have produced mainly broadcloths; and when Norden wrote in 1594 the 'best whites in England' were made in Coggeshall.[9] By 1720, how-

---

[1] *Commons Debates, 1621,* vii, 251.
[2] *V.C.H. Hampshire,* v, 451.
[3] Ibid., v. 486.
[4] *Tour,* i, 289.
[5] *V.C.H. Berkshire,* i, 394.
[6] Heaton, op. cit., pp. 86–8.
[7] *Cal. Pat. Edward VI,* v, 9–10; *1553–4,* p. 386.
[8] Hist. MSS. Comm. *Portland MSS.* iii, 548.
[9] *Norden's Description of Essex,* p. 9.

ever, little remained of the woollen cloth manufacture in Essex; and in Coggeshall, where it was still carried on, the industry was 'very much decayed'. But a large worsted manufacture had taken root in the county; and this and the spinning of 'great quantities of yarn' which were 'sent to London for the fringe makers and Spitalfield weavers', now occupied the majority of the industrial population.[1]

The arrival of the new draperies during the early years of Elizabeth's reign opened a new chapter in the history of the East Anglia wool-textile industry. Worsted had long been the principal manufacture of the Norfolk textile industry, and as early as the fourteenth century it had also been made in Essex and Suffolk.[2] But compared with the production of cloth in England, the output of worsted had never been anything but small. Indeed, the worsted trade had for some time been in difficulties[3] when the Walloons and Dutchmen arrived with their manufacture of the new draperies to give it a fresh lease of life. Though the Protestant immigrants settled in other places besides East Anglia, the largest proportion of them went to this region; and as increasing numbers of Englishmen took up the new manufacture, the worsted industry continued to grow and flourish there until the early decades of the eighteenth century.[4]

Norwich was the chief seat of the new industry; and in the last years of Elizabeth's reign the city was manufacturing bayes, sayes, russells, chamletts, grograines, damasks, callimancoes, mockadoes and many other types of 'stuff'.[5] By this time the manufacture of the traditional worsted seems to have been all but extinct.[6] Next in importance to Norwich was Colchester, which concentrated mainly upon the production of bayes, sayes and perpetuanas; and a further large manufacture of bayes was carried on at Bocking.[7] But the new industry established itself

---

[1] *V.C.H. Essex*, ii, 398–9.
[2] G. Unwin, *Studies in Economic History* (1927), p. 263.   [3] *Supra*, p. 44.
[4] *V.C.H. Essex*, ii, 331–3, 386–90; Unwin, op. cit., p. 291. For the decline of the East Anglia worsted industry in the eighteenth century, see M. F. Lloyd Prichard, 'The Decline of Norwich', *Econ. Hist. Rev.* 2nd ser. iii (1951), 371–7; *V.C.H. Essex*, ii, 400–1.
[5] P.R.O. E.134/44–5 Elizabeth I. Mich. 1; N. J. Williams, 'Two Documents concerning the New Draperies', *Econ. Hist. Rev.* 2nd ser. iv (1952), 354–7.
[6] Allison, *thesis*, p. 588.
[7] P.R.O. E.134/15 James I. Mich. 31; Hist. MSS. Comm. *House of Lords MSS.* iii,

all along the border of Essex and Suffolk. Sudbury, which made chiefly sayes, was the main Suffolk centre, and may almost be considered as an outlying part of the Essex district.[1]

Further north, in the West Riding, the wool-textile industry in the sixteenth and seventeenth centuries was concerned very largely with the manufacture of coarse woollens. The chief varieties of cloth produced were kersies, broadcloths, dozens, penistones, and straights. More kersies were made than any other type of cloth. Their manufacture was centred on Halifax, while broadcloths were made mainly in the vicinity of Leeds.[2]

Little is known of the origins of the worsted industry in Yorkshire. Coverlets or 'chalons', which seem to have been types of worsted, were made in the county during the fourteenth century; and there was a small manufacture of 'cushions', coverlets and carpets, and a larger manufacture of knitted stockings, in the late sixteenth and early seventeenth centuries. But up to the end of the Commonwealth the worsted industry in Yorkshire never attracted much attention, and never for a moment did it look like rivalling the woollen industry. Even after 1660, progress was at first only gradual; but by 1688 the output of bayes in Yorkshire was sufficiently great to justify the inclusion of this fabric in a short list of cloths on which subsidy and ulnage were paid; and by the early years of the eighteenth century a considerable manufacture of shalloons, serges and other varieties of worsted had become established in many parts of the West Riding.[3]

This development was in accordance with the general trend of events in manufacturing regions all over England, the West Riding industry being affected by factors similar to those which had led to the rise of the worsted manufacture in other industrial areas. Consumer-countries had begun to produce their own cheap varieties of cloth; and now that few markets remained to be won from rival English manufacturers,[4] there seemed little prospect of much future development in the manufacture of

386–8; Hist. MSS. Comm. *Buckingham MSS.* p. 49; *H. of C. Journals*, xii. 79; ibid., xiii, 720; *V.C.H. Essex*, ii, 386, 394–9.
[1] Unwin, op. cit., pp. 291, 295–7.
[2] Heaton, *Yorkshire Woollen and Worsted Industries*, passim.
[3] Ibid., pp. 264–8.
[4] See P.R.O. S.P. 14/111/69.

kersies and other such low-grade woollens. Industrialization in Germany during the first few decades of the seventeenth century adversely affected the West Riding industry. The low-grade broadlist kersies, which had previously been exported in great numbers to the German market, went out of demand; and only by improvements in technique did the Yorkshire clothiers manage to avert major disaster.[1] At the beginning of Charles II's reign the largest market for English kersies was in France; but following the imposition of progressively increasing tariffs during the 1660's, the French market for this commodity violently contracted and never materially recovered.[2] There was good reason for the West Riding manufacturers to complain in 1676 that trade was very bad, and that kersies now fetched only half the price of former times.[3]

Apart from developing new markets or applying cost-reducing innovations, there was only one sound method by which the Yorkshire manufacturers might hope to increase substantially their sales of woollens, and that was by improving their workmanship. The West Riding clothiers had done this in the early decades of the seventeenth century; but manufacturing standards could not be raised indefinitely when the clothiers were confronted with a wool supply that was deteriorating in quality. Not only was the wool of Lincolnshire, Leicestershire and other midland counties growing longer and coarser, but, as far as the West Riding woollen industry was concerned, it was also becoming scarcer; and as increasing quantities of it went to the worsted industry in East Anglia and other parts of England, the more difficult it became for the Yorkshire manufacturers to obtain the grades of wool that they required. As their supplies of better-quality raw material began to dry up, the West Riding clothiers were compelled to draw more and more heavily upon the cheaper and inferior grades of wool from the northern counties, Scotland, Ireland and elsewhere.[4] Using such raw material they had little chance of breaking down resistance in the foreign market.

[1] P.R.O. E.134/14 Charles I. Mich. 20, 21.
[2] M. Priestley, 'Anglo-French Trade and the Unfavourable Balance Controversy, 1660–1685', *Econ. Hist. Rev.* 2nd ser. iv (1951), 45–7; Heaton, op. cit., pp. 250–1.
[3] P.R.O. E.134/28 Charles II. Mich. 29.
[4] P. J. Bowden, *Econ. Hist. Rev.* 2nd ser. ix (1956), 47, 54–5.

But while the Yorkshire clothiers were obtaining supplies of short-staple wool from far afield, there were abundant supplies of long-staple wool close at hand, and while their products were meeting with stubborn markets abroad, exports of English worsted were booming. The next step was obvious; and by the middle of the eighteenth century the West Riding worsted industry was proving a formidable rival to that of East Anglia.

To the west of the Pennines, there were important centres of the woollen industry at Manchester, Salford, Rochdale, Bury and Bolton, in Lancashire, and Kendal, in Westmorland. Situated in very poor wool-growing country it is not surprising that the fabrics produced in this region were coarser than those made elsewhere in the kingdom. In the sixteenth and early seventeenth centuries the chief articles of manufacture were 'cottons', friezes and rugs.[1] By the beginning of Charles I's reign, fabrics known as 'bayes' and 'minikins' were also being produced in Lancashire. These, however, were not genuine new draperies. They were the old types of woollen cloth freshly labelled so as to attract the foreign buyer. Far from being worsted fabrics, they were 'in themselves only cottons and only differenced in the fullinge and thickening of them'.[2]

After the Restoration, the coarse woollen industry in the north-west of England, like that in the West Riding of Yorkshire, experienced a long period of stagnation due to the fall in overseas demand;[3] and here, as in other industrial regions, the manufacture of woollens was partially replaced by the production of other types of fabric. In Kendal, the manufacture of linsey-woolseys was taken up, and was evidently of some size in 1702.[4] In Lancashire, the cotton industry was developed; and so rapid was its progress that by the end of the eighteenth century it had displaced the woollen industry in the county, except in the Pennine districts and round about Rochdale.[5]

IV

As with the woollen industry in other parts of the country, the west of England broadcloth manufacture owed its origin to, and

---

[1] *Statutes of the Realm*, 5 and 6 Edward VI, c. 6; *V.C.H. Lancashire*, ii, 296; P.R.O. E.134/9 James I. Mich. 29; B.M. Add. MS. 34325, fols. 14–16.
[2] P.R.O. E.134/3–4 Charles I. Hil. 23.
[3] Heaton, op. cit., p. 251.   [4] *H. of C. Journals*, xiii, 747.
[5] Heaton, op. cit., p. 257.

its type of product was in the first instance determined by, supplies of locally grown raw material. During the first few decades of the sixteenth century the wool which was worked up into broadcloth still came very largely from within the confines of the broadcloth region itself and particularly from nearby growers. Thomas Horton, the Bradford-on-Avon clothier mentioned in Leland's *Itinerary*, purchased not long before his death £30 worth of wool from a Wiltshire farmer.[1] Some years later, in 1546, a Wickwar clothmaker made a long-term agreement for a supply of raw material with a grower from Bleadon, Somerset.[2] Somewhat earlier, another Gloucestershire clothier, from Minchinhampton, purchased 549 stones of wool from a Wiltshire gentleman.[3] As the West Country cloth manufacture expanded, however, the wool grown within the region proved insufficient for the combined needs of industry and the wool export trade, and the clothiers found it necessary to supplement it with supplies drawn from farther afield. By 1530 some Gloucestershire clothiers had started to use Leicestershire wool in their manufacture;[4] while during the following decade the Honiton district of Devon was tapped by clothiers from South Wiltshire,[5] although possibly not for the first time.

In the second half of the sixteenth century and the first quarter of the seventeenth the broadcloth-manufacturing counties still continued to draw upon themselves and each other for their supplies of raw material.[6] But, though the broadcloth industry had reached its zenith by about 1550, it now became necessary for it to draw more heavily on distant sources of supply. This was due partly to the fact that there was not the same incentive to farmers to produce wool in the second half of the sixteenth century as there had been in the first, and partly to the fact that the deterioration in the quality of some of the wool grown in the counties of Oxford and Worcester, and to a lesser extent in Gloucester, meant that increasing quantities of locally grown wool were becoming unsuitable for the manu-

[1] P.R.O. C.1/642/40; Ramsay, op. cit., p. 6.
[2] P.R.O. C.1/1186/2.
[3] P.R.O. Req. 2/3/100.
[4] P.R.O. C.1/642/9; C.1/790/17.
[5] P.R.O. C.1/1117/33.
[6] See, for example, P.R.O. Req. 2/171/24; Req. 2/206/29.

facture of fine broadcloth.[1] Other sources of supply had therefore to be exploited. As the wool-export trade passed away, the
entire wool production of Herefordshire, Shropshire, Staffordshire and the Midlands became available for the use of the home
manufacture; and a large part of the finest of this raw material
was seized upon to feed the western broadcloth industry. The
wools of Herefordshire and its two northern neighbours were
used largely by the clothiers of Worcester City;[2] but considerable
quantities of these wools also found their way to Gloucestershire
and Somerset, often through the operations of wealthy middlemen.[3] Some of the largest Wiltshire and Somerset clothiers
travelled as far north as Warwickshire and Northamptonshire in
search of raw material, making their purchases from growers or
from dealers on the spot.[4] But the majority of the broadcloth
manufacturers were supplied with the wools grown in distant
shires by middlemen at their own local markets, particularly
that at Cirencester. This great wool mart was situated within
easy reach of the Gloucestershire and Wiltshire clothiers; and
in 1577 it was being regularly frequented by dealers from the
counties of Warwick, Oxford, Buckingham, Leicester and
Northampton: the last named county alone sending to it a few
years earlier some thirty or forty packs of wool each week. But
this influx of raw material from central England was apparently
already beginning to diminish;[5] and with the change in the
character of the Midlands wool more and more of it found its
way to East Anglia and the West Riding where it was worked up
into worsted and coarse woollens, for which it was better
adapted.[6]

The West Country clothiers had therefore to seek out fresh

[1] In 1586, West Country clothiers were complaining: 'the grosenes of wolles in
England' hath 'much encreased . . . within theis tenne yeres or theiraboutes'
(B.M. Lansd. MS. 48/66).
[2] Society of Antiquaries Library, *Prattinton MSS.* v, fol. 173; *A.P.C. 1616–17*, p. 35;
V.C.H. Worcester, ii, 283; P.R.O. S.P. 14/80/13.
[3] P.R.O. Req. 2/113/13; Req. 2/163/96; S.P. 14/80/13. Herefordshire wool had
sometimes been sold at Cirencester in the late fifteenth century (Ramsay, op. cit.,
p. 7).
[4] P.R.O. E.133/6/833; Req. 2/45/100. In 1577 the Wiltshire clothiers stated: 'the
woolles growinge within this our Shire ys not suffycient for the drapinge and
workinge of the inhabytantes of our sayde Shire by xx[ti] thowsande toddes at the
leaste yerlye' (P.R.O. S.P. 12/114/27).
[5] P.R.O. S.P. 12/114/39, 40. See also Req. 2/25/163; Req. 2/202/2; Req.
2/203/2.
[6] P. J. Bowden, *Econ. Hist. Rev.* 2nd ser. ix (1956), 49–50.

sources of supply. These they found mainly in the south of England and in South Wales. By the beginning of the seventeenth century most of the finest wool grown in Dorset was being spun into yarn within the county for sale to the clothiers of Wiltshire and Somerset,[1] while the decline of the local cloth-making industry in Hampshire made further supplies of raw material available. Probably high-quality Hampshire wool had been used in the manufacture of fine broadcloth in earlier years, but even the best of the Dorsetshire wool seems to have been considered too coarse for this purpose in the fifteenth and early sixteenth centuries. The use of such inferior raw material may have been unavoidable in view of the growing deficiency in the supply of suitable fine wool, but it could have done nothing to enhance the reputation of English broadcloth abroad. Similarly, the wool of South Wales was not of the best quality.[2] In the mid-sixteenth century most of this wool had been manufactured into cottons and friezes by the local cloth industries of Carmarthenshire and Pembrokeshire. But between then and the end of the century these industries experienced a substantial decline, and the amount of wool available for export correspondingly increased. From Michaelmas, 1566, to Michaelmas, 1567, Milford and its member ports exported only 1,560 stones of wool to England, but by 1592–3 this figure had risen to 7,990 stones. Milford was the chief port of despatch; but Cardiff and Carmarthen also shipped wool to England, and less frequently, the North Wales ports of Beaumaris and Caernarvon. Somewhat over one-half of these exports went to Bristol, and the remainder to northern ports in Somerset and Devon.[3] Shipments of Welsh wool to England continued in the seventeenth century, but in the later decades appear to have become less important, probably owing to the demands of the woollen industry of North Wales.[4]

For their supplies of short-staple wool the comparatively small number of worsted manufacturers in the West Country doubtless tapped the same geographical sources as their neighbours

---

[1] P.R.O. E.134/6 James I. East. 30.
[2] Welsh wool in general was of an inferior quality. See P.R.O. C.3/200/90; Prothero, op. cit., p. 139; A. L. Rowse, *The England of Elizabeth* (1951), p. 77.
[3] E. A. Lewis, *Welsh Port Books 1550–1603* (Cymmrod. Rec. Ser. xii, 1927), pp. xxxii–xxxiv, 86–91, 156–9; P.R.O. S.P. 14/122/130; S.P. 14/123/28, 54.
[4] Rowse, op. cit., p. 77.

who made broadcloths and kersies, while for their long-staple wool they relied largely upon the Midlands.[1] As the production of worsted in the west of England and in the south-western serge region expanded, the market at Circencester did an increasingly important business in long wool. Before the end of the seventeenth century a large wool-combing trade had sprung up at Cirencester, Tetbury and elsewhere along the Gloucester-shire-Wiltshire border to accommodate the industries in the two areas. Much of the wool which was brought to the Cirencester market was purchased by the wool-combers living in the locality. After combing and sometimes spinning, it was then 'carried into the Western Parts as far as Exeter and there sold at a good Price'.[2]

The raw material used by the south-western cloth industry during the sixteenth century came largely from local sources, though wool grown in nearby areas, including South Wales, was also sometimes used.[3] The inferior fabrics produced in Dorset and Cornwall were made from the coarsest local wools, the better quality wools being sold, often spun into yarn, to manu-facturers of neighbouring counties. In the early seventeenth century the best Dorsetshire yarn was being made into Wiltshire and Somerset broadcloths and Reading kersies, while much Cornish yarn was being purchased by dealers from Tiverton and other towns for use in the Devonshire kersey manufacture.[4] Already, in the late sixteenth century the growing shortage of locally grown wool was leading Devon and Somerset clothiers to use increasing quantities of Cornish, Dorset and Welsh raw material in their manufacture. Most of the Welsh wool was imported by the clothiers themselves, but sometimes it was brought across by growers and dealers from Glamorgan.[5]

As the manufacture of bayes and serges spread rapidly throughout the region in the early years of the seventeenth century it became necessary to tap more distant sources of raw

[1] But considerable quantities of Irish long and short-staple wool were imported at Bristol in the late seventeenth century, and Irish yarn was a popular raw material with some of the West Country woollen and worsted manufacturers in the eighteenth century. See *H. of C. Journals*, xv, 533, 544, 547; ibid., xvi, 111, 115, 119, 127, 575, 595.
[2] Ibid., xv, 477; ibid., xvi, 111; Defoe, *The Complete English Tradesman*, ii, 279–80; Defoe, *Tour*, i, 282; ibid., ii, 432.
[3] Westcote, op. cit., p. 60; P.R.O. C.1/1176/1; C.1/1233/2–5; C.1/1300/92–3; C.3/6/108; E. 134/6 James I. East. 30.
[4] P.R.O. E.134/20 James I. East. 10; E.134/12 Charles I. East. 41.
[5] P.R.O. C.1/1300/92–3; C.3/6/108.

material supply. By 1630, Gloucestershire, Worcestershire, Warwickshire and Ireland were providing wool for manufacture into woollens and worsteds, whilst further supplies of raw material were obtained from the wool market in London.[1] As the century progressed and the serge manufacture expanded, the south-western industry drew more heavily upon these sources of supply and at the same time tapped new ones in the Midlands and south-east England.

The wools grown in Gloucestershire, Worcestershire and the adjoining midland counties were brought to the south-western industrial region by two main routes: down the Severn, and overland via Circencester. Gloucester shipped wool to Bristol, Bridgwater and Barnstaple, while Bristol sent wool to Bridgwater and Minehead.[2] By the end of the century the coastal traffic in wool from Gloucester had assumed considerable proportions. In 1691, for example, the port shipped about 23,700 stones of wool, of which almost 16,600 stones went to Bridgwater, and the remainder to Bristol.[3]

A miscellaneous collection of wool came from London.[4] It was sent to the south-western manufacturing region by waggon or by shipment along the coast. Exeter was the importing centre for the coastal trade; and in addition to receiving wool from London, it imported fair-sized amounts of Kentish and Sussex wool from Rye, and smaller quantities from Faversham and Dover.[5]

It was from Ireland, however, that the south-western industry appears to have drawn the largest part of its extra-regional wool supplies in the last quarter of the seventeenth century. During this period, exports of Irish wool to England rapidly increased. From 1678 to 1681 the average annual import into England of Irish wool was roughly 178,000 stones;[6] by 1702 it had risen to

[1] Westcote, op. cit., p. 60; K.A.O. U.269/A.418/5, fol. 7ᵇ; U.269/A.418/6, fol. 5; U.269/A.418/8; U.269/A.424.

[2] T. S. Willan, *The English Coasting Trade, 1600–1750* (Manchester, 1938), pp. 168–75. The shipments from Bristol probably included Welsh and Irish wool as well as Gloucestershire and Midlands wool. Bristol also had a considerable coastal trade in wool with Gloucester (ibid., pp. 90–1).

[3] Ibid., p. 90.

[4] Some of this may have been Midlands and Lincolnshire wool (see P.R.O. Req. 2/174/14), but the bulk of it probably came from the home counties, particularly Kent.

[5] Hoskins, op. cit., p. 35; Willan, op. cit., p. 161.

[6] Calculated from the revenue received for licences to export Irish wool (Hist. MSS. Comm. *Ormonde MSS*. N.S. iv, 665–76).

412,000. Of this amount, approximately 230,000 stones, or 56 per cent. passed through the south-western ports of Minehead, Bideford, Barnstaple, Bristol and Bridgwater. Liverpool and Chester took the remainder.[1] By 1706, total imports of Irish wool had more than doubled since 1702, and the proportion passing through the south-western ports had risen to two-thirds.[2]

Irish long-staple wool made up a large proportion of the import into the south-western region; and without it, neither the Devon and Somerset serge manufacture, nor indeed the English worsted industry as a whole could have experienced the great expansion that was so striking a feature of the post-Restoration period. For the manufacture of worsted fabrics in England was necessarily limited by the available supplies of long-staple wool; and though the native production of long wool continued to increase throughout the century, eventually, with the very rapid growth of the worsted manufacture, it began to fall short of potential demand. The need of the English worsted manufacture for more raw material became strong at a time when changes in the Irish wool supply were resulting in the production in Ireland of increasing quantities of long-staple wool.[3] That the south-western serge manufacture was able to monopolize the largest part of this wool for itself was due both to its geographical situation and to the economic policy of the English government.[4] But the benefits of the Irish long-wool trade extended far beyond the south-western region; and the worsted industry elsewhere in England greatly gained: not only by a limited use of the Irish raw material, but also by the increased supplies of English long-staple wool which became available.

Much of the wool which was used in the Berkshire and Hampshire cloth manufacture was obtained from local growers. In the early years of the sixteenth century Thomas Baker, a Winchester clothier, contracted for a regular supply of wool from one Hampshire grower and made single purchases of wool from others.[5] Similarly, Gilbert Freman, who lived in Abingdon, purchased the entire wool-clip of a Berkshire gentleman in 1540

[1] Hist. MSS. Comm. *House of Lords MSS.* N.S. v, 334.
[2] Ibid., N.S. vii, 233.
[3] P. J. Bowden, *Econ. Hist. Rev.* 2nd ser. ix (1956), 53, n. 3.
[4] Infra, pp. 207–8.
[5] P.R.O. C.1/290/3; C.1/386/43.

for manufacture into cloth or yarn.[1] But the fleeces grown in the two counties did not always suffice, once demands on them by the wool-export trade and the West Country industry had been met; and the clothiers also bought wool from growers and dealers of neighbouring areas and from wool middlemen in London.[2] Buckinghamshire, in particular, became important during the later years of the sixteenth century as a source of raw material supply; and in 1616 it was liberally estimated that 140,000 tods of wool yearly went from the county to the manufacturing towns of Reading, Newbury and Basingstoke.[3] Other counties also supplied wool, and Dorset provided yarn.

Away to the east, the sources of wool supply tapped by the clothiers of Sussex, Surrey and Kent were again largely local. The Surrey cloth manufacturers obtained some raw material from Sussex, while the London wool market was also visited.[4] Somewhat exceptional must have been the case of Thomas Streate, a Guildford clothier. Streate probably manufactured good-quality cloth; and at the beginning of the seventeenth century he 'vsed the helpe of one Xpofer Owen . . . who dwelleth in the Cyttie of Coventrie' to obtain his wool.[5]

The development of the worsted industry in parts of southeastern England raised no major problems of raw material supply. In Kent, where a number of alien 'new drapers' settled, there were supplies of both long and short-staple wool on hand, and most of the raw material that was used was apparently grown within the county or obtained from London.[6] In Southampton (and probably the other worsted centres in Hampshire and Berkshire), yarn made from long Buckinghamshire and Oxfordshire combing wool constituted the warp; while at first, Hampshire and Berkshire wool was used for the weft.[7] But later, in the early seventeenth century, yarn manufactured from Devonshire and Cornish wool was found to be more suitable for the weft of certain types of fabric; and it was purchased by

[1] P.R.O. Req. 2/2/14. See also P.R.O. C.1/981/95.
[2] P.R.O. C.1/237/3; C.1/286/37; C.1/822/52; Req. 2/5/56; Req. 2/17/16; Req. 2/30/56.
[3] *Commons Debates, 1621*, vii, 499.
[4] P.R.O. C.1/396/40; C.1/1099/9–10.
[5] Advocates' Library, the National Library of Scotland, Edinburgh. ADV. MSS. 34. 2. 15 (MS. dated 9th September, 1602).
[6] See Advocates' Library, ADV. MSS. 34. 2. 15. (MS. dated 20th October, 1602); Willan, op. cit., pp. 88, 140.
[7] P.R.O. S.P. 12/250/47.

F

representatives of the town in the markets of Devon and
Cornwall.[1] In 1627–8 Southampton was importing wool from
Plymouth, and at the end of the century shipments of wool were
received from Cowes and Rye.[2]

In Essex, a large part of the raw material used in the production of woollen cloth in the early sixteenth century was
grown locally or in Suffolk.[3] Norfolk also provided some wool.[4]
During the second half of the century many cloth manufacturers
probably still relied upon the same sources of supply. But by
1560 the Coggeshall clothiers were making their fine white
broadcloths from the superior March wools of Shropshire and
Staffordshire; and the London dealers who supplied them also
provided the Dedham clothiers with raw material.[5]

Much of the woollen cloth produced in Suffolk during the
Tudor and Stuart periods was of a coarse, or somewhat coarse,
texture, and was made from inferior or medium-quality wool.[6]
The wool grown in East Anglia was generally coarse, while that
grown in Lincolnshire was steadily deteriorating; and it was
from these areas that the Suffolk cloth manufacturers seem to
have drawn the bulk of their wool supplies. In the late sixteenth
and seventeenth centuries the Suffolk woollen industry also
obtained raw material from the counties of Buckingham,
Northampton and Leicester.[7] Some of this may have been good-
quality wool; but the Suffolk clothiers also purchased Midlands
wool that did not find a ready market at Norwich, either
because it was 'tarry and rotten', or because it was in other ways
unsuitable for the worsted manufacture.[8]

Part of the raw material used by the East Anglia worsted
industry was obtained locally. In the early sixteenth century
Norfolk wool had been almost the only type used in the old
worsted manufacture,[9] and from time to time its export in a raw
state or as yarn was prohibited in an endeavour to protect the

[1] *A.P.C. 1601–4*, pp. 347–8.
[2] Willan, op. cit., pp. 151–3.
[3] P.R.O. C.1/390/30; C.1/449/6; C.1/1489/115.
[4] Allison, *Econ. Hist. Rev.* 2nd ser. xi (1958), 107–8.
[5] P.R.O. E.133/1/36; S.P. 12/114/47; Req. 2/32/14; Req. 2/93/20.
[6] P.R.O. S.P. 12/106/48.
[7] P.R.O. C.1/1311/70–1; Req. 2/61/93; Req. 2/80/45; E.133/6/833; Advocates'
Library, ADV. MSS. 34. 2. 15. (MS. dated 16th December, 1602); Lumley MS.
2305; L.A.O. MM. VI/5/8, 18; Allison, *Econ. Hist. Rev.* 2nd ser. xi (1958), 107–8.
[8] Hist. MSS. Comm. *Various MSS.* iii, 96.
[9] *Statutes of the Realm*, 33 Henry VIII, c. 16.

declining local industry against its foreign competitors by denying them supplies of raw material.[1] Even forty years after the arrival of the new draperies it still supplied a large part of the raw material used in Norwich. Essex and Suffolk wools were generally too short to be suitable for the manufacture of full worsted; but with the shorter Norfolk wool they were made into yarn for the weft of the new draperies.[2] By about 1570, however, supplies of locally grown raw material had proved insufficient for the requirements of the expanding eastern industry, and it became necessary to supplement, and eventually replace,[3] them with supplies drawn from elsewhere. Three main sources of supply were developed. These were Lincolnshire, the Midlands, and the London wool market.

The Norfolk manufacturers, being mainly in a small way of business, obtained a large part of their supplies of Midlands and Lincolnshire wool from dealers at their local markets, and, together with the Suffolk and Essex manufacturers, they obtained further supplies at Stourbridge Fair.[4] Owing to its size and geographical position, the Norfolk worsted industry was the chief consumer of Lincolnshire and Northamptonshire long-staple, whilst the Essex manufacture was fed with large quantities of wool from Buckinghamshire.[5] Most of the Lincolnshire wool was transported to the manufacturing and distributing centres by packhorse or waggon, but during the seventeenth century considerable quantities of it were also shipped along the coast. In the year ending Christmas, 1624, for example, Boston shipped coast-wise approximately 12,990 stones of wool, of which 7,990 stones went to King's Lynn and 2,880 to Brandon.[6] King's Lynn was a 'greate place for woolle broking',[7]

---

[1] Ibid., 6 Henry VIII, c. 12; ibid., 33 Henry VIII, c. 16; ibid., 1 Edward VI, c. 6; ibid., 1 & 2 Philip and Mary, c. 14.

[2] *Tudor Economic Documents*, i, 195; P.R.O. E.134/44–5 Elizabeth I. Mich. 1.

[3] Supra, p. 35. In 1624 the Norfolk wool growers unsuccessfully endeavoured to obtain the passage of an Act of Parliament prohibiting worsted weavers from using other than Norfolk wool (Allison, *thesis*, p. 689).

[4] P.R.O. Req. 2/169/12; S.P. 12/114/40; S.P. 14/80/13; Hist. MSS. Comm. *Various MSS.* iii, 96–7; *H. of C. Journals*, xiii, 784; *V.C.H. Northampton*, ii, 332; *V.C.H. Cambridge*, ii, 87; Defoe, *Tour*, i, 84. Stourbridge Fair was a great mart for cloth as well as for wool (*Tour*, i, 80–3). It does not appear to have been of very great importance as a wool market until the second half of the seventeenth century, though it was frequented by clothiers in the sixteenth (P.R.O. S.P. 12/114/40).

[5] *H. of C. Journals*, xiii, 720.

[6] Willan, op. cit., pp. 88, 123.

[7] Advocates' Library, ADV. MSS. 34.2.15 (MS. dated 16th December, 1602).

and probably some of this wool was purchased by dealers for sale to manufacturers farther inland. Later in the century changes seem to have taken place in the port-to-port trade, with London and Colchester taking more than three-quarters of the wool shipped from Boston in 1685–6.[1] Fifty years later, however, King's Lynn was again the main centre of import.[2]

Besides receiving shipments of wool from Lincolnshire and making purchases of wool at Stourbridge Fair and in the inland counties, the Essex manufacturers also drew heavily upon London for their raw material. Many thousands of sheep were brought yearly to the London meat market and slaughtered by the carcass butchers to feed the capital's growing population. Much fell wool thus came to the London market. This was bought up by the fellmongers, wool dealers and Staplers of Southwark, Barnaby Street and Leaden Hall. One large part of it was resold to the blanket makers of Witney,[3] and another to the bayes makers of Essex. That for the bayes manufacture was usually carried north by the Colchester carriers who weekly brought the manufactured goods to London.[4] In addition to obtaining fell wool from London the Essex manufacturers also acquired fleece wool from the same source. Probably most of this wool was sent by land carriage, but some of it was shipped along the coast. By the end of the seventeenth century there was a considerable coastal trade in wool between London and Colchester.[5] Thus in the year ending Christmas, 1685, London shipped 19,550 stones of wool to the Essex port, this amounting to just over seventy per cent. of Colchester's total import of the raw material. Other ports to send wool were, in order of importance, Cowes, Faversham, Boston, Great Yarmouth, Newcastle and Southwold.[6]

---

[1] Willan, op. cit., p. 124.

[2] King's Lynn received 371 packs out of a total of 604 shipped from Boston in 1736 (ibid., p. 88).

[3] R. Plot, *The Natural History of Oxfordshire* (1677), pp. 279–80.

[4] P.R.O. P.C. 2/47, fols. 30–1; *H. of C. Journals*, xiii, 570, 720, 783–4; *Tudor Economic Documents*, i, 195; R. B. Westerfield, *Middlemen in English Business* (1915), p. 259; Defoe, *The Complete English Tradesman*, ii, 277. Fell wool was also used, though to a lesser extent, by the Norfolk worsted industry. The Northampton glovers supplied part of the raw material (P.R.O. Req. 2/169/12).

[5] In the early eighteenth century two Colchester packet boats were 'going weekly from Wivenhoe to London with Bays, Says and Perpetuanas and from London to Wivenhoe with wooll to be manufactured at Colchester' (*Statutes of the Realm*, 13 Anne, c. 20, sec. 19).

[6] Willan, op. cit., pp. 89, 136. In the same year Colchester shipped 63 packs of coarse locks to London (ibid., p. 136).

The fairly wide area from which the Essex industry was drawing its wool supplies at this period suggests that the manufacturers in the county were finding it difficult to obtain sufficient raw material for their requirements. Such a view is confirmed by a petition from the manufacturers of Colchester to the House of Commons in 1699, which pointed out that the making of bayes, sayes and perpetuanas in the town had 'lain under great discouragement for about seven years last, by the scarcity of wool';[1] and this followed a petition of 1698 in which the Essex manufacturers asked that Colchester should be made a port for the importation of Irish wool.[2] The request was not granted. But not many years afterwards the Colchester manufacturers were receiving considerable quantities of Irish yarn which were brought overland from Bristol.

The Norwich manufacturers also began using large quantities of Irish yarn. Much of this was received via London, to which town it was taken by land carriage from Bristol.[3] A large coastal trade in this commodity sprang up between London and Great Yarmouth; and in 1733 the Norfolk manufacturers obtained 34,250 stones of Irish worsted yarn by this route. In the same year Great Yarmouth imported 770 stones of yarn from Hull.[4] The Norfolk industry was drawing its supplies of raw material from far afield; and even early in the seventeenth century yarn had been obtained from Essex, Suffolk and other nearby counties.[5] Defoe found 'almost the whole counties of Cambridge, Bedford and Hertford' employed in making yarn for the Norwich manufacturers, who also imported 'many thousand packs of yarn' from as far north as Westmorland. When Defoe wrote, much of this yarn was made from wool that the Norwich manufacturers — some of them now big men — sent out for spinning.[6] But this would seem to have been a comparatively recent development. During the early seventeenth century the spinners of the neighbouring counties worked mainly with locally grown wool; and much of the yarn that they spun was

[1] Hist. MSS. Comm. *House of Lords MSS.* N.S. iii, 386.
[2] *H. of C. Journals*, xii, 79.
[3] B.M. Add. MS. 33344, fol. 67; Defoe, *The Complete English Tradesman*, ii, 276–7.
[4] Willan, op. cit., 93–4.
[5] *A.P.C. July 1621–May 1623*, p. 486. See also *V.C.H. Essex*, ii, 398; Unwin, op. cit., pp. 294, 298.
[6] *The Complete English Tradesman*, ii, 276.

taken by dealers to markets in Norfolk, where it was sold to the manufacturers of worsted fabrics.[1]

The West Riding woollen industry obtained its wool supplies from a number of areas. In the first half of the sixteenth century probably the largest part of the raw material used by the West Riding industry was grown in Yorkshire; and before their dissolution there were many monastic houses in the county, besides individual farmers, to help satisfy the demand. In 1525, for example, a clothier from Bradford purchased £20 worth of wool from the prior of St. Oswald's.[2] But Yorkshire wool alone was not sufficient to supply the needs of the expanding West Riding industry; and while some of the wealthier clothiers travelled to Derbyshire, Lincolnshire and Nottinghamshire for their raw material, the smaller manufacturers sometimes obtained the wool grown in neighbouring counties from dealers at their local markets.[3]

During the remainder of the sixteenth century and throughout the seventeenth, the West Riding woollen industry continued to draw heavily upon Yorkshire[4] and the adjacent counties for its supplies of raw material, while at the same time it tapped more distant sources of supply. By 1619 the market and manufacturing towns of Halifax, Leeds and Wakefield were taking a large part of the wool grown in the four northern counties; and these areas continued to supply the West Riding industry with raw material for many years to come. Wool was brought regularly to the Wakefield market from Kendal and Rochdale among other places, while dealers

[1] *A.P.C. July 1621–May 1623*, pp. 295–6, 329, 445–56, 486–8. Bedfordshire, and probably the other neighbouring counties, also supplied raw wool to the Norwich industry (P.R.O. E.134/44–5 Elizabeth I. Mich. 1).

[2] P.R.O. C.1/637/4. The monastic houses in Lincolnshire also supplied wool to the West Riding manufacturers. See J. E. T. Rogers, *A History of Agriculture and Prices in England* (Oxford, 1882), iii, 232; iv, 323.

[3] P.R.O. C.1/718/11; C.1/746/31; C.1/747/12; C.1/793/24; C.1/1329/15; C.3/7/107.

[4] According to Henry Best, the dealers who bought wool from the East Riding farmers carried 'it into the West, towards Leeds, Hallifax' (*Rural Economy in Yorkshire in 1641*, p. 26). Much of the wool grown in the North Riding was sold in the wool market at Ripon, which was greatly frequented by the Leeds clothiers in the sixteenth and seventeenth centuries (Heaton, op. cit., p. 119). The wool grown in the West Riding, however, was generally of a poorer quality than that produced elsewhere in the county and, as the local industry developed, some of it was sold to the Lancashire clothiers who manufactured it into the coarsest types of cloth (Hist. MSS. Comm. *14th Report*, part iv, p. 573).

carried Northumberland wool to Richmond, Ripon and Leeds for sale to the Yorkshire manufacturers.[1]

The wool grown in the northern counties was of the poorest quality, and, like some of that produced in Yorkshire, it was suitable for the manufacture of only the very coarsest cloths. It was, however, no worse than Scottish wool, which by 1621 was also being used by the West Riding industry. The wools of Scotland and the northern counties were held in very low esteem by many Yorkshire manufacturers and at first Irish wool was judged to be little better.[2] But improvements in the breed of sheep in Ireland and the deterioration in the quality of the English wool supply led the West Riding clothiers to revise their opinions. By 1698 men who knew something about the business were advancing the view that Irish wool was 'generally better than the English', besides being considerably cheaper;[3] and in 1707 the Yorkshire manufacturers found the Irish raw material to be of such 'great advantage' to their trade that they requested Parliament to make Lancaster a centre for its import, it being 'much nearer and more convenient . . . than the tollerated ports'.[4]

For making their better-quality kersies and broadcloths the West Riding manufacturers employed mainly Lincolnshire or Midlands wool; and they used this either by itself or mixed it with the coarser northern wool — the mixture making the cloths 'more durable and more saleable' than when made from northern wool alone.[5] The textile industries of East Anglia and the West of England took most of the finest and longest wool produced in Lincolnshire and the midland counties; and the West Riding clothiers used only the coarser grades of short-staple wool grown in these areas. This, however, was superior to that produced in Yorkshire and the northernmost counties.

The transference of wool to the West Riding from areas situated south of Yorkshire was carried on in several ways. As the northern industry expanded, direct purchase of wool by

---

[1] B.M. Add. MS. 34324, fol. 15; P.R.O. S.P. 12/117/38; *H. of C. Journals*, xiii, 501; S. H. Waters, *Wakefield in the Seventeenth Century* (1933), p. 135.
[2] P.R.O. E.134/14 Charles I. Mich. 21; *H. of C. Journals*, i, 653; Defoe, *The Complete English Tradesman*, ii, 280.
[3] Hist. MSS. Comm. *House of Lords MSS*. N.S. iii, 109.
[4] *H. of C. Journals*, xv, 242.
[5] P.R.O. S.P. 14/111/72; E.134/14 Charles I. Mich. 21.

clothiers became more common. Depositions in a law-suit of 1638 show many of the West Riding manufacturers making journeys into the wool-growing districts of Lincolnshire and Leicestershire in order to purchase wool,[1] and growers who lived in the north of Lincolnshire sometimes brought wool to the Doncaster market.[2] But the wool middleman still remained a vital link between the West Riding industry and its supplies of raw material. In the second quarter of the seventeenth century wool was brought regularly to the Doncaster wool market from the counties of Nottingham, Derby, Lincoln, Leicester and Warwick, as well as from Yorkshire;[3] and doubtless the other large West Riding markets were similarly attended.

The great bulk of home-grown wool that went to the West Riding for manufacture was transported there by land carriage. But by the end of the seventeenth century there was a rapidly growing coastal trade in the raw material between some of the east coast ports and Hull. Only Boston appears to have shipped wool to Hull in the early seventeenth century, and this trade was of small importance. In 1684, however, the Yorkshire port received wool from King's Lynn, Colchester, Great Yarmouth, Woodbridge and London. The largest shipments at this time were from King's Lynn. In 1684 these amounted to 14,100 stones; and in 1685, out of a total of 13,900 stones shipped from King's Lynn, Hull took all but 60. The West Riding industry drew more heavily upon Norfolk for its supplies of raw material in the eighteenth century. In the year ending Christmas, 1735, King's Lynn sent out almost 43,800 stones of wool, all of which were bound for Hull; and the Yorkshire port also received considerable quantities of Norfolk wool from Great Yarmouth and Wells. But by this time there was scarcely a port along the east coast shipping wool that did not send some at least to Hull. London, which does not appear to have sent much wool to the West Riding during most of the seventeenth century, became an increasingly important source of supply in the eighteenth; and during the year ending Christmas, 1732, it shipped 3,231 bags of wool to Hull. At the same time, 587 packs of wool were sent

---

[1] P.R.O. E.134/14 Charles I. Mich. 20, 21; Req. 2/118/37.
[2] P.R.O. E.134/18 Charles I. East. 9, 19; E.134/17 Charles I. Mich. 8.
[3] P.R.O. E.134/17 Charles I. Mich. 8. See also P.R.O. S.P. 14/80/13; *V.C.H. Northampton*, ii, 332.

from Grimsby and smaller quantities from other Lincolnshire ports. Suffolk wool was shipped from Ipswich, Aldeburgh and Woodbridge, and northern wool from Alnmouth and Berwick.[1] The Yorkshire coarse-woollen industry thus drew supplies of raw material through Hull from many sources; but probably a not insignificant proportion of the wool shipped from Norfolk, Lincolnshire and London was used by the worsted industry, which took firm root in the West Riding after the Restoration.

In the north-west of England the woollen industry in the sixteenth and seventeenth centuries relied largely upon the northern counties and Ireland for its raw material. The coarsest of the northern wool seems to have sufficed for the Kendal industry, it being stated in 1619 that Kendal 'converteth not into Cottons the fortith part' of the wool grown in Cumberland, Westmorland and Northumberland, 'and that only the refuse'. The better types of northern wool were used by the clothiers of Lancashire and the West Riding;[2] and in addition, the manufacturers of the former county drew upon Yorkshire for some of their supplies.[3]

Although Ireland did not become a major source of wool supply for the Lancashire industry until some way through the seventeenth century, Irish wool was being sold in Lancashire at least as early as 1530, and Irish yarn by 1590.[4] Towards the end of the seventeenth century very large quantities of Irish wool were being imported at Liverpool and smaller quantities at Chester.[5] English merchants went to Ireland, bought wool, and sent it across to Liverpool. Here it was sometimes warehoused until sent for by agents, who sold it at Bolton, Bury and other places.[6]

Besides drawing upon Ireland and the northern counties of England for supplies of raw material, the Lancashire clothiers also obtained wool from Scotland, the Midlands and Lincolnshire.[7] But none of these areas appears to have been drawn upon

[1] Willan, op. cit., pp. 88–9, 120–1.
[2] B.M. Add. MS. 34324, fol. 15.
[3] Hist. MSS. Comm. *14th Report*, part iv, 573; P.R.O. C.1/639/43.
[4] See P.R.O. D.L. 1/5/M.2; D.L. 1/8/T.2; Req. 2/110/32; S.P. 15/27/35.
[5] Supra, p. 62.
[6] P.R.O. E.134/26 Charles II. East. 15. The bulk of the Irish wool used in the West Riding industry must also have come through Liverpool and Chester.
[7] P.R.O. S.P. 14/80/13; L.A.O. HEN. 3/2; *Commons Debates, 1621,* vii, 497; Defoe, *The Complete English Tradesman,* ii, 280.

until the seventeenth century, and none seems to have been of primary importance as a source of wool supply for the Lancashire industry.

V

We have now surveyed the most important wool-manufacturing areas in England during the sixteenth and seventeenth centuries, and have looked at the sources of wool supply from the standpoint of demand. Viewed from the supply side, the two most striking features of the wool supply are seen to be firstly, the changes in the distribution of the Midlands[1] wool, and secondly, the increase in the import of wool from Ireland and Spain.

In the early decades of the sixteenth century a large part of the wool grown in the Midlands was exported; but by the third quarter of the century the export trade had become of little significance, and most of this wool now went to the fine broadcloth manufacture of the West of England. As the Midlands wool changed in character, its distribution also changed; and by the early years of the seventeenth century a considerable proportion of it was being supplied to the eastern worsted industry and the northern coarse-woollen manufacture. The East Anglian industry, in particular, drew more and more heavily upon the inland counties for its supplies of raw material; and by the end of the seventeenth century the English fine woollen industry was probably taking the smallest part of the Midlands wool; the coarse-woollen manufacture a larger part, and the worsted industry most of all.

Not only did the increase in the production of long-staple wool in central England give an impetus to the manufacture of worsted fabrics in East Anglia and other industrial areas, it also facilitated the establishment of the worsted industry in the Midlands region itself. Here, there had been several important seats of the cloth manufacture in the twelfth and thirteenth centuries;[2] but most of these had subsequently declined. Only Northampton and Coventry could put forward any serious claim to be considered as cloth-producing centres in the sixteenth century; and even in these places the woollen manu-

---

[1] Including Lincolnshire.
[2] E. Lipson, *The History of the English Woollen and Worsted Industries* (1921), pp. 220–2.

facture had practically disappeared by the early decades of the seventeenth.[1] In the later years of the seventeenth century, however, the wool-textile industry in these and other midland towns was revived by the development of the worsted manufacture. Stockings were made in Leicestershire, Rutland and Northamptonshire, as well as in the neighbouring counties of Derby and Nottingham; while shalloons, tammies and serges were also produced, particularly at Coventry and round about Kettering.[2]

The change in the character of the English wool supply stimulated the rise of the worsted manufacture, both in the Midlands, where lack of adequate water power for fulling mills militated against the economic production of woollens, and in other areas where the cloth industry was well-established, but depressed. At the same time it proved detrimental to the woollen manufacture, especially in the West of England, and made necessary the import of fine wool from Spain. As for the large increase in the import of Irish wool during the seventeenth century, this was due partly to the economic policy of the English government, and partly to the rapidly growing demands for raw material by the English worsted industry.

Though the changing character and distribution of Midlands wool and the growing importance of Irish and Spanish wool were the most notable features of the English textile industry's wool supply during the sixteenth and seventeenth centuries, there were yet other aspects worthy of mention. The part played by Cirencester as a distribution centre for wool grown in and about the Midlands has already been considered,[3] and nothing further need be added. London acted in a similar capacity, receiving and sending out many types of wool, particularly that grown in the south and east of England;[4] and probably long before the end of the seventeenth century the capital had become more

---

[1] See *V.C.H. Northampton*, ii, 332–6; *V.C.H. Warwick*, ii, 251–6.

[2] *Records of the Borough of Leicester, 1603–1688*, ed. H. Stocks, p. 536; *H. of C. Journals*, xi, 475; *V.C.H. Rutland*, i, 237; *V.C.H. Northampton*, ii, 332–4; *V.C.H. Derby*, ii, 321, 367, 371; *V.C.H. Nottingham*, ii, 285, 293, 358; *V.C.H. Warwick*, ii, 256. Bayes were made in Coventry as early as 1595 (ibid., p. 252). Tammies were also made in Rutland and at Mansfield in Nottinghamshire (*V.C.H. Rutland*, i, 237; *V.C.H. Nottingham*, ii, 293).

[3] Supra, pp. 58, 60.

[4] See, for example, P.R.O. E.134/5 George I. Trin. 5; E.134/6 George I. East. 13; *H. of C. Journals*, xiii, 783–4.

important in this role than Cirencester. Not only was London the chief centre of the wool-stapling trade, with its headquarters at Leaden Hall and Barnaby Street, it was also the most important distributing point for woollen manufactures and the largest port in the kingdom. Wool was brought to the capital by dealers, was sold, and then carried west and north, usually in the same waggons as arrived weekly with manufactured goods. Shipments of wool were received from a number of ports on the south and east coasts; and at least three important manufacturing areas obtained supplies of wool from London by sea.[1] In the eighteenth century, London's coastal trade greatly increased, and the capital became even more important as a centre for the distribution of wool.

Another notable feature of the wool supply in the sixteenth and seventeenth centuries was the increase in the transmission of wool along the coast. Such a development is what one would expect at a time when the internal wool market was continually expanding. Yet though the coastal traffic in wool had assumed considerable proportions by the end of the seventeenth century, it was even then somewhat smaller than one might have anticipated. There was good reason why the coastwise trade was not large during the late sixteenth and early seventeenth centuries, when the purchase of wool was restricted by legislation,[2] and why the only substantial shipments of wool during this period were those imported from South Wales by the clothiers themselves.[3] But merchants were free to deal in wool after 1620; and as it was often considerably cheaper to send wool along the coast than overland, it may seem surprising that sea-transport was not utilized to a greater extent.

Reliable figures showing the relative costs of transporting wool by land and by water during the sixteenth and seventeenth centuries are not easy to obtain.[4] Original data on the subject

---

[1] Willan, *The English Coasting Trade, 1600–1750*, passim.

[2] Infra, pp. 115–18.

[3] Infra, p. 59.

[4] A few isolated figures (other than those given in the text and footnotes following) have been obtained of the costs of transporting wool. These, however, are not very reliable; and as the wool concerned was carried between different places, the relative costs of the two forms of transport cannot be compared. Most of these figures relate to the costs of transporting Irish wool or yarn. In 1698 one wool dealer stated that the cost of bringing a stone of Irish wool to England amounted to 3s. or 37½ per cent. of its prime cost (Hist. MSS. Comm. *House of Lords MSS.* N.S. iii, 109). Another contemporary ventured that Irish wool could be bought at 9d. per

appear to be almost non-existent, and the figures given by contemporaries cannot be accepted as being altogether trustworthy. John Haynes, who favoured a prohibition of the port-to-port trade in wool, may be suspected of playing down the differences in relative costs when he stated in 1706 that the cost of sending a pack of wool from London to Exeter by land carriage was not more than 13s. and by water carriage, 11s.;[1] and he then proceeded to make further comparisons showing that the cost of transporting wool by land was little dearer than it was by sea.[2] Evidence relating to later years, however, tends to confirm the view that the differences in costs were much greater than Haynes alleged. In 1741, John Eyes, surveyor, giving evidence before a Committee which was considering a petition for extending the Calder navigation to Halifax, declared that the water carriage of a ton of wool, from Halifax to Wakefield would be 9s. as compared with 15s. for land carriage.[3] In 1800, a Committee of the House of Lords was told that the carriage of a pack of wool from Exeter to Leeds via London was 29s. 3d. if sent by land from London to Leeds, and 21s. 3d. if sent by sea from London to Leeds.[4] The difference in the cost of the two forms of transport at this time was therefore considerable.

Water carriage being cheaper, why was it not more popular in the seventeenth century? Haynes supplied part of the answer when he stated:

> I presume the greatest disproportion between the Sea and land carriage is so small, that it will not pay for insurance in time of War, or counterballance the hazard of the Sea in time of Peace. Over and above all which, we are still to remember that the Sea

lb. 'including the charge of freight' at 'one penny per pound or a ninth part' (B.M. Add. MS. 4761/34, fol. 189). In 1732 the Commissioners of Trade computed the cost of transporting a pack of Irish wool from Bristol to Colchester or Norwich 'at near fifteen per cent upon the prime cost of the wooll', and the cost of transporting a pack of Irish yarn between the same places 'to be no less than five per cent at a medium upon the prime cost of ye yarne' (B.M. Add. MS. 33344, fols. 67–67b). For other costs of transport, see Hist. MSS. Comm. *Various MSS.* iii, 96; P.R.O. C.1/423/2–3; *H. of C. Journals*, xvi, 137.

[1] *A View of the Present State of the Clothing Trade in England*, p. 65.

[2] Haynes continued: 'Again a Pack of wool sent from London to Colchester by Sea, will cost for carriage three shillings and sixpence, and the land carriage is but four shillings and sixpence. The wool that goes from London to Selby and so to Wakefield or Leeds, will cost for Freight, Cocket and other incident Charges twelve shillings per Pack, and by land carriage fifteen shillings or under' (ibid., pp. 65–6).

[3] T. S. Willan, *River Navigation in England, 1600–1750* (Manchester, 1936), p. 121.

[4] C. T. Clay, 'Notes on the Importation of English Wool into Ireland as Affected by the Union', *Thoresby Society Publications*, xxvi, 157.

carriage unavoidably damages the wool by the Fogs, wet etc. to which 'tis not expos'd in the land carriage.[1]

To the reasons given by Haynes it may be added that land carriage was often much quicker and more convenient than water carriage, and that until the inland navigation system was properly developed it was in many cases to remain so.

[1] *A View of the Present State of the Clothing Trade in England*, p. 66. Complaints were sometimes made by manufacturers that their wool was spoilt by salt water getting into it (P.R.O. C.3/199/28; *The Letter Books of Joseph Holroyd and Sam Hill*, ed. H. Heaton (1914), p. 39). Even in 1800 the finer sorts of wool were usually transported by land (Clay, op. cit., p. 147).

Chapter III

THE MARKETING OF WOOL

I

Among the most notable features of English economic development during the sixteenth and seventeenth centuries was a trend towards greater regional specialization. Increasingly, the barriers of local self-sufficiency were being broken down. In the wool-textile industry, wool-producing districts and cloth-manufacturing centres became more sharply defined as the internal wool market expanded. The widening of the market owed something to improvements in the means of communication, but more largely it was due to the rise of classes of professional middlemen and carriers, whose activities came to play an increasingly important role in the evolution of the domestic economy.

The profits to be gained from the purchase and sale of wool had long led men to participate in this trade. Originally, most English wool had been bought by alien merchants for shipment abroad. But the business of riding round and collecting wool from individual farmers and monastic houses was a troublesome one for the foreign exporter, and the middleman wool dealer made his appearance at an early date. By the end of the fourteenth century both Staplers[1] and Italians, though continuing to buy some of their wool direct from the growers, were obtaining a large part of their supplies from these woolmen. In the fifteenth century, with the decline of demesne farming and the growth of peasant agriculture, the woolmen formed one of the wealthiest and most important trading groups in the country, supplying not only the export trade, but also the native cloth industry with wool. Some of these middlemen were merchants from London and other large towns, who dealt in wool among

[1] i.e. members of the English Company of the Merchants of the Staple.

other commodities; but for the most part the woolmen lived in the country districts where they made their purchases. One such district was the Cotswolds — noted for its production of fine-quality wool — where the memory of the woolmen is still preserved in some of the most beautiful churches of England.[1] The correspondence of John Johnson the Stapler[2] shows that some of these dealers were still carrying on a substantial wool trade in the 1540's; but by then, their business being primarily that of supplying wool for export, their importance and numbers had considerably diminished.

Though the woolmen had conducted a subsidiary trade in wool with the native clothiers in the fifteenth century, and continued to do so in the sixteenth, they do not appear to have concentrated as a body on serving the needs of the home industry as the export trade declined. In the first place the size of the transactions which they could conduct with the English clothiers was probably too small. In supplying the export trade with wool the woolmen were accustomed to making bargains in terms of hundreds or even thousands of pounds; but few native manufacturers appear to have been prepared to buy more than £150 worth of wool at a single purchase.[3] Moreover, it was only in the middle years of the sixteenth century that the internal market for wool began to develop on a wider-than-regional basis; and until it did, the wealthier clothiers — who alone of the manufacturers could have provided the woolmen with any considerable custom — were generally able to obtain the larger part of their wool supplies direct from nearby growers, and so experienced no great need for the middlemen's services.

A further reason why the woolmen did not concentrate their attention upon supplying raw material to the home industry may have been the greater attraction of other, more profitable, fields of investment. Besides dealing in wool, the middlemen frequently engaged in other economic activities; and of these, two in particular — those of growing wool and of manu-facturing it — enjoyed a remarkable boom during the first half of the sixteenth century. As the export trade declined, therefore,

---

[1] E. Power, 'The Wool Trade in the Fifteenth Century', *Studies in English Trade in the Fifteenth Century*, ed. E. Power and M. M. Postan (1933), pp. 52–4.
[2] See *Cal. L.P.F.D. Henry VIII*, xix–xxi, passim.
[3] Power and Postan, op. cit., pp. 54–5; P.R.O. C.1/286/37; C.1/370/96; C.1/561/49.

the woolmen may well have turned more and more to these other sources of income. Some, like Richard Waymman of Witney, Oxfordshire, apparently engaged in a little depopulation.[1] Others, like Thomas Busshe, son of John Busshe one of the great woolmen of the *Cely Papers*, entered into the land market in a big way.[2] Again, providing that he commanded the necessary capital, there were no great difficulties in the way of the woolman who wished to become a cloth merchant or entrepreneur on a large scale. Instead of selling the wool which he purchased he could 'exchange' it with the native clothiers for cloth, and in this way gain control over the manufacture and sale of the clothier's product. Such 'exchanges' sometimes took place. In 1496, for example, William Dormer, a Buckinghamshire woolman, delivered 69 sacks 8 tods of 'good and mydell woll of the growyng of Bucks' to William Brograve, who in payment was to make delivery by instalments of 126 'brode clothes of puke colour'.[3] The cloths delivered, they could then, of course, be sold by Dormer. Later, after the mid-sixteenth century, the cloth trade became a less rewarding field for enterprise, but there was a growing traffic in imported wool; and as the home hat industry expanded, the merchants of London, especially the haberdashers, turned more and more to dealing in wools from Spain and other foreign parts.[4]

Though the woolmen were the most important group of wool middlemen at the beginning of the sixteenth century, they were almost certainly outnumbered by the smaller common dealers who were to be found in all parts of the country. Frequently known as 'wool broggers', these often appear to have combined their wool-dealing activities with agriculture and sometimes with other occupations. The increase in the number of these middlemen which undoubtedly took place in the early decades of the sixteenth century, was both a natural consequence of, and a contributory factor in, the expansion of the home cloth manufacture. For it was the wool broggers who kept the small manu-

---

[1] I. S. Leadam, *Domesday of Inclosures* (1897), p. 381.
[2] Power and Postan, op. cit., p. 54.
[3] P.R.O. C.1/308/15. See also C.1/322/19; Finch, op. cit., p. 8. Cloth being an easily marketable commodity, it was also sometimes accepted by wool sellers in lieu of money from manufacturers who defaulted in making payment for wool. See P.R.O. Req. 2/184/48; C.1/364/19.
[4] P. J. Bowden, *Econ. Hist. Rev.* 2nd ser. ix (1956), 56–7.

facturers regularly supplied with raw material, and it was to these dealers that the wealthier clothiers occasionally turned when their stocks of wool ran low in the last six months of the wool-growing year. The transactions of the smallest of these middlemen were too trifling for them to become the subject of costly litigation, but the dealings of some of the more important members of the group may be found in the records of the Courts of Chancery and Requests. While bargains involving one hundred stones of wool or more were occasionally made,[1] the brogger was essentially a retailer of wool, often buying as well as selling in small quantities. His main customers were the poorer manufacturers and, as the size of the transactions concluded with them was small and the number of sales large, a moderate amount of ready cash quickly turned over was all that was required for his business.

Already an essential link between the wool grower and the small manufacturer the middleman became yet more indispensable as his wool-sorting functions developed and the internal wool market expanded. Wool sorting, in the modern sense, became increasingly necessary after about 1570 as English fleeces became more diverse and the varieties of English textiles more numerous. Moreover, as during the late sixteenth and seventeenth centuries the geographical pattern of industrial specialization became more sharply defined, so an extra-regional market for wool came into being, and to the smaller manufacturers were added others, moderately wealthy, who found their trade much facilitated by a third hand placed between themselves and distant growers.

It was here that new and important classes of middlemen appeared on the scene. There were three such classes. First in importance were the Staplers, the majority of whom turned to the internal wool trade after the loss of Calais in 1558.[2] Next came a group of dealers who had connexions with one branch or another of the leather industry. These included glovers, white tawyers, fellmongers, leather sellers and tanners. Finally there were the 'brogging clothiers': manufacturers who resold either all or part of the wool which they purchased.

---

[1] P.R.O. C.1/584/42; C.1/705/20; C.1/718/11; C.1/747/12; C.1/790/17; C.1/1186/33; C.1/1214/12; C.1/1233/2-5.

[2] Infra, pp. 159-60, 167.

The trade of a typical Stapler in the second half of the six-teenth century may be illustrated by that of Richard Baynes, whose business transactions were a subject of frequent litigation. Most Staplers appear to have lived part of the time in a fine wool producing district, and part of the time in London; and Baynes, whose home was in Newport, Shropshire, was no excep-tion. His trade was very largely, if not entirely, in the fine 'March' wool of Shropshire and Staffordshire; and while his factor made purchases from the numerous small wool growers who predominated in these two counties, he himself dealt with the larger business. Some of the wool which he bought was sold to clothiers from Somerset, but Baynes' best customers were the Essex clothiers, particularly those of Coggeshall and Dedham.[1] Some of these purchased wool from Baynes in London; others travelled to his house in Shropshire for the purpose. 'March' wool was not easy to collect: as one contemporary put it, 'the parcelles be so smale where suche wolles growes and aske so longe tyme in gatheringe';[2] and most of the purchases made by Baynes probably weighed less than 10 or 20 stones apiece.[3] Larger amounts of wool could be bought from the wealthier wool growers, and in 1588 Baynes was recorded as buying 600 stones in London from a Wolverhampton dealer named Thomas Huntbache, who was acting on behalf of Sir Walter Leveston.[4] But wealthy wool growers were relatively few in this part of the country, and consequently purchases of such a size, even by the larger middlemen, tended to be rare. In this respect the Staplers who dealt in 'March' wool appear to have differed from their fellows who made their purchases in the Midlands. When, however, it came to selling wool, these merchants, like the rest of the Staplers, seem to have bargained almost entirely in wholesale quantities. Sometimes a sale might be made of as little as a dozen stones of wool,[5] but usually the Staplers' transactions with the manufacturers appear to have been of a much larger magnitude. The sale of 400 stones of fine wool which Richard

---

[1] P.R.O. E.133/136; E.134/7 Elizabeth I. Hil. 1; Req. 2/32/14; Req. 2/35/58; Req. 2/93/20; Req. 2/113/13; Req. 2/163/96; Req. 2/175/19; Req. 2/176/21; S.P. 12/114/47.
[2] P.R.O. S.P. 12/149/34.
[3] Some of the purchases made by Baynes' factor weighed no more than a stone (P.R.O. E.134/7 Elizabeth I. Hil. 1).
[4] P.R.O. Req. 2/175/19.   [5] P.R.O. S.P. 12/114/47.

Baynes made to a Somerset clothier in 1581[1] was certainly somewhat larger than the average, but sales by Staplers of between 50 and 200 stones of wool apiece were very common.[2]

The second group of middlemen — the glovers, fellmongers, leather sellers etc. — came to deal in wool through their interest in sheep skins, which they bought as a normal part of their business.[3] When purchased from the farmers these skins were covered by a growth of fell wool, and this had first to be removed before the pelts could be put through the various processes of manufacture. As the wool was of no use to the leather industry it was then sold (sometimes sorted according to quality) to wool dealers and manufacturers.[4] From selling superfluous fell wool to dealing in fleece wool was but a short step to take; and in the second half of the sixteenth century the trade in fleece wool of a few of the members of this group appears to have been as large as that conducted by many of the Staplers.

The glovers of the central and east Midlands, and those of Northampton in particular, were great wool dealers; and as early as 1545 John Dickeson, a Northampton glover, was contracting to supply £120 worth of wool to Matthew King, one of the capitalists of the Wiltshire cloth industry.[5] Another glover to carry on a large business in wool was Thomas Adkins, probably Bailiff of Northampton in 1579 and Mayor in 1600.[6] In September, 1586, Adkins bought 220 stones of wool from John Isham of Lamport (co. Northants.).[7] His purchases in 1587 were said to incude one of 400 stones from John Freeman, a Northamptonshire gentleman, and another of a similar amount from 'Mr. Brickmylles', a Leicestershire grower. In the following year he was stated to have obtained 1,160 stones of wool from Sir Thomas Tresham of Rushton (co. Northants.), and 400 stones from Anthony Shuckborough Esq., of Warwickshire.[8] Further transactions by Adkins after this date included the sale of a

[1] P.R.O. Req. 2/113/13.
[2] See P.R.O. E.133/1/36; S.P. 12/114/47; Req. 2/32/14; Req. 2/80/45; Req. 2/93/20; Req. 2/163/96; Req. 2/202/2.
[3] See P.R.O. C.1/348/37; C.1/394/3; C.1/1124/20.
[4] P.R.O. C.1/584/42; C.1/1148/4; C.1/1231/23–5; C.1/1311/70–1; Req. 2/104/60; Req. 2/169/12.
[5] P.R.O. Req. 2/16/21.   [6] Finch, op. cit., p. 19, n. 3.
[7] Ibid., p. 19.   [8] P.R.O. E.133/6/833.

considerable quantity of fell and fleece wool to Simon Bowde of Norwich,[1] and a purchase made in partnership with another Northampton glover of 800 stones of wool, priced at £533 6s. 8d., from Sir Edward Montague.[2]

The fellmongers, who do not appear to have figured prominently as wool dealers in the sixteenth century, came more to the fore in the seventeenth. By 1650 there were few fellmongers who did not deal in fleece wool: a business which they had come to regard as being 'as incident to their trade' as the buying and selling of sheep skins.[3] The fellmongers of Southwark and Bermondsey undoubtedly conducted the largest trade in wool,[4] but there were other important groups of these dealers in Coventry and in the counties of Buckingham and Oxford.[5] The towns of Gainsborough and Hungerford also had their fellmongers, some of whom sold 'divers great quantities of wooll' in the markets of Doncaster and Newbury respectively.[6]

Many of the 'brogging clothiers' who bought and sold wool for profit seem to have been wealthy or moderately wealthy men.[7] In the latter half of the sixteenth century the number of such clothiers was probably not very large, and these generally appear to have retained some interest in the manufacture of cloth. George Rugle of Lavenham, for example, who was alleged in 1593 to have resold more than 1,000 stones of wool, was 'a great occupier in makyng of cloth'.[8] In the seventeenth century, however, the indications are that large numbers of clothiers dealt in wool, some completely abandoning their manufacture in favour of the trade.[9] The depressed state of the cloth industry may have been partly responsible for this development, which involved not only the most capitalistic clothiers but small entrepreneurs and independent weavers as well.[10] A further factor, whose influence must have been very considerable, was

[1] P.R.O. Req. 2/169/12. For further on Simon Bowde, see infra, pp. 130, 132, 141.
[2] P.R.O. Req. 2/45/100.
[3] *Cal. S.P. Dom. 1651–2*, p. 470.
[4] See P.R.O. Req. 2/37/46; S.P. 16/515/140.
[5] *Cal. S.P. Dom. 1651*, pp. 198–9; *1651–2*, pp. 470, 471.
[6] P.R.O. E.134/17 Charles I. Mich. 8; E.134/11 Charles I. East. 27. The glovers of Lincoln City also sold wool at Doncaster market (B.M. Add. MS. 43849, fol. 6ᵇ; P.R.O. E.134/17 Charles I. Mich. 8).
[7] See P.R.O. S.P. 12/115/40; S.P. 14/80/13.
[8] P.R.O. E.133/8/1124.
[9] *Cal. S.P. Dom. 1651*, pp. 248–9.
[10] P.R.O. E.134/4 Charles I. East. 36; Ramsay, op. cit., p. 126.

the increasing diversity of the English wool supply. Fleeces which might formerly have been worked up in their entirety had now to be sorted fibre by fibre, and wool for which individual manufacturers could find no use would naturally be sold.

In addition to the clothiers, fellmongers, glovers and Staplers, numerous other persons were attracted to the wool trade in late Tudor and Stuart times. In 1577 it was stated: 'it is . . . a common practize in the wooll contries, that euerie man that will dothe, and is suffered to buy wooll and sell it againe, as well he that is not worthe xl⁸ as he that is worthe vᶜ li';[1] and that appears to have been no great exaggeration, even at a time when the general liberty to trade in wool was restrained by legislation. Yeomen like Roger Sedgewick,[2] and husbandmen like John Issacke,[3] were considerable wool dealers, and many others conducted a lesser trade.[4] Merchants and artisans of all descriptions sometimes dealt in wool, and there were even parsons who tried their hand at the business.[5] Country gentlemen, who had found wool growing to be a very lucrative occupation in the sixteenth century, found wool dealing hardly less profitable in the seventeenth, and numbers of them joined the Staple Company[6] or traded independently of the organization.[7]

The attraction of the wool trade for so many different classes of person suggests that there were few better investments available in Tudor and Stuart England. In the late seventeenth century, one dealer stated that he 'always proposed to get 1s. a stone' profit, this amounting to a little over 9 per cent. of the total cost of wool and transport.[8] Other contemporary sources also suggest that about 1s. or 10 per cent. was a dealer's average profit-margin on wool sold at 11s. or 12s. per stone.[9] Richard Best, a Yorkshire carrier in the reign of James I, 'got a great

---

[1] P.R.O. S.P. 12/114/33.

[2] P.R.O. Req. 2/109/3; Req. 2/122/32; Req. 2/243/53; E.133/3/399; E.134/9 Elizabeth I. Hil. 3; S.P. 12/114/42.

[3] P.R.O. E.133/3/545; Req. 2/111/28.

[4] An estimate made in June, 1577, of the amounts of wool sold by different dealers in the market at Cirencester, credited a Warwickshire husbandman with selling 80 stones weekly, and two Leicestershire husbandmen each with selling 60 stones (P.R.O. S.P. 12/114/41).

[5] P.R.O. Req. 2/206/3.   [6] B.M. Add. MS. 43849, passim.

[7] K.A.O. U.442/E.4, fols. 7ᵇ–8; *V.C.H. Derbyshire*, ii, 346.

[8] Hist. MSS. Comm. *House of Lords MSS*. N.S. iii, 109.

[9] P.R.O. Req. 2/169/12; *H. of C. Journals*, xii, 277.

estate with that and selling wool at Halifax, which he brought upon his own horses',[1] and doubtless there were others like him. At the end of the seventeenth century industrialists with profits to invest might put them into the wool trade. Information 'that there was a great deal of money to be got in that Trade' led Anthony Smoult, a London sweetmaker and distiller, to forsake his old business in order to deal in wool. 'Having neither skill nor knowledge therein' he took into partnership a London journeyman wool-stapler named Michael Howard to attend to the practical side of affairs.[2] But though some fortunes were made in the wool trade, not everyone who engaged in it prospered. Wool dealing did not make the fortune of Henry James of Briston (co. Norfolk), who died in 1618 with household goods worth only £2 16s. 2d., and it had been precarious for Francis Aylemer of Buxton, in the same county, who had little at his death in 1601 apart from hopeful and desperate debts amounting to £60.[3]

Increasingly, those who prospered were dealers able to start out in a large way of business. Ever since the last decades of the sixteenth century the day of the small and unspecialized wool broggers had been gradually coming to an end. The widening of the internal wool market and the increasing diversity of English fleeces were factors too great for them to contend with; and in the eighteenth century the home trade in wool came to be conducted very largely by big and specialist merchants, the broggers being employed in the country as agents for them and the wealthy manufacturers.[4]

II

The procedure adopted in the purchase and sale of wool varied considerably. Growers might dispose of their clip to clothiers or to middlemen, while tarry wool and locks were sometimes sold to local inhabitants for domestic use.[5] Ignoring transactions of the latter type, the majority of growers normally disposed of their entire wool crop each year to a single buyer or partnership of buyers. The larger growers sometimes supplied several

---

[1] *Rural Economy in Yorkshire in 1641*, p. 26.
[2] P.R.O. E.134/6 George I. Hil. 9.   [3] Allison, *thesis*, p. 364.
[4] R. B. Westerfield, *Middlemen in English Business* (1915), p. 266. See also B.M. Lansd. MS. 28/26; ibid. 114/25; P.R.O. S.P. 12/113/19; S.P. 12/114/40, for instances of broggers acting as agents in the sixteenth century.
[5] Supra, p. 4, n. 2.

different demands during the year, but in such cases the amounts of wool involved were usually substantial. Sir Roger Townshend of East Rainham sold his wool in 1625 to 165 Norfolk men and women — presumably worsted manufacturers — in quantities of one or two stones each, but he did not normally engage in such small transactions[1] and neither did the class of sheep farmer which he represented.

Many growers sold their wool by contract. It is impossible to measure the relative importance of advance agreements as compared with on-the-spot transactions, but they were certainly very common. There were several different kinds of contract, and these may be divided into two main categories: those for a single delivery of wool; and those for a regular supply of the raw material.

Contracts of the first type were made at all times of the year, and at anything from a day to a year ahead of the date specified for delivery. Thus, in May, 1551, a London middleman sold a large quantity of wool to a Newbury clothier and promised to make delivery to him in London ten days later.[2] In November, 1591, a Northamptonshire grower sold wool worth £105 to a London merchant, who agreed to collect the wool at Dingley during the following August.[3] Most agreements of this kind were made between April and June, when wealthy clothiers and middlemen travelled around the country purchasing wool from farmers before it was shorn. In some of these cases the growers contracted to supply a specified weight of wool,[4] while in others they agreed to supply their entire clip.[5] Usually the price to be paid for such wool was agreed upon when the bargain was made, but occasionally it was made dependent upon the current market price at the time of delivery.[6] A payment, either token, partial or complete, was usually made by the buyer to seal the bargain.[7] The small and medium growers frequently entered

[1] Allison, *Econ. Hist. Rev.* 2nd ser. xi (1958), 107.
[2] P.R.O. Req. 2/17/16.
[3] P.R.O. Req. 2/212/72.
[4] P.R.O. Req. 2/204/48; Req. 2/206/29.
[5] P.R.O. Req. 2/2/14; Req. 2/171/24. See also P.R.O. C.1/584/42, for an agreement between a glover and a wool dealer for a year's supply of fell wool; C.1/1148/4, for a similar agreement between a glover and a clothier.
[6] P.R.O. Req. 2/2/14.
[7] See, for example, P.R.O. S.P. 12/113/19; S.P. 15/9/56; *B.M. Pamphlets,* 712, g. 16/3, pp. 13–14.

into contracts before sheep-shearing time, but the larger growers usually preferred to keep their produce until later in the wool-growing year in order to benefit from the seasonal rise in price.[1] This latter practice was adopted, for example, by Sir John Hatcher and Sir Nicholas Saunderson, both early seventeenth-century Lincolnshire gentlemen, who on occasion held their wool until the following spring before disposing of it.[2] Some growers kept their wool even longer, storing it in years of low prices and selling when prices rose. One such grower was Townshend, who had two or three years' clips in his wool-house in 1479–83. Normally, in such instances, old wool was sold first.[3]

Contracts for the regular delivery of wool were of two main varieties. First, there were those contracts for the supply of wool at the current market price. These might be written or unwritten agreements, made for a specified number of years, or for life. They might relate to a definite quantity of wool or to a grower's entire clip. A rather unusual sort of agreement was that made in 1581 between Thomas Wynde of South Wotton (co. Norfolk), and Roger Sedgewick of St. Ives (co. Hunts.), whereby Wynde promised to sell Sedgewick all his wool for three or four years until the supply reached the value of £119 17s. od.[4] A less binding arrangement was the tacit understanding whereby a grower sold his clip to the same buyer every year, although not pledged in any way to do so. In the 1630's Sir George Heneage — having supplied wool in previous years to various local Lincolnshire dealers and to Suffolk, West Riding and Lancashire manufacturers and middlemen — appears to have come to some such understanding with Tempest Pollard, gentleman of Wakefield.[5] At about the same time, Hatcher of Careby, whose previous customers had been equally various, began to supply his clip regularly to Thomas Reynolds of Colchester, although there is no evidence that he was under any legal obligation to do so.[6]

[1] B.M. Lansd. MS. 114/25; ibid. 28/26; P.R.O. S.P. 12/114/28, 32. Stated Henry Best: 'Wee solde our woll (this yeare) to a Beverley-man the 1st Aprill, and had for it 8s. a stone, besides 12d. in earnest; and if wee had kept it for a fortnight longer might have had 9s. 6d. if not 10s. a stone' (*Rural Economy in Yorkshire in 1641*, p. 30).
[2] L.A.O. H.97/22/1, 2; Lumley MS. 2305.
[3] Allison, *Econ. Hist. Rev.* 2nd ser. xi (1958), 107.
[4] P.R.O. Req. 2/122/32. See also P.R.O. C.1/192/58.
[5] L.A.O. HEN.3/2.   [6] L.A.O. H.97/22/1, 2.

The second, and in some ways more interesting, types of long-term contract were those made for the supply of wool at a fixed total price, or at a fixed price per stone. Thus in the early years of Elizabeth I's reign, Nicholas Maryn, vicar of Morval parish in Cornwall, entered into a long-term contract to supply John Bone, a local dealer, with all his tithe wool, excepting that grown by sheep on glebe lands, in return for the payment of a yearly 'rent' of £6 13s. 4d.[1] This type of agreement does not appear to have been very common; but in the early years of the sixteenth century, contracts were frequently made for the supply of wool at a fixed price per stone.

Typical of such agreements was that made in 1504 between Richard Tanty of Chipping Norton and George Somerfeld, a Gloucestershire grower, whereby Somerfeld contracted to supply the Oxfordshire man with all the wool that he grew during the remainder of his life at a fixed price of 5s. 8d. per stone.[2] This type of agreement seems to have been most common in the West of England, where the cloth industry was most capitalistic, but similar arrangements were sometimes made in other parts of the country.[3] Such agreements were appropriate only in an era of more stable prices; and when the price of wool rapidly increased, some growers refused to make delivery at the terms agreed upon,[4] while others withheld the largest part of their clip to sell elsewhere.[5] The buyers thereupon endeavoured to obtain legal redress, and as not all these contracts had been drawn up in writing, a number of actions was brought in the Court of Chancery,[6] where equity cases were heard. Contracts for the supply of wool at a fixed price continued to be made after the mid-sixteenth century. But the growers were now more wary; and in 1600, one prominent Midlands grower, on being asked to sell his wool to the Corporation of Leicester, replied that he was willing to do so, either at a fixed price for seven

---

[1] P.R.O. C.3/19/14.   [2] P.R.O. C.1/449/17.
[3] P.R.O. C.1/578/15; C.1/1122/8–9; C.1/1229/62–4.
[4] P.R.O. C.1/386/43; C.1/396/40; C.1/449/17.
[5] One Devonshire clothier accused a Somersetshire gentleman of doing this, adding that in a previous year when the market price had been lower than the contract price, the grower had purchased wool and resold it to him 'vnder the coloure of the wull comynge and growing of his owne shepe' (P.R.O. C.1/1176/1).
[6] P.R.O. C.1/1117/33; C.1/1122/8–9, 27; C./1/1176/1; C.1/1186/2; C.1/1201/24; C.1/1279/45–7.

years, or, if they gave bond 'to become his chapmen for life', at the best current price.[1]

It was not only long-term contracts at fixed prices, however, which were broken through rapid movements in the price of wool. The carrying out of contracts for single deliveries of wool was also sometimes affected. Between 1544 and 1551 several such agreements were broken because the price of wool had risen after the date of the bargain and before the date specified for delivery.[2] But it was not always the sellers who went back on their bargains. When the price of wool suddenly fell, as in 1518 and 1551, some buyers refused to accept the delivery of wool which they had ordered previously.[3]

A broken agreement for the supply of wool could prove both costly and inconvenient to the party offended against, particularly the buyer. Quite apart from the unnecessary trouble and expense involved in travelling to collect the wool,[4] arrangements which middlemen might make for the disposal of the raw material and manufacturers might make for the hiring of labour or the delivery of cloth were also upset by non-delivery. In one such case an Abingdon wool dealer and yarn manufacturer named Gilbert Freman claimed that he had 'made Bargaynes withe dyuars persones for to serue them bothe of woll and yarne and bounde hymselfe in severall obligacions to seuerall persones for the delyuere of the said woll and yarne', which obligations had been forfeit.[5] In another case, a Banbury clothier alleged that he had 'to his greate costes and charges . . . waged and hyred dyuers and sondre persons for one hole yere . . . for the makinge of cloth' from wool which he had not received.[6] Another clothier estimated 'hurte and Damage of xl^li';[7] while one dealer who had made a sale of 15 tods of wool to a

[1] *Records of the Borough of Leicester, 1509–1603*, ed. M. Bateson, p. 417.
[2] P.R.O. C.1/1107/4; C.1/1148/4; Req. 2/5/56; Req. 2/16/21; Req. 2/17/16. Similarly, in the years 1525–6 and 1589–91, the rise in the price of wool led some growers to break their contracts. See P.R.O. Req. 2/3/100; Req. 2/204/48.
[3] P.R.O. C.1/584/42; C.1/1311/70–1.
[4] One Somerset clothier claimed that he and his carriers had travelled over a hundred miles to obtain wool which a grower had agreed to supply, only to find that it had been sold to 'persons vnknowne' (P.R.O. C.1/951/13). In another case, a Newbury clothier 'hyryd a cart purposely to come to London' to collect wool which was not delivered (P.R.O. Req. 2/17/16).
[5] P.R.O. Req. 2/2/14. For 'obligations' see infra, p. 102.
[6] P.R.O. C.1/1148/4.
[7] P.R.O. C.1/1214/12. See also P.R.O. C.1/981/95.

Wiltshire clothier, gave him forty shillings to release the bargain.[1]

After a sale of wool had been made, the wool was normally weighed, packed and delivered to the buyer. In the case of an on-the-spot transaction, the first operation at least was performed immediately. But where there was an advance agreement for the supply of wool, all three operations were carried out at some future date, which was usually specified at the time of the bargain. The weighing of wool could be a tricky business, and not infrequently accusations were made of sharp practices. In one dispute it was alleged that the buyer 'did not way the . . . woll indefferentlie . . . and did kepe vp the scale with his hosen';[2] and a number of ingenious devices were also allegedly used with intent to swindle.[3] In some instances, therefore, wool was weighed in the presence of 'indifferent' men, who saw to it that there was fair play.[4] Disputes also arose over the weighing of damp wool, which, if weighed in the normal way, gave an advantage to the seller.[5]

When the wool had been weighed, it might be packed in canvas, and if delivery was to be made at some later date, each pack was then marked with the 'marke or signature' of the buyer. The canvas was of some value, and in cases where it was supplied by the seller, it was normally returned to him, or payment was made for it by the buyer.[6]

After weighing and packing, wool which was purchased at a grower's house was either taken away immediately or, most often when it was bought by a dealer, left there for collection at some future date. In the latter case the wool might be locked up in the grower's wool-house, and the key given to the buyer as a precaution against the wool being tampered with in his absence.[7] Wool that was bought in the country was seldom delivered to the purchaser elsewhere than at the grower's house, it being 'the order and vse amongeste clothyers [and dealers] to weye the wooll they buy in the countrie and fetche the same where the

---

[1] P.R.O. Req. 2/45/100.   [2] P.R.O. Req. 2/49/37.
[3] See B.M. Lansd. MS. 152, fols. 223-4.
[4] P.R.O. C.3/200/90; Req. 2/49/37.
[5] P.R.O. Req. 2/394/76.
[6] P.R.O. C.1/423/2-3; C.1/718/11; C.1/1198/20; Req. 2/113/13; E.134/9 Elizabeth I. Hil. 3.
[7] P.R.O. C.3/200/90.

seller thereof dothe pyle the same'.[1] The clothiers and middlemen themselves frequently came with transport to fetch wool from the grower's house.[2] If the buyer had not, or could not spare, the means of transport, it could be hired. One Gloucestershire clothier, for instance, went to collect wool from a Wiltshire gentleman with 'as many carttes and horses as stood hym in xl^s'.[3] Sometimes, carriers were employed to fetch wool. In 1523, for example, one Rutland dealer was indebted to a local husbandman 'in the some of xlvj^s for carying of certain lodes of woll to Cristowe and other placies to his greit labor and coste'.[4]

Clothiers usually lost little time in fetching wool from the grower's house. In most cases the entire purchase was collected at one time. But a clothier buying a large quantity of wool from a grower might prefer to collect it in several instalments. Thus in 1526 a West Country manufacturer purchased 549 stones of wool from a Wiltshire gentleman, and made arrangements to fetch it in three instalments, namely at the Feast of St. Bartholomew (24th August), at the Feast of All Saints (1st November), and at the Feast of the Purification (2nd February).[5]

More frequently than the clothiers, the middlemen left wool in the growers' hands and collected it later in the year when wool prices had risen. The complaint was often made that dealers 'resort to the growers and bargaine with them for their woulles at higher prices than the prices of the cuntrie ben whear they dwell geving only but a smal somme of monie in earneste the woulle to be receaved at their pleasures afore the next sheare'.[6] Sometimes the middlemen bought wool by earnest, and sold 'the same remayning in the growers handes'.[7] After wool had been delivered by the grower, the dealer or his hired carrier might take it straight to market.[8] At other times, wool might be taken to an inn.[9] But most frequently it was carried to the dealer's house or warehouse.

---

[1] P.R.O. Req. 2/206/29.   [2] P.R.O. C.1/951/13.
[3] P.R.O. Req. 2/3/100.
[4] P.R.O. Req. 2/2/161. See also P.R.O. E.134/9 Elizabeth I. Hil. 3.
[5] P.R.O. Req. 2/3/100.   [6] P.R.O. S.P. 12/113/19.
[7] Ibid. See also P.R.O. C.1/894/42; Req. 2/45/100.
[8] P.R.O. C.1/718/11.
[9] P.R.O. E.134/9 Elizabeth I. Hil. 3.

Leaden Hall, where the Staplers sold much of their wool, was not only a market; it was also the largest wool warehouse in the kingdom. Rooms in the Hall were rented by the Staple Company from the City of London, and these in turn were sub-let to members of the Company and sometimes to outsiders for storage purposes.[1] But not all the wool that was brought to London was housed in Leaden Hall. A room in a private dwelling could be rented for the purpose.[2] By the end of the seventeenth century there were many wool warehouses in Southwark and Bermondsey; and a London dealer who was not able to rent one of these might convert part of his own dwelling-house into a storage place for wool.[3]

The middlemen sold their wool in either an assorted or an unsorted condition. During the sixteenth century most dealers sold wool in the fleece; but from about 1570 onward the middlemen's wool-sorting functions began to assume increasing importance. After sorting (if it was sorted), wool might be stored by a dealer for a number of months, or sold almost immediately. The arrangements made between middlemen and manufacturers for the sale and delivery of wool varied considerably. Most often, wool was sold by direct personal arrangement, usually in the market or at the dealer's house or warehouse. Where an advance agreement was made for the supply of wool, the middleman generally undertook to make delivery, either at the clothier's house or somewhere else conveniently situated. One large Shropshire dealer, for instance, sold wool to a Shepton Mallet clothier at Shrewsbury, and later sent his servants to deliver the wool at Bristol.[4] In the early years of Elizabeth's reign, many of the wealthiest Coggeshall clothiers made a regular practice every June of travelling to Shropshire and arranging with local middlemen for a supply of 'March' wool. George Lee, who was a Stapler and came from Shrewsbury, conducted a large trade with these clothiers; and at about Bartholomewtide each year he forwarded their wool to 'the Sygne of the Mayden Hedde in Seynt Gyles within the Fylde' in the county of Middlesex.[5] Wool which was present at the time of a transaction was

[1] P. J. Bowden, 'The Home Market in Wool, 1500–1700', *Yorkshire Bulletin of Economic and Social Research*, viii (1956), 134.
[2] P.R.O. C.1/603/31.   [3] P.R.O. E.134/6 George I. Hil. 9.
[4] P.R.O. Req. 2/113/13.   [5] P.R.O. E.133/1/36.

usually taken away immediately by the clothier; but if the manufacturer had not the means of transport with him, the wool might be left with the dealer and collected at a later date.[1]

Wool could, of course, be ordered by letter, but this method of purchase appears to have been little practised in the sixteenth century, though it became increasingly common in the seventeenth. When it was adopted, the clothier sent directions as to the quality and quantity of wool required, and the dealer dispatched the order.[2] Of the practice, which later became very common, of sending samples of wool by mail to prospective buyers, no evidence has been found. Wool was sometimes sold by sample,[3] but in such cases both buyer and seller were present at the time of the agreement. Even this kind of arrangement, however, does not appear to have been very common; and in most arrangements a verbal description of type of wool to be supplied was sufficient.

The increase in the transaction of business by letter lessened the importance of the public market as a meeting place for buyers and sellers of wool; but in the sixteenth and seventeenth centuries a very large volume of wool was sold through this medium. Every town of any size held at least one market a week for the sale of general commodities; and in manufacturing areas and wool-growing districts some towns held a special market for the sale of wool and yarn. Large quantities of wool passed through the most important of these markets. In 1577 it was estimated that 40 or 50 horse packs of wool a week were sold at Halifax,[4] and this amount was certainly increased in later years. Of another West Riding town, Doncaster, it was stated in 1642 that there were 'sometymes fortie sometymes three score and sometymes fower score packes of wooll sould in the markett . . . in one day',[5] each pack averaging 16 stones in weight.[6] Cirencester's trade was even larger; and Defoe was

---

[1] P.R.O. Req. 2/17/16.
[2] Advocates' Library, ADV. MS. 34.2.15/ 9th Sept. 1602; *The Letter Books of Joseph Holroyd and Sam Hill*, ed. H. Heaton (1914), passim.
[3] P.R.O. C.1/1124/20; S.P. 12/149/34.
[4] P.R.O. S.P. 12/114/39. At the same time it was estimated that 500 tods of wool a month were sold at Chard.
[5] i.e. on a special market day for wool. In Doncaster the wool market was held every Saturday.
[6] P.R.O. E.134/18 Charles I. East. 19.

informed that roughly 5,000 packs of wool a year were sold there.[1]

Probably the largest part of the wool that was sold in public markets was sold by dealers. The smaller growers sometimes brought their wool to market; but often they could not spare the time, especially when the nearest market town was some distance away. Time could be saved if one grower marketed another grower's clip with his own.[2] But probably more often than not the smaller growers sold their wool at home. The gentlemen farmers and great sheep masters seldom brought their wool to market. They refused to sell wool 'in such smale parcells as ye poore are able to buy it', but transacted the bulk of their business at home with wealthy clothiers and middle-men.[3] The largest growers did not always do this; and a number of them, like Sir Walter Leveston and Sir Edward Montague, sometimes employed agents to dispose of their produce.[4]

When wool was sold in a public market, however, certain regulations governing the conduct of the market were supposed to be complied with. Commodities which were sold in the market, such as wool, woollen yarn, meat and cheese, had to be weighed at the common beam by official weighers, and a payment was exacted for the service.

But the business of ensuring that traders abided by these regulations was a troublesome one for Corporations to undertake, and in a large number of cases the market tolls were farmed out to private individuals for the payment of a yearly rent. In some towns the tolls levied on wool accounted for by far the most substantial item of market revenue, though the individual duty was never large. In the market at Doncaster, $\frac{1}{2}$d. per stone was charged for the weighing of wool.[5] This toll was payable by the seller but it was usual 'for the buyer thereof to take the same for the weight upon the credditt of the seller'.[6] Large wool sellers usually obtained better terms from the Doncaster officials, and generally paid only 6d. for the weighing of a pack of 15 or 16 stones.[7] At the nearby market in Wake-

[1] *Tour*, ii, 432.
[2] P.R.O. Req. 2/25/251.
[3] P.R.O. S.P. 12/90/38; S.P. 12/261/63.
[4] P.R.O. C.1/642/9; Req. 2/175/19; Hist. MSS. Comm. *Buccleuch MSS*. iii, 198.
[5] P.R.O. E.134/17 Charles I. Mich. 8.
[6] P.R.O. E.134/18 Charles I. East. 19.
[7] P.R.O. E.134/17 Charles I. Mich. 8.

field, 4d. per pack was charged.[1] In the market at Newbury, Berkshire, 1d. per tod was levied for the weighing of wool if it was sold to an inhabitant of the borough; but if it was sold to an outsider, 2d. per tod was charged, the payment of the duty being equally divided between the buyer and the seller. Here also, the toll was 6d. if wool was sold by the pack.[2]

These tolls caused considerable irritation to a number of traders,[3] and as the seventeenth century progressed it became increasingly difficult for market authorities to collect them. Some traders refused outright to pay the tolls;[4] others evaded making payment by resorting to dwellings adjoining a market in order to weigh their wool with private weights.[5] Some of the greatest offenders were prosecuted, but these were exceptions. As the Lord Mayor and Aldermen of London pointed out in 1692, it was not 'reasonable to bring such a multitude of actions at law for such small sums as those Duties for weighing'.[6] Market regulations were therefore often disregarded with impunity; and when the depressed state of the cloth trade is also considered, it is not surprising that complaints were frequently made in the seventeenth century of a fall in the receipt of market tolls for the weighing of wool.[7]

III

From beginning to end the medieval wool export trade had rested on a credit basis.[8] The part played by credit in the internal wool trade in the sixteenth and seventeenth centuries was hardly less important, though it was somewhat more complex. Throughout the wool-textile industry, from the purchase of sheep to the

---

[1] S. H. Waters, *Wakefield in the Seventeenth Century* (1933), p. 135.
[2] P.R.O. E.134/11 Charles I. East. 27.
[3] See P.R.O. E.134/20 James I. East. 10; E.134/18 Charles I. East. 19.
[4] P.R.O. E.134/11 Charles I. East. 27; E.134/17 Charles I. Mich. 8; Hist. MSS. Comm. *House of Lords MSS.* iii, 301.
[5] P.R.O. E.134/4 Charles I. East. 36; S.P. 16/164/19; Hist. MSS. Comm. *Various MSS.* iv, 242; B. H. Cunnington, *Some Annals of the Borough of Devizes* (1925), i, pt. ii, 117, 168, 199.
[6] Hist. MSS. Comm. *House of Lords MSS.* iii, 301. See also B.M. Add. MS. 43849, fols. 12ᵇ, 15ᵇ, 19, 22; *Stow's Survey of London* (edn. 1603), ed. C. L. Kingsford (1908), i, 155–6; W. Bohun, *Privilegia Londini* (1702), p. 18.
[7] P.R.O. E.134/4 Charles I. East. 36; Hist. MSS. Comm. *House of Lords MSS.* iii, 301–2; Cunnington, op. cit., i, pt. ii, 85, 130; *V.C.H. Buckingham*, ii, 128.
[8] E. Power, 'The Wool Trade in the Fifteenth Century', *Studies in English Trade in the Fifteenth Century*, ed. E. Power and M. M. Postan, p. 62.

H

sale of cloth, credit was frequently given at every stage. Sometimes it took the shape of a direct loan at interest; but normally it assumed the form of book credit granted in many cases, though not always, by the seller to the buyer. Each of the three classes concerned in the wool trade — the growers, manufacturers and middlemen — contained within its ranks both creditors and debtors, who gave or received credit according to their substance and immediate needs; and whilst no generalizations can be made about the financial transactions of any one class as a whole, they can be made about sections within each class.

Numerous among the wool growers were the husbandmen or 'petty breeders'. These small farmers, often living close to the margin of subsistence, needed money with which to get in their harvests, to pay their rents, or simply to meet normal, everyday expenses. Not being able to wait any length of time for payment, the small growers usually sold their wool at, or shortly after shearing time for cash or, if in more desperate need of money, accepted part-payment in advance and the remainder on delivery.[1]

The larger tenant farmers, with their greater reserves of capital, were better placed to act as creditors to the wool buyers, and they normally sold their wool on credit or for cash. Occasionally, however, they were paid in advance — sometimes by clothiers, less frequently by middlemen. The dealers often sealed bargains with payments of earnest, but the greater part of the credit in these and other transactions was usually supplied by the growers.[2]

The really large-scale sheep farmers were in an even stronger position. They could delay the sale of wool until market conditions were most favourable, and they gave extensive credit to their customers, especially the dealers. Numbered among these 'men of great estate having both groundes and Stocke of their owne'[3] were Sir William Spencer, Sir Thomas Tresham, Sir Edward Montague, Andrew Nowell Esq., and Edward Beau-

---

[1] B.M. Lansd. MS. 28/26; ibid. 65/49; ibid. 114/25. P.R.O. S.P. 14/80/13; S.P. 16/515/139; *B.M. Pamphlets*, 712, g. 16/3, pp. 8, 22; E. Rozer, *Reasons shewing the desires of the Clothiers and Woollen Manufacturers of England . . . Against Ingrossing and Transporting of Wooll and Fullers Earth* (1648).

[2] P. J. Bowden, *Yorkshire Bulletin of Economic and Social Research*, viii (1956), 138–9.

[3] P.R.O. S.P. 14/80/13.

mont, gentleman: all great sheep breeders in the Midlands.[1] In Norfolk in the late fifteenth century, most of Townshend's sales of wool (and sheep) allowed payment to be made over a period of several years.[2] The payments were usually made in due course, but on several occasions Townshend had to discharge his sheep-reeve from accounting for small sums that were overdue from middlemen.[3]

Within the manufacturing side of the wool-textile industry there were likewise considerable differences in wealth and credit-worthiness. At the apex of the industry was a numerically small group of capitalist merchant-manufacturers or rich clothiers, of whom the famous Jack of Newbury and William Stumpe of Malmesbury were outstanding examples, whose employees were numbered in hundreds and who mixed on terms of social equality with the landed gentry and aristocracy. These clothiers purchased large stocks of wool at shearing time, often making their 'whole yeares provision before hand'.[4] Whether they gave or received credit for wool or paid cash, depended largely upon the state of the cloth export trade, for the larger clothiers often gave long credit to the merchant exporters, and were paid by them when the cloth was sold. When cloth exports were booming the merchants made payment with the minimum of delay, and as often as not the rich manufacturers paid for all or part of their wool in advance or, failing that, made payment for it on delivery. But the trading capital of even the wealthiest clothiers was not unlimited, and the heavy losses which were often sustained during a serious depression of trade,[5] in addition to the enforced slowness of merchants in making payment for cloth, inevitably affected the manufacturers' ability to give credit for wool. Unless trade were exceptionally bad, however, the rich clothiers made ready payment for at least part of the wool that they purchased, and in the seventeenth century, when the cloth trade was frequently depressed, they appear generally to have paid for wool on delivery.[6]

---

[1] P.R.O. Req. 2/45/100; Req. 2/176/45; Req. 2/179/46; Hist. MSS. Comm. *Buccleuch MSS.* iii, 12; Hist. MSS. Comm. *Various MSS.* iii, 96; M. Finch, op. cit.

[2] Allison, *thesis*, p. 205.

[3] Allison, *Econ. Hist. Rev.* 2nd ser. xi (1958), 108.

[4] P.R.O. S.P. 14/80/13; *B.M. Pamphlets*, 712, g. 16/3, p. 8.

[5] See *A Discourse upon Usury*, ed. R. H. Tawney (1925), p. 49.

[6] Rozer, op. cit.; *B.M. Pamphlets*, 712, g. 16/3, p. 8; *A Dialogue Between Dick Brazenface the Card-maker and Tim Meanwell the Clothier*, p. 8.

Beneath the rich clothiers and above the small producers was a considerable body of 'meaner clothiers' who, though often manual workers, were also employers of labour. Typical of such men were the more substantial West Riding manufacturer and the average Suffolk clothier. These normally purchased several months' stocks of wool from the growers at shearing time and relied largely on the local wool market for supplies of raw material later in the year. Though these manufacturers preferred to pay ready money for the wool which they purchased, their ability to do so was limited both by the amount of their capital and by the length of credit that they gave the cloth buyers.[1] In order to have cash available for the purchase of wool, the clothiers endeavoured to 'so order it, as to have their money due at shear time; which debts when they cannot receive, they procure money upon their credit, or their goods by pawn'.[2] But as the seventeenth century progressed, it became increasingly difficult for the clothiers to regulate the date of payment for cloth, and the period of credit allowed in the cloth trade became longer. Part of the outcry against the Blackwell Hall factors[3] arose because 'through the management of the Factor, who constrains the Clothier to give Credit to the persons who buy his Cloth', the clothier 'was forced to take up his wool upon credit at dearer rates'. It was added: 'If the Clothier had money to buy at Shearing-time, by turning his Stock, he would be able to purchase again at Michaelmas; but wanting some money then, the Wool-broggers buy up all before him.'[4] But even in the sixteenth and early seventeenth centuries the 'meaner clothiers' often purchased wool on credit from the middlemen and larger growers;[5] and when an exporter or draper defaulted in making payment for cloth, it was not always only the clothier who went unpaid.[6]

More numerous than the 'meaner clothiers' were the small

---

[1] *B.M. Pamphlets*, 712, g. 16/3, p. 8. The amount of capital and the length of credit were, of course, inter-related. See J. Haynes, *A View of the Present State of the Clothing Trade in England* (1706), pp. 9–10.

[2] Rozer, op. cit.

[3] Infra, pp. 182–3.

[4] *H. of C. Journals*, xii, 277. See also *The Clothiers Complaint, or reasons for passing the Bill against the Blackwell Hall Factors* (1692), p. 10.

[5] P.R.O. S.P. 16/282/130.

[6] P.R.O. C.1/793/24; Req. 2/54/39. Similarly, when wool buyers defaulted, wool sellers were sometimes unable to discharge their debts. See P.R.O. C.1/1311/70; C.1/1318/5.

independent producers, whose main stronghold was the north of England but who were to be found even in districts where the woollen industry was most capitalistic — men who bought in the market a small supply of wool or yarn for ready money or on credit, and 'who make every week a coarse kersy, and are compelled to sell the same at the week-end, and with the money received for the same provide both stuff wherewith to make another the week following, and also victuals to sustain themselves'.[1]

In the reign of James I, it was estimated that there were 'about two or three hundreth poore Clothmakers within' the parish of Halifax 'which make and returne a carsey weekely'.[2] The small West Riding manufacturer bought his wool in the market, and with the assistance of four workers, who might all be members of his family, was able to carry through the carding, spinning and weaving of a kersey in a week.[3] In the West Country there was a greater division of labour among the small producers:

> First the gentleman farmer, or husbandman, sends his wool to the market, which is bought either by the comber or spinster, and they, the next week, bring it thither in yarn, which the weaver buys: and the market following brings that thither again in cloth.[4]

Necessity drove the small manufacturers to sell their cloth for ready money, or for payment in advance,[5] though in the seventeenth century they found it increasingly difficult to obtain cash for their goods.[6] The lengthening of the period of credit in the cloth trade undoubtedly contributed towards the decline in the number of these small producers, and at the same time made them more dependent upon the advances of the wool and yarn middlemen.[7]

The part played by the wool middlemen in the financing of the wool trade has already been touched on in the preceding pages, where it has been shown that the dealers most commonly

[1] Quoted R. B. Westerfield, *Middlemen in English Business* (1915), p. 287. See also *V.C.H. Yorkshire*, ii, 415; P.R.O. S.P. 14/80/15.
[2] P.R.O. E.134/11 James I. Mich. 9.
[3] Heaton, op. cit., p. 96.
[4] T. Westcote, *A View of Devonshire in 1630* (edn. 1845), p. 61. See also P.R.O. S.P. 14/80/13.
[5] P.R.O. E.134/14 Charles I. Mich. 20; S.P. 14/80/13; Hist. MSS. Comm. 4. *Fifth Report*, p. 38; Finch, op. cit., p. 8.
[6] P.R.O. E.134/14 Charles I. Mich. 21; Hist. MSS. Comm. 3. *Fourth Report*, p. 62.
[7] See Haynes, *A View of the Present State of the Clothing Trade in England*, p. 84; *Reasons for Restraining the Factors of Blackwell Hal from dealing in Spanish and English Wooll; The Languishing State of our Woollen Manufacture, Humbly Represented to the Parliament; The Blackwell Hall Factors Case.*

purchased wool from the smaller growers for ready money, and
from the larger growers on credit. Normally, a dealer relied
upon his own resources when paying ready money for wool; but
if he wished to pay cash for wool priced in excess of his trading
capital he might — subject to the law on usury — do so with
money borrowed at interest. Up to 1571, except for a short
period between 1545 and 1552, the taking of interest was forbidden, and this must have restricted the use of borrowed
capital in the wool trade.[1] By the Act[2] passed in 1571, a lender
was allowed to receive up to a maximum of 10 per cent. interest,
and following this enactment the direct loan at interest appears
to have become more common.[3] According to a statement made
in 1590, the profits to be gained from the wool trade were so
great that some dealers were willing to pay rates of interest in
excess of the legal maximum in order to obtain loans.[4] Alternatively to borrowing money, dealers sometimes joined in temporary partnership or joint stock in order to make larger than normal purchases.[5] This might be done so as to spread any possible risk
of loss, or because, when the wool so bought was the subject of a
credit transaction, the grower was not satisfied that a single dealer
could give 'to his lykinge sufficiente assurance for payment'.[6]

In their transactions with the clothiers the middlemen were
frequently, though not always, the creditors. The smaller
dealers, who purchased much of their wool from the 'petty
breeders', sometimes sold on short credit to the poorer manufacturers, but were probably more often paid by them in ready
money.[7] Cash sales by the larger dealers were not uncommon,[8]
and the middlemen sometimes accepted advance payment for
wool from the wealthy clothiers.[9] But most of the business of the
substantial dealers was conducted with the 'meaner clothiers',
to whom they usually gave credit. The time allowed for payment varied, the normal period being between three and six

---

[1] For an example, see P.R.O. C.1/1229/62.
[2] *Statutes of the Realm*, 13 Elizabeth I, c. 8.
[3] B.M. Lansd. MS. 114/25; P.R.O. Req. 2/122/9; S.P. 16/503/43; Hist. MSS.
Comm. *Various MSS.* iii, 96.
[4] B.M. Lansd. MS. 114/25.
[5] P.R.O. C.1/718/11; Req. 2/45/100; B.M. Add. MS. 34324, fol. 15ᵇ; *Cal. S.P.
Dom. 1650*, p. 408.
[6] P.R.O. Req. 2/45/100.   [7] See *B.M. Pamphlets*, 712, g. 16/3, p. 22.
[8] P.R.O. C.1/580/32; Req. 2/37/46; Req. 2/169/12.
[9] P.R.O. C.1/1214/12; Req. 2/16/21; Req. 2/113/13.

months. As, however, the larger dealers purchased much of their wool on credit, and often, it seems, on longer credit than they allowed the manufacturers,[1] it was, in effect, the wool growers who financed many of these transactions.

When a seller gave credit for wool he received a higher price for it than he would have done had he accepted payment in ready money. The price of wool sold on credit thus contained an element of interest 'in respecte of the forbearinge and gevinge daie of paiment of the saide money'.[2] In the sixteenth century this interest charge was normally disguised as part of the principal, but after the Act of 1571, and particularly towards the end of our period, it was sometimes recorded as a separate item.[3] This sale of time was naturally favoured by those growers and middlemen who could afford to wait for payment. Dealers found that they could 'make a better reckeninge of theire monye this waye then by putting of it owte after x^{li} in the C^{li}'; and it was usually in order 'to buye wooll for redye monye to sell againe at dayes' that they sometimes borrowed money at shearing time.[4] The rate of interest charged on these credit sales varied, being anything from about 8 to 40 per cent. per annum of the cash price.[5] In the second half of the sixteenth century, when the rate was probably at its highest, the normal charge appears to have been about 20 per cent., so that wool sold on three months' credit would have cost the buyer an additional 5 per cent. in interest. Likewise, when a wool seller received credit for wool, its price was adjusted in order to take this into account; and in one such transaction a seller agreed to supply wool 'a grote better chepe in every todd' than the current market price at the time of delivery.[6]

IV

Credit dealing naturally involved some risk; and when large, or comparatively large amounts of wool were the subject of credit

---

[1] Sometimes dealers bought wool on credit and sold it for ready money. See P.R.O. Req. 2/45/100; Req. 2/49/37.
[2] P.R.O. Req. 2/226/84.   [3] See P.R.O. E.134/6 George I. Mich. 42.
[4] B.M. Lansd. MS. 28/26; P.R.O. S.P. 12/149/34.
[5] For examples, see P.R.O. Req. 2/54/39; Req. 2/111/28; Req. 2/122/9; Req. 2/206/3; S.P. 12/149/34; E.134/6 George I. Mich. 42; B.M. Lansd. MS.28/26; ibid. 114/25; *Reasons for preserving the Publick Market of Blackwell Hal, and restraining the Factors from dealing in Wool: Humbly offer'd to the Parliament.*
[6] P.R.O. Req. 2/2/14.

transactions, the creditor usually took precautions to ensure that the debtor would carry out his side of the bargain. In Tudor times,[1] in return for the advance of wool or money, a debtor normally gave to his creditor a form of bond commonly known as a 'bill obligatory' or 'speciality' which was an acknowledgement of obligation already incurred. This bill, or bond, was normally enforceable at law,[2] and obliged the debtor to carry out the condition of the bond before a specified date in the future. The bond thus gave the creditor security for his advance of wool or money, and as such often gave security for a greater sum than the advance itself. This was not always the case, however. Indeed, during the first half of the sixteenth century the most common type of bond used in the wool trade appears to have been one which gave security for a sum equivalent to the debt incurred.[3] But even in the early sixteenth century the security given by a bond was not always equivalent to the amount of the debt. Sometimes it was a little more, and there were cases when it was exactly or approximately twice or three times as much.[4]

Though bonds were frequently used as instruments of credit in the wool trade during the first half of the sixteenth century, they were used to probably an even greater extent in the second half, when financial machinery became more highly organized. Certainly, during Elizabeth's reign the degree of security stipulated in such bonds became fairly well standardized and creditors secured a greater amount of protection against default. It is true that some creditors still accepted bonds which gave no additional security above the amount of the debt;[5] but these cases were relatively few. In the vast majority of instances, creditors obtained security for greater sums than those owing to them, frequently for exactly twice as much. Bonds which gave security for a little more or a little less than twice the amount of

---

[1] Little definite can be said at present about practice in Stuart times.

[2] But common-law courts would not enforce a bond which had not been sealed by the debtor, nor one which could not be exhibited in the court as evidence of debt. In such cases, an action in the Court of Chancery was the obvious course for the creditor to take. See for example, P.R.O. C.1/966/59.

[3] P.R.O. C.1/857/3–4; C.1/240/75; C.1/273/35; C.1/286/37; C.1/597/34; C.1/641/37; C.1/642/9, 40; C.1/790/17; C.1/966/59.

[4] P.R.O. C.1/290/30; C.1/339/10–11; C.1/766/1; C.1/793/24; C.1/1111/60; C.1/1176/1; C.1/1398/52; Req. 2/3/153.

[5] P.R.O. C.3/268/77; Req. 2/41/61; Req. 2/142/22.

the debt were also very common.[1] In such cases there was a very simple explanation why the security was not exactly twice the amount of the debt. Contemporaries preferred to deal with round figures, and after a debt had been doubled, the bond was usually made out to the nearest round number.

But even these precautions did not always satisfy the creditors, particularly in cases where the debtor's ability to carry out the condition of the bond was thought to be questionable, or where he was not well-known. Some creditors therefore required that a bond should be underwritten by one or more sureties,[2] capable of making full compensation should the debtor default. As failure to carry out the condition of a bond left a surety open to prosecution, the business of underwriting was often performed by relatives or friends of the debtor. A more unusual case was that in which a creditor was bound as his debtor's surety to a third party in order to obtain the repayment of his own debt.[3]

The possibility of default was always present and, especially where there were no family connexions between the debtor and his surety, the latter sometimes covered his own risk by taking a 'counter-bond'[4] from the debtor. Thus in 1595 John Loe and Thomas Hopkins, two London feltmakers, purchased 12 bags of Spanish wool priced at £136 19s. 4d. from Nicholas Lynge, a salter. At the request of Loe and Hopkins, George Smith, a haberdasher of London, became bound 'joyntlie and seuerallie' with them 'unto Nicholas Lynge by their seuerall Billes obligatorye for the sure payment of the said full some of cxxxvj^{li} xix^s iiij^d at the daies and tymes agreed vpon. And for the discharge and savinge harmelesse of George Smythe being onelie bound as suretie' Loe and Hopkins 'did then (as in good equitie they ought to do) become bounde by their bonde obligatorie vnder their handes and seales vnto George Smythe in the some of CC^{li} with condicion therevpon endorsed that' Loe and Hopkins 'shoulde not onelie well and trewlie paye vnto Nicholas Lynge the saide full some of Cxxxvj^{li} xix^s iiij^d at the daies and tymes limytted by the said former bill. But also sholde and wolde

---

[1] For examples, see P.R.O. Req. 2/25/59; Req. 2/49/37; Req. 2/104/60; Req. 2/122/9; Req. 2/163/96; Req. 2/176/21; Req. 2/226/84. That double value bond-taking was a common practice in Shakespeare's day is suggested by Macbeth: 'I'll make assurance double sure, And take a bond of fate' (*Macbeth*, Act IV, Scene I).

[2] See, for example, P.R.O. Req. 2/61/93; Req. 2/174/14; Req. 2/204/48.

[3] P,R,O, Req. 2/5/79.   [4] This term is used in P.R.O. Req. 2/118/37,

thereof clerelie discharge or save harmeless George Smyth against Nicholas Lynge'.[1] In another case, John Fanstone, a Dorsetshire gentleman, made a credit purchase in 1592 of £31 worth of wool on behalf of John Cowper, a neighbouring parson. Fanstone became bound as a surety for payment and 'for his securitie' it was decided that he 'showld keepe Cowpers goods and rentes in his handes'.[2]

When the condition of a bond had been performed, the bond was cancelled, normally by return to the erstwhile debtor, or by means of an acquittance.[3] Sometimes wool was paid for in a number of instalments, in which case there might be a separate bond made out for the payment of each instalment, or alternatively, one bond made out for the payment of the entire debt. Where there were several bonds, these were cancelled one by one as the payments were made. But where there was only one bond, the payment of each instalment was endorsed on the back of the bond, which was kept by the creditor until the entire debt had been wiped out.[4] Should the debtor fail to perform the condition of the bond, the creditor was legally able to enforce payment of the full security stated in the bond;[5] and should the debtor be unable to make payment himself, the sureties, if any, might be called upon to do so. Similarly, where two or more debtors were jointly bound, compensation for default by one debtor might be extracted from the others.

But the creditor did not always resort to legal proceedings when the condition of a bond was not performed. If he were willing to forbear, the debtor might be required to enter into a new bond which gave the creditor a greater amount of security than the old.[6] Alternatively, and presumably subject to the law

---

[1] P.R.O. Req. 2/41/61.   [2] P.R.O. Req. 2/206/3.

[3] Bonds were also cancelled by slashing. See H. R. Trevor-Roper, 'The Elizabethan Aristocracy: An Anatomy Anatomized', *Econ. Hist. Rev.* 2nd ser. iii (1951), 281; P.R.O. Req. 2/160/81.

[4] Where credit transactions involving similar amounts of wool were regularly conducted between the same buyer and seller, a bond might be left in the hands of the creditor, and the date at which it became enforceable deferred by a legally valid document every time the debtor incurred a fresh obligation. See P.R.O. C.3/268/77.

[5] A court of law might give judgment for the payment of the full security stated in the bond, plus costs of prosecution, though the debtor might afterwards compound with the creditor for the payment of a lesser sum. See P.R.O. Req. 2/118/28.

[6] See, for example, P.R.O. C.1/286/37. At the same time, and particularly where a long extension of credit was allowed, the sum to be repaid might also be increased. In 1518, an Essex clothier alleged that he had been forced to enter into bonds for the payment of twice the original price of wool (P.R.O. C.1/390/30).

on usury, the date of the old bond was deferred and a new bond was issued as security for the payment of interest. In the last decade of the sixteenth century Zachary Maye, having failed to make payment for wool priced at £125, agreed to pay his creditor 'for the forebearinge of his money . . . after the rate of Tenne pounds in the hundrethe'; and he 'entred into a bonde of xxx[li] for the payment of xv[li] for the interest of the saide some of cxxv[li] to be paid at fowre six monethes by iij[li]xv[s] at a tyme'.[1] Sometimes a creditor might agree to accept repayment of principal, plus interest, in the form of an annuity.[2] At other times wool sellers accepted cloth from clothiers and hats from feltmakers who defaulted in making payment for wool.[3]

Bills obligatory were by far the most common form of security for debts in the Tudor wool trade, and only one instance has been found of a mortgage being used for the purpose.[4] Though by the end of the Stuart period the bill obligatory had probably been ousted by the inland bill of exchange, there is no evidence that this process had begun before 1600. Bonds were in great use among nearly all classes of the community in sixteenth-century England, and those that were given as security for payment of the price of wool were sometimes assigned by creditors to pay their own debts. In the 1580's Richard Baynes purchased £50 worth of wool on credit from Sir Walter Leveston, and gave him a bond as security for payment. Leveston later became indebted to Nicholas Barbourne, a Staffordshire gentleman, and Baynes 'vppon a dischardge to hime . . . from the said Sir Walter of the said fyftye poundes became indebted by Bill in wrytinge vnto the said Nicholas Barbourne in the like some of fyftye poundes to be paied att certayne daies therein expressed'.[5] Sometimes creditors were willing to accept debts owing to their debtors in payment for wool. Thus, William Ryvett, who sold £100 worth of wool on credit to Philip Bassett in 1584, agreed to accept a debt of £72 due to Bassett by Richard Frend, a Sudbury clothier, in part-payment, Bassett to be bound with a

[1] P.R.O. Req. 2/65/6. See also P.R.O. Req. 2/176/21.
[2] P.R.O. Req. 2/202/2.
[3] P.R.O. C.1/364/19; Req. 2/54/39; Req. 2/184/48.
[4] In the early sixteenth century, William Hylle, Merchant of the Staple of Calais, gave Edward Lightfoote a mortgage upon shops in St. Andrews, Cornhill, as security for the delivery of woolfells (P.R.O. C.1/550/42).
[5] P.R.O. Req. 2/175/19. See also P.R.O. C.1/857/3.

surety for the payment of the remaining £28.[1] The practice of transferring debts appears to have been a common one. A bond for a good debt could be assigned at the full value of the debt, while a bond for a doubtful debt might be sold at a discount.[2]

Bonds appear to have been seldom drawn up as security for the payment of sums of less than £3 or £4. The business was probably too troublesome and costly; and, in any case, the period of credit allowed in the wool trade for the payment of small debts was often very short. But even when a creditor did not take a bond from his debtor, he usually endeavoured to obtain some degree of security by other means. In many cases, spectators were called upon to witness a bargain; and sureties often agreed to guarantee payment, without entering into a written undertaking of any kind. Thus in the later years of Henry VIII's reign, Thomas Alsop purchased £27 worth of wool on credit from a grower, and his brothers, John and Lawrence, 'promised . . . that if Thomas did faulte to pay the said xxvij poundes at the dayes before lymitted that then they the said John and Lawrence would content and pay the same sume and euery peny therof'.[3] In another instance, a grower sold 19 stones of wool on credit to three dealers. Two of the middlemen 'dyd dwelle in a foren countie' and were completely unknown to the seller; and it was agreed that the third dealer, a local man, should 'confesse hymself to be onely dettor' for the wool.[4] In cases like these there was, of course, a greater risk of default and less chance of remedy than when bonds were taken as security. But though the common-law courts would not enforce the payment of debts of which there was no written evidence, the equity courts could, and sometimes did.[5]

---

[1] P.R.O. Req. 2/174/14.   [2] P.R.O. C.1/688/31.
[3] P.R.O. C.1/747/12.   [4] P.R.O. C.1/893/30.
[5] The Courts of Chancery and Requests were quite often the scene of disputes concerning the purchase and sale of wool, and actions were brought by plaintiffs who, for one reason or another, were unable or unwilling to take their cases to a court of common law. But though the two courts served a useful purpose in that they redressed genuine grievances which the common law could not, they too often impeded, rather than furthered, the cause of justice. The Court of Requests, in particular, from being the 'poor man's court' at its inception, appears to have become by the end of the sixteenth century a refuge for defaulting debtors of all social classes.

Chapter IV

REGULATION BY ACT OF PARLIAMENT

I

When the sixteenth century commenced, the exportation of
English wool, which throughout the Middle Ages had been the
basis of the country's export trade, was steadily giving way to
that of cloth. The change from raw wool exporter to cloth
exporter had been proceeding since the early years of the fourteenth century, when England had exported more than 30,000
sacks of wool a year and only about 5,000 cloths. But the transition had been a slow one, and by the end of the fifteenth century
the wool-export trade, though declining, was still of considerable
proportions.

During the fourteenth and fifteenth centuries the immense
importance of this trade to the Netherlands had led, in the
interests of royal finance and mercantile convenience, to the
evolution of the staple system and to the formation of the
Company of the Merchants of the Staple with a practical
monopoly of the English wool-export trade north of the Alps.
After various experiments the Staple had been settled finally
by the beginning of the fifteenth century at Calais.

The trade gave the government a diplomatic lever in its
negotiations with foreign powers, and provided the Crown with
one of its most valuable sources of revenue by the custom and
subsidy levied on the export of wool: these payments normally
amounting to 40s. per sack for native exporters and 53s. 4d. per
sack for aliens. Through the Staple the Crown had found it
possible to anticipate its revenue by loans raised on the security
of the customs and to enforce its bullion regulations; in addition,
by the 'Acts of Retainer' it had made the Company responsible
for the payment of the garrison and for other expenses incurred
in the upkeep of Calais, allowing the Staplers to recoup

themselves from the customs due on the wool which they exported.[1]

It was no wonder then that the government's interest in the trade was so great and that the overwhelming bulk of wool exports went to Calais. But exceptions had nearly always been made to this general rule. From early times the government had allowed the coarse low-valued wools of Scotland, on the one hand, and the four northern counties of England,[2] on the other, to be shipped direct to the Netherlands. This privilege had been permitted to the merchants of Berwick and Newcastle-upon-Tyne respectively. The government had usually stipulated that exportation should be to the ports of Bruges and Middleburgh, but sometimes shipment was allowed to any part of the Netherlands. Here, the towns which specialized in the manufacture of cheap cloths supplied a good market for the coarse wool, which because of its low value was made subject to a relatively small export tax of ten shillings per sack. The Newcastle men highly valued their licence, and they periodically obtained its renewal throughout the sixteenth century whenever a new monarch ascended the English throne.

In 1523, letters patent were granted to the citizens of York authorizing them to export from Hull certain types of Yorkshire wool and fells paying the same custom and subsidy as the merchants of Newcastle. But this grant was not destined to last for long. There was constant trouble concerning it with the Staplers, particularly over the export of the finer Yorkswold wool, and it was also criticized by the Yorkshire clothiers on the ground that it caused a shortage of locally-grown raw material.[3] In 1529, the privilege was accordingly annulled by Act of Parliament.[4]

The Staplers' objections to the infringement of their monopoly was not new; they had constantly complained throughout the fifteenth century of the licence granted to the

[1] For the evolution of the Staple system, see E. Power, *The Wool Trade in English Medieval History* (Oxford, 1941); E. Power, 'The Wool Trade in the Fifteenth Century', *Studies in English Trade in the Fifteenth Century*, ed. E. Power and M. M. Postan (1933), pp. 30–91; *The Ordinance Book of the Merchants of the Staple*, ed. E. E. Rich (Cambridge, 1937).

[2] Northumberland, Westmorland, Cumberland and Durham, together with parts of the North Riding.

[3] *York Civic Records*, Vol. 3 (Yorkshire Archaeological Society Record Series (1942), cvi), 91–4, 98, 100–1, 104, 106, 110.

[4] *Statutes of the Realm*, 21 Henry VIII, c. 17.

Newcastle merchants, stating that advantage was taken of it to export the finer wools of the neighbouring counties.[1] But with the sixteenth century the efforts of the Staplers to get coarse as well as fine wool under their control appear to have abated, and they seem to have become resigned to the exportation from the northern port.

Of much more concern to the Staplers were the royal licences for the export of finer wool, especially those granted to Italians for shipment through the Straits of Gibraltar. Since early times these had caused a never-ending source of dispute between the Company and the government; but the fees for the licences and the loans which their recipients sometimes made to the Crown were sufficient to ensure that these shipments continued. The Staplers blamed the competition of such licensees for the decline of their trade, through which in 1525, much to their cost, they had been unable to carry out the Act of Retainer entered into in 1515.[2] But this competition the Company had always experienced, and the fundamental reasons for the decline in the staple trade were not to be found there but in the expansion of the English cloth industry and in the increasing competitiveness of Spanish wool in the Netherlands market.

The expansion of the home cloth manufacture had a two-fold effect upon the foreign demand for English wool. First, the growing claims of the native clothiers for the raw material lessened the supply available for export, at the same time raising its price. Rising wool prices, on top of already heavy export duties, made it increasingly difficult for the Staplers to meet the competition of the Spaniards, who in 1494 had established a staple for their own wool at Bruges. The Spanish wool was cheap and plentiful,[3] and moreover Bruges had certain advantages over Calais as a staple town. A further factor in the decline of overseas demand for fine wool may well have been the deterioration in the quality of the English fine-wool supply. The effect of these various influences was to cause the Netherlanders to turn more and more to the weaving of Spanish wool alone or, by

[1] Power and Postan, op. cit., p. 43.
[2] Rich, op. cit., p. 10.
[3] But the price of Spanish wool was also rising in the early sixteenth century (E. J. Hamilton, *American Treasure and the Price Revolution in Spain, 1501–1650*, Harvard Economic Studies, xliii (1934), p. 285). It was almost certainly the upward trend in the price of Spanish wool, rather than exchange depreciation, which caused a temporary revival in English wool shipments in the early 1540's.

using it with longer and coarser English raw material, to concentrate upon the manufacture of the new draperies. Secondly,
this switch to a different type of product was brought about, in
part, by the encroachment of English cloth exports on the continental market of the Flemish and Dutch woollen manufacturers, who had formerly relied upon the Staplers for much of
their raw material supply.[1]

II

In England, the rise in the price of wool had far-reaching
implications for agricultural organization, hastening the transition from the medieval to the modern world. Since the twelfth
and thirteenth centuries, consolidation and enclosure of open-
field holdings and common land — sometimes for arable use,
sometimes for pasture — had been very gradually transforming
the face of the countryside. From the middle years of the
fifteenth century, the movement towards enclosure for pasture
farming quickened in response to the ever-increasing demand
for wool; it was given a further impulse by the partial restraint
imposed upon the exportation of corn.[2]

The change over from arable to pasture farming, although in
many cases accomplished without disturbance, was too often
accompanied by the eviction of tenants and the depopulation of
villages, when the wealthier landed interests, in seeking to
participate to the uttermost in the large profits to be made from
wool, turned acre after acre into a sheep-run. The Tudor
government made ceaseless endeavours to stop depopulation,
and to this end employed all the weapons at its disposal.
Between 1489 and 1597 eleven Acts of Parliament were passed
having as their object the prevention of depopulation.[3] These
Acts were not strictly enforced, for their administration lay in
the hands of those most opposed to them, and the government
resorted to other measures[4] with little apparent success.

[1] P.R.O. S.P. 10/13/81; B.M. Lansd. MS. 113/21; Hist. MSS. Comm. *Salisbury
MSS.* xiv, 55; Rich, op. cit., pp. 13–18; *Tudor Economic Documents,* ed. R. H. Tawney
and E. Power (1924), iii, 102, 114.
[2] See supra, pp. 4–5.
[3] These were all repealed by Statute 21 James I, c. 25, except 39 Elizabeth, c. 2,
which was repealed by the Statute Law Revision Act of 1863.
[4] The Privy Council intervened on a number of occasions and offenders were
sometimes dealt with by the Prerogative Courts. Eight Royal Commissions were
appointed: the first in 1517, the last in 1636.

The reasons for the government's concern were varied: apart from a genuine dislike of economic oppression, it argued that depopulation enfeebled the military strength of the State, was financially disadvantageous to the Crown, and turned loose in the country large numbers of vagrants whose idleness was a menace to the social order; in addition, it was felt that the accompanying increase in pasture was politically dangerous, tending, as it did, to make the country dependent upon foreign powers for supplies of corn.

In the event, the pull of economic forces succeeded where moral sermons and government measures failed. With the increased profitability of corn growing in the second half of the sixteenth century, the retreat from arable was halted. Enclosure activity continued, but much of it was now undertaken with an eye to more efficient tillage. After the mid-sixteenth century very few villages were completely depopulated; indeed, total depopulations were becoming rare by 1520. The Royal Commission appointed in 1548 found instances of houses destroyed and fields enclosed, but they were single houses and relatively small areas of land.[1] Nevertheless, it was during the latter years of the 1540's that public sentiment against landlords and graziers reached its height. Regarded as the main causes of rising prices and agricultural distress, they incurred the wrath of churchmen and social reformers and the hostility of a disgruntled peasantry. A Statute passed in 1533 had sought to curb the growth of large-scale pasture farming by making it an offence to keep flocks of more than 2,400 sheep.[2] In March, 1549, an Act in similar vein granted Edward VI the proceeds of a poll tax on sheep coupled with a special levy on home-produced cloth. The sheep tax aroused widespread resentment amongst landlords and graziers; both it and the relief on cloth proved cumbersome to collect, and within a year the attempt to reduce the profitability of sheep farming by taxation was abandoned.[3] Shortly afterwards, external events achieved what government legislation and administrative action had failed to do.

---

[1] M. W. Beresford, *The Lost Villages of England* (1954), pp. 142, 148.
[2] *Statutes of the Realm*, 25 Henry VIII, c. 13. 'Two thousand' counted in long hundreds of 120.
[3] M. W. Beresford, 'The Poll Tax and Census of Sheep, 1549', *Agric. Hist. Rev.*i (1953), 9–15; ii (1954), 15–29.

I

III

During the 1540's the boom in cloth exports was in no small measure responsible for the failure of the government's agrarian policy. In its final stages, this boom was probably stimulated by exchange depreciation consequent upon currency debasement.[1] In 1550, when shortcloths[2] exported from London numbered almost 133,000, there were complaints of overproduction as it became increasingly obvious that the advantages of exchange depreciation were being swallowed up by rising domestic prices. The merchants, who benefited most from devaluation, were in favour of letting things take their natural course; but the inflation at home and heavy debts abroad forced the government in 1551 to call down the currency, leaving sticky internal prices to fall as best they could to the new equilibrium level. Through the exchange appreciation the export industries received a violent set-back. The number of shortcloths exported from London fell to less than 113,000 in 1551, and to 85,000 in 1552;[3] whilst the Staplers complained that high internal wool prices prevented them selling at a profit abroad.[4]

Almost inevitably, strong pressure from vested interests upon the government accompanied the contraction, demanding that measures should be taken to restrain competition and to enable the cutting down of costs in order to meet the changed situation. Such pressure came chiefly from the mercantile and established manufacturing classes, and was a direct attack upon those clothiers who had been drawn into production by the preceding boom and upon the wool middlemen who served them; it was also, less directly, an assault upon the wool growers as a whole. The most forceful pressure came from the merchants — both Adventurers and Staplers — who at this time were performing valuable services for the debt-ridden government by meeting its obligations to foreign bankers.[5] This fact, allied to a conservative

---

[1] The coin issue of 1544 contained only half its weight in fine silver, in 1545 the proportion was only one-third, whilst some coins issued in the reign of Edward VI were only one-quarter fine.

[2] The shortcloth was a fictional 'cloth' of 24 yards into which different types of woollens were translated according to a standard table for purposes of customs assessment (Supple, op. cit., p. 257).

[3] Fisher, *Econ. Hist. Rev.* x (1940), 96, 103; G. Unwin, *Studies in Economic History* (1927), p. 148.

[4] Rich, op. cit., p. 162.

[5] *A.P.C. 1552-4*, pp. 199, 207, 267, 275, 278.

economic policy, led to official endorsement of the demands of the merchants and of those interests which coincided with them. Enough members of the Commons, especially those die-hards who had sourly viewed the rise of a new industrial class, shared the government's feelings to facilitate in 1552 the passage of a comprehensive and restrictive code for the regulation of the woollen industry.

The restrictionist policy which was given legislative form in this and in the following years is best known by the measures to maintain the quality of English woollens and to confine the cloth industry to the towns. But this endeavour to adapt the cloth manufacture to its shrinking foreign markets had other important aspects which, as will be shown, strongly coincided with the interests of the wool-exporting merchants.

The increase in the price of wool during the later 'forties had been proportionately greater than for cloth,[1] and it was in the foreign market for English wool that the adverse effects of the depreciations were first sharply felt. The contraction in their market abroad had doubtless led some of the Staplers by 1549 to traffic illegally in their wool at home;[2] and in 1550 it had caused the Staple Company to agitate for, and succeed in obtaining greater control over the operations of wool winding and packing.[3] But there was little relief to be hoped for there, when the chief reason for the lack of wool sales abroad was the disparity between English and Spanish wool prices. Of this the Staplers were well aware, and they pressed for stringent measures against their competitors who bought wool at home as a remedy to the situation.

The Staplers had never taken kindly to buyers competing with them for the supplies of English wool. Their earliest objections had been against the export licensees, but with the growth of the home cloth industry the main weight of their attacks gradually shifted elsewhere. About 1527 they were

---

[1] *Cal. S.P. Dom. Add. 1547–65*, pp. 420–1.

[2] See below and infra, pp. 159–60.

[3] In May, 1550, a proclamation was issued ordering that 'henceforth none wind or fold wools unless admitted thereto by the master and wardens of the company of woolmen of London, who are to give testimonials of admittance under the seal of the Mayor of the Staple; also that all such, before working take an oath before the said mayor to wind and fold without deceit, or putting in anything, or mingling worse wools. . . . No grower of wool, henceforth to employ any person without a certificate to fold or wind' (*Tudor and Stuart Proclamations*, ed. R. Steele, No. 380).

complaining of the scarceness of wool which, they said, was 'in the handes of rich graysiers, brogers and engrossers and by them enhaunced and lifted to such price that nether Stapler nor clothier is able to obtain his living theirupon'.[1] The wealthier cloth manufacturers, who could dispense with the wool middle-men's services, took a similar line. In 1531, when both wool and cloth-export trades were depressed, an Act of Parliament was passed,[2] reviving for ten years the lapsed legislation of 1489[3] which had forbidden common dealers to purchase or to make contracts for wool in a large number of counties[4] between shearing time and the following Feast of the Assumption; a further clause forbade the purchase of wool for aliens. Although informations were laid on this Act,[5] its enforcement probably lasted little longer than the slump which produced it. In 1546 similar transitory legislation[6] was passed embracing roughly the same geographical area.[7] But a loophole was left for the brog-ger's activities, the grower being permitted to sell his wool to anyone in the open market providing that clothiers and Staplers were given the first option of purchase. The part which the Staple Company played in the passing of the 1546 Act is at least suspect, for a few months earlier it had been called upon to pay off some of the government's foreign debts.[8] In 1551 the Staplers were arguing that if the English cloth manufacture expanded during the ensuing twelve years at a rate equal to the previous

---

[1] *Tudor Economic Documents*, ii, 27.

[2] *Statutes of the Realm*, 22 Henry VIII, c. 1.

[3] 4 Henry VII, c. 11. A similar Act had been passed in 1465 (4 Edward IV, c. 4).

[4] The counties listed in the Act of 1489 were: Berkshire, Oxford, Gloucester, Hereford, Shropshire, Worcester, Wiltshire, Somerset, Dorset, Hampshire, Essex, Hertford, Cambridge, Norfolk, Suffolk, Kent, Surrey and Sussex. To these the 1531 Act added Buckingham, Northampton, Leicester, Huntingdon, Warwick, Lincoln, Derby, Rutland, Nottingham and Yorkshire.

[5] P.R.O. E.36/139, fol. 18.

[6] *Statutes of the Realm*, 37 Henry VIII, c. 15. This Act forbade wool to be con-tracted for, or bought, between shearing time and the Feast of the Purification by any persons but clothiers or Merchants of the Staple, upon pain of a penalty equal to double the value of the wool purchased. It also repeated the prohibition con-cerning trading in wool on behalf of alien merchants. Originally made to endure until the end of the following Parliament this legislation was re-affirmed by Edward VI in the first year of his reign (B.M. Tit. MS. B. II. 4), and in 1549 a proclamation was issued ordering that offenders should be punished by imprisonment (B.M. Harl. MS. 4943).

[7] The 1546 Act included Bedford, but not Berkshire and Oxford. The two latter counties were added by proclamation in March, 1546, together with Middlesex and Stafford (*Cal. L.P.F.D. Henry VIII*, xxi, pt. 1, p. 63).

[8] *A.P.C. 1542–7*, pp. 237, 330.

twelve, then there would not be even enough wool for the English clothiers, let alone for exportation.[1] By 1552, therefore, they had good cause to applaud the steps taken which would diminish the home consumption of wool and to press their own claims for preferment.

The obvious objective of the Staplers, to bring down the home price of wool, could have been accomplished by diminishing the demand for the raw material or by increasing its supply. The first alternative was the only acceptable solution: for strong public opinion forbade the latter, and indeed more often than not, contemporary opinion associated an increase in the wool supply with engrossing and a rise, instead of a fall, in its price.[2] According to how it was viewed, such a fall in the price of wool would have two other favourable consequences: first, it would make arable farming relatively more profitable and so lead to reconversion from pasture; and secondly, it would give manufacturers a better chance to meet the depression by cutting down their costs of production, and was, because of technological reasons, in fact the only way in which any drastic reduction in costs could be effected.[3]

The most obvious way to lessen the demand for wool was to revive in more stringent form the 1546 legislation against wool broggers; not only would this reduce a competition for wool supplies which was objectionable to Staplers and wealthy clothiers alike, but by cutting off many small cloth producers from the source of their raw material supply, would be a further restraint upon the spread of industrialization. A Bill on wool was accordingly included with the other restrictive measures of 1552, and with them was given the sanction of the Statute Book.

IV

Referred to in the preamble as 'an Act to bring down the price of wool',[4] the anti-middleman legislation of 1552 went as far as it could to meet the wishes of the pressure groups. By it, complete liberty of buying wool was allowed only to manufacturers and

---

[1] P.R.O. S.P. 10/13/80.
[2] *Tudor Economic Documents*, iii, 52, 319.
[3] Employers might also achieve a substantial saving in costs by drastically cutting wages.
[4] *Statutes of the Realm*, 5 & 6 Edward VI, c. 7, subsequently referred to as 'the 1552 Act' unless otherwise specified.

Merchants of the Staple: the latter to ship all staple wool to Calais. A counterpart to the triumph of economic nationalism in the cloth-exporting trade[1] found its place in the wool trade by the enactment which forbade any alien merchant to buy wool between shearing time and the Feast of the Purification — and it could not have been for any lack of effort on the Staplers' part that the restraint was not complete. The penalty for any of these offences was stipulated at an amount double in value to the wool bought, half of which was to go to the informer and the other half to the Crown.

With the decline of their trade the Staplers had increasingly specialized in exporting, on the one hand, the very finest grades of wool and, on the other, the longer and coarser types of staple.[2] But the very coarse northern wools were of little interest to them, and by the Act the merchants of Newcastle were permitted to continue buying them for exportation. However, clips, even from fine-woolled sheep, contained a certain amount of wool unsuitable for the Staple, and this refuse wool and locks the Staplers were authorized to sell within the realm to any cloth or yarn manufacturer, providing that it was 'shotte and packed by the woolpacker, declaringe of what packinge or contrey the refuse or lockes be, and writinge upon the Clothes wherin the saide refuse woolles ys packed in great letters as they doe upon the wolles that ys shipped to Callice'.

The wool growers' interests, already injured by the restraint which the Act placed upon dealers and alien merchants, received a further set-back by the next clause, which forbade any grower to keep his wool unsold for longer than one year providing that he had received an offer for it at the current market-price; and a penalty for any offence was laid down at ten shillings for every tod of wool unsold, half to the informer and half to the Crown.

Perhaps it may seem strange that such an Act, so apparently opposed to the landed interests, should be passed under a government of great and 'rapacious' landlords.[3] Part of the

---

[1] In return for the financial services of the Merchant Adventurers, the government in 1552 abolished the privileges of the Hansards. See Unwin, *Studies*, pp. 146–147, 149–50; Fisher, *Econ. Hist. Rev.* x (1940), 108–9.

[2] P. J. Bowden, *Econ. Hist. Rev.* 2nd ser. ix (1956), 48, n. 5.

[3] See R. H. Tawney, *The Agrarian Problem in the Sixteenth Century* (1912), pp. 14, 352; A. F. Pollard, *England under Protector Somerset* (1900), p. 271.

explanation must be that the rapacity of England's rulers at this time has been exaggerated. However self-seeking the administration of Northumberland may have been, its agrarian policy was in fact no more anti-social than that of other Tudor governments. Indeed, at the same time as legislation was being passed on the wool trade, fresh measures were being taken against depopulation.[1] The government may also have believed that the effects of the legislation would not be unduly harmful to the wealthier landowners. At this stage in the development of the wool trade relatively little capital was in the hands of the wool broggers. Although these dealers supplied one of the most important markets for the small growers' wool, the more wealthy growers relied mainly upon the Staplers and the more capitalistic clothiers for their sales, and, to a lesser extent, upon the alien merchants. Again, it may also be supposed that the keeping of wool over long periods by growers was unlikely to assume very significant proportions unless its price became abnormally depressed. For only the wealthier growers, who were numerically few, could afford to keep their capital locked up in stocks of wool over considerable periods; and in any case, wool kept in store for a year or more could become rotten and moth-eaten and so lose much in market value.[2]

Nevertheless, it could not be denied that the Act was disadvantageous, even though in different degrees, to large wool growers as well as small, and it is apparent that there were doubts in the mind of the government as to what the results of the legislation would be. It could not be taken as certain that the wealthy landed interests would not suffer substantial damage or, for that matter, that the cloth manufacture would not be greatly disrupted; and it was probably because of this uncertainty that a clause was added to make the Act repealable by royal proclamation. A further reason for the inclusion of this rider may have been that the Crown desired to use the power which it gave as a bribe or a threat: a threat, for instance, to hold over the heads of the Staplers to ensure their future compliance — which they gave during the following decade — in the matter of paying off its foreign debts.[3] Whatever the original motive

---

[1] M. W. Beresford, *Agric. Hist. Rev.* ii (1954), 21–2.
[2] P.R.O. S.P. 16/21/66.
[3] *A.P.C. 1556–8,* p. 414; *Cal. Pat. 1555–7,* pp. 81–2; W. R. Scott, *Joint Stock Companies to 1720* (Cambridge, 1910), i, 28.

had been, it was long forgotten when, nearly seventy years later, the royal prerogative was first used to annul the power of the Act; but in the meantime other ways had been found of setting it aside.

v

Much Tudor legislation on economic matters had two features in common. One was a conservatism which — by impeding the most profitable form of agriculture, by obstructing the mobility of labour, by prohibiting the middleman trade in certain food-stuffs and raw materials — endeavoured to maintain the old order in the face of growing industrialization and the expansion of markets. The other feature — most notable in the regulation of the cloth industry — was a failure, when laying down uniform standards to be observed, to make due allowance for significant differences in local and regional conditions.

From the very beginning, the effective enforcement of such restrictive legislation was found to be difficult, if not impossible. Sooner or later the government recognized the need to mitigate the harshness of the law, and to this end it discriminated in particular instances and sanctioned limited and regulated dispensations in more general cases.

The legislation on the wool trade was no better and no worse than the typical enactments of its period. Its defects were the same and its consequences similar. Already an essential link between the small manufacturer and his supply of raw material, the wool middleman became yet more indispensable as his wool-sorting functions developed and the internal wool market expanded.

As early as 1547 legislation was passed, permitting Norfolk the services of wool dealers. The reasons for this exemption were given in the preamble of the Act,[1] which stated that the poor spinners of Norfolk (and the city of Norwich) were dependent upon 'retaylers of wolles' for supplies of their raw material. From them wool was obtainable by 'eight-pennyworth and twelve-pennyworthe at one time': quantities which were too paltry for growers to deal in. Following the 1546 Act, it was

---

[1] *Statutes of the Realm*, 1 Edward VI, c. 6. This Act also made perpetual Statute 33 Henry VIII, c. 16, which forbade the sale of worsted yarn in Norfolk to any person but weavers, and which prohibited its export.

stated, these dealers had ceased to frequent the Norfolk markets, with the result that many of the inhabitants of the county 'be now unoccupied . . . and a greate number of them enforced to begge for lacke of worke'. It was therefore enacted that any inhabitant of the county should be allowed to buy Norfolk wool — which was the main, if not the only source of supply for the manufacture of worsteds at this time[1] — in order to retail it at the common markets or other open places within the county. There was little objection which the vested interests could raise to this, for most Norfolk wool was unsuitable for the manufacture of broadcloth and was too coarse for the Staple;[2] whilst from the government's point of view there was much to be gained by keeping these small independent spinners contented and occupied.

The exemption which Norfolk obtained — ratified in 1552 — led, during the following twenty years, to an agitation for similar privileges from those other parts of the country where the small manufacturer predominated. During this period a number of Bills was introduced into Parliament with this intention, but only one — that relating to Halifax — was successful. In 1547 a Bill for buying wool in Devon and Cornwall, and in 1548 a Bill for Devon alone, had been introduced into the Commons only to be thrown out. In 1553 and 1554 Bills 'to repeal divers Branches' of the 1552 Act were also unsuccessful. In 1555 a Bill to extend the privileges of Norfolk got no further than a first reading; and in 1563 a proposal for the resale of coarse wools in Norfolk and Suffolk, after a successful passage through the Lords, was dropped following amendment by the Lower House. The greatest agitation, however, came from the North Country, and resulted in six Bills being introduced into Parliament between 1555 and 1566. One, introduced in 1562 for wool to be bought in Lancashire and Yorkshire for sale in fairs and markets, was rejected after a first reading. Most of the other Bills — including one in 1563 for the licensing of dealers by J.P.'s to buy wools in six of the northern counties — had a slightly longer existence, but all of them, save one, ultimately suffered the same fate.[3]

---

[1] See supra, pp. 35, 64.
[2] P.R.O. E.134/44–5 Elizabeth I. Mich. 1.
[3] *H. of C. Journals*, i, 2, 4, 29, 34, 43, 44, 68, 70, 71–2, 73, 74, 77, 78, 79.

In parliamentary eyes only the parish of Halifax vindicated
its claims for special consideration. The reasons for this were
given in the picturesque and oft-quoted preamble to the Act[1]
passed in 1555:

> Forasmuch as the Paryshe of Halyfax and other places theronto
> adjoyning being planted in the grete wastes and moores where the
> fertilite of grounde ys not apte to bring forthe any corne nor good
> grasse but in rare places, and by exceeding and great Industrye of
> thinhabitantes: and the same Inhabitantes altogether doo lyve by
> Clothemaking, and the greate parte of them neither gette the corne
> nor is hable to kepe a Horse to carry woolles, nor yet to bye muche
> wooll at once, but hathe ever used onely to repayre to the Towne
> of Halyfaxe, and some other nigh theronto, and ther to buy upon
> the woolldriver some a stone some two and some three or foure,
> according to their Habilitie and to carye the same to their Houses
> some iii, iiij, v, and vj myles of, upon their Headdes and Backes,
> and so to make and converte the same eyther into yarne or clothe,
> and to sell the same, and so to buy more wooll of the wooldryver
> . . . which nowe are like to bee undone and dryven to Beggary by
> reason of the late Estatute made that takethe awaye the wool-
> dryver. . . .

It was therefore enacted that any inhabitant of the parish
could buy wool providing that it was sold only at the town of
Halifax to poor manufacturers of that and of adjoining
parishes. Sale was forbidden to traders and to those wealthier
clothiers — of which Halifax had a small number — who were
in a position to obtain their own raw material direct from the
growers. To check the abuse of this privilege, it was decided
that a penalty of double the value of the wool involved should
be imposed — in a Court of Record or at Quarter Sessions —
upon any dealer who under its protection sold wool elsewhere
than at Halifax, and upon any purchaser who resold wool
obtained through the working of the Act.

The concessions secured by the small-manufacturer strong-
holds of Halifax and Norfolk were fundamental to the well-
being of those localities. Without wool middlemen their
industrial structures were in danger of collapse. Other local
concessions, made later in the century, had not the same
significance. Their prime object was to increase the prosperity

---

[1] *Statutes of the Realm*, 2 & 3 Philip and Mary, c. 13.

of the towns which received them rather than to remove a restraint on wool dealing which had been found particularly burdensome. This is shown, for example, by a Statute passed in 1576, which authorized any person to buy wool and yarn at New Woodstock in Oxfordshire, upon the usual market and fair days, to dispose of as he wished.[1] The reasons for this Act were stated to be that New Woodstock, which had formerly been 'chiefly supported by access of the Queen's noble progenitors unto their manor of Woodstock', had fallen into great poverty; and it was thought that the measure enacted would help to attract trade and industry to the borough. Similar privileges were granted by letters patent to the town of Leicester in 1599 and to Grantham, in Lincolnshire, in 1604.[2] Finally, in 1589, Parliament passed an Act authorizing the citizens of Lincoln to buy Lincolnshire wool to sell again at any places within the realm, providing that one-quarter of the wool so bought was manufactured within the precincts of the city for the relief of the poor.[3]

VI

An effective enforcement of the 1552 Act could not fail to be prejudicial to wool growers and small manufacturers. It could also mean hardship to those men who, previous to the legislation, had made some part of their livelihood from dealing in wool — a trade now legally denied to them. The consequences of the restraint were not so serious for those dealers who had other occupations to turn to, but to the Company of Woolmen[4] the matter was one of more urgent import.

These woolmen (otherwise known as wool winders or wool packers) had a history stretching back several hundred years. Becoming more important as the wool-export trade developed, they had a craft gild of their own in the fifteenth century and obtained a grant of incorporation from Henry VIII in 1522.[5] The prosperity of the wool packers was bound up very closely

[1] *Statutes of the Realm*, 18 Elizabeth I, c. 21.
[2] P.R.O. S.P. 38/6/22nd May, 1599; S.P. 38/7/29th May, 1604.
[3] This Act is not printed in *Statutes of the Realm*, but proof that it was passed may be found in P.R.O. S.P. 14/108/34.
[4] Not to be confused with the prosperous wool middlemen of the fifteenth century.
[5] *Cal. L.P.F.D. Henry VIII*, iii, pt. 2, no. 2385.

with the fortunes of the export trade, for their livelihood depended primarily upon the amount of wool which passed through their hands for export. Such a business could hardly hope to escape statutory regulation, and by the beginning of the sixteenth century the wool packers' functions had been clearly defined by legislation. Winding and packing wool for export, valuing it and casting out refuse wool were the chief of these. In addition, they were warned to be on the alert for fraudulent trade practices, and were employed by buyers as a check on the sellers and by the royal officials and the Staple at the ports as a check on the merchants. During the fifteenth century, the further to prevent frauds, it had been enacted that wool should be packed in the county of growth.[1] Of necessity, therefore, the wool winders' trade entailed a considerable amount of travel, particularly in the months following the June clipping. But even in good years, the bulk of this employment as a full-time occupation was over in six months,[2] and many wool winders had supplemented it by engaging in the business of wool dealing.

Whilst the wool-export trade was still flourishing, much of this business had been done with alien buyers. The Staplers' objections to this had led in 1473 to transitory legislation being passed forbidding any wool packer to buy or sell wool and woolfells within the realm for himself or for any other person.[3] In 1489, 1531 and 1546 further measures were enacted forbidding dealing on behalf of alien merchants.[4] The effects of this legislation, combined with the growth of the home cloth industry, brought about a change in the direction of this side of the wool packers' business. By the mid-sixteenth century it was no longer alien merchants, but English manufacturers, who were the winders' most important customers for wool. Especially was this so in London, where that port's increasing monopoly of wool shipments[5] had concentrated the members of the Company. Here they sold wool 'to the Clothiers repayringe to London, and to Cappers and Hat-makers and others occupienge

---

[1] Power and Postan, op. cit., pp. 56–7.   [2] P.R.O. S.P. 12/90/37.
[3] Postan and Power, op. cit., p. 58.
[4] *Statutes of the Realm*, 4 Henry VII, c. 11; ibid., 22 Henry VIII, c. 1; ibid., 37 Henry VIII, c. 15.
[5] By 1565 only London, Boston and Hull were left to the staple trade, and London easily outdistanced the other two (Rich, op. cit., pp. 97–8).

wolle inhabitinge and dwellinge in and aboute the same Citie'.[1]
Such dealings, falling into the same category as the trade of the
wool broggers, had been declared unlawful. But previous to
1552 the Acts which had restrained such activities had always
left dealers some freedom to take part in them during the latter
part of the wool-growing year: a slack time for wool winding
and packing. Thus it was that some of the strongest — and
certainly the best organized — protests at the introduction of
the 1552 Bill came from the wool packers, and their objections
against it were laid before the Commons.[2] But nothing in the
case put forward by the Company could secure favoured
treatment for its members or prevent the Bill from becoming
law.

The disadvantage which this restraint placed upon the
Company was accentuated during the following years by the
continued decline in the wool-export trade which, dragging
down the Company's chief support, had fallen by 1570 to
almost insignificant proportions.[3] Nor was this diminution in
the Company's trade compensated by a corresponding amount
of employment in winding wool for the home market, although
some of its members were bound to turn to this as an alternative
means of livelihood. When, in earlier years, the great bulk of
English wool had been worked-up abroad, the Company had
been assured of a fairly exclusive position in its business by the
fact that every aspect concerned with the export of wool
(including winding and packing) was regulated by statute and
carefully watched over by officials. But, apart from insisting that
fraudulent trade practices should be avoided,[4] there was no
necessity for the government to duplicate these regulations —
which had been made chiefly for the specific purpose of facilitat-
ing the collection of export custom — for the winding of wool to
be used at home. The operations involved in winding and packing wool for home consumption appear to have been no more
than semi-skilled in character, and growers apparently often

---

[1] P.R.O. S.P. 12/90/37.   [2] *H. of C. Journals*, i, 21.   [3] Infra, p. 162.
[4] Fleeces that were wound unwashed or were wound around heavy objects such
as lead and stones, naturally gained much in weight. Such practices were forbidden
in 1532 (*Statutes of the Realm*, 23 Henry VIII, c. 17), and a penalty of sixpence for
every fleece wound in this manner was imposed upon any offender. This Act was
renewed in subsequent Parliaments until in 1571 it was made perpetual by Statute
13 Elizabeth, c. 25.

employed part-time and unspecialized winders. Neither, it seems, was the practice of hiring non-members of the Company limited entirely to the home trade: if the Staplers are to be believed it had also intruded into the winding of wool for export. It was inevitable that the Company of Woolmen should deprecate the encroachments by outsiders upon the trade of its members, and that the Staplers should lament this as being the cause of much falsehood in the winding and packing of wool. In response to complaints from these two bodies the Crown issued five proclamations between 1545 and 1604 for the reform of the abuses cited and for the regulation of the trade,[1] but with little effect.

Although the Company of Woolmen succeeded in obtaining proclamations against interlopers in 1550 and 1562,[2] in the latter year it was again unsuccessful in persuading Parliament to pass a Bill authorizing its members to buy and sell wool within the realm.[3] But doubtless this failure did not prevent some of them from engaging in illicit wool dealing; for after the middle of the 1560's the wool-export trade shrank to such an extent that a handful of packers could have managed it with ease. Certainly, it could not sustain 'the nomber of Two Hunderithe and Foure skore Parsons vsinge the trade of Wolmen within the Citie of London besides theire famelies wifes and children in nomber to geather nyne hunderithe parsons at the leaste'.[4] This the Company pointed out in a petition to the Lord Treasurer in 1572, after again unsuccessfully attempting to obtain parliamentary sanction to a Bill authorizing them to engage in wool dealing.[5] It was a sorry picture, of unemployment and of household goods being sold to pay for food, which the woolmen painted of themselves; soon, they claimed, it would be one of 'vtter beggerye vnles some spedy remidy therein be had'. The plea that the Company should be granted a licence to

---

[1] *Tudor and Stuart Proclamations*, Nos. 276 (1545), 380 (1550), 570 (1562), 883 (1596), 992 (1604).

[2] Ibid., Nos. 380, 570. These stated that no person was to wind wool without licence under seal of the Company of Woolmen under pain of being stood in the pillory with a fleece of wool around his neck. A further proclamation, in 1604, stated that offenders would incur this penalty and, in addition, ten days' imprisonment (ibid., No. 992).

[3] *H. of C. Journals*, i, 65.

[4] P.R.O. S.P. 12/90/37. The date of this document is uncertain.

[5] *H. of C. Journals*, i, 89.

buy and sell wool within the realm was disregarded. Not that this prevented some wool winders from engaging in such a profitable trade. During the 'seventies a number of patents authorizing a limited middleman trade in wool was granted by the Crown. The usual course adopted by the recipients of such grants was to sub-let them piecemeal to dealers who, at a price, were thus able to legalize their activities. A few wool winders were amongst the dealers who traded under the protection of a patentee's licence, but they were a small minority of the Company. Nevertheless, a considerable number of wool winders continued to deal in wool irrespective of such protection and in defiant violation of the law.[1]

[1] See P.R.O. S.P. 12/114/39, 42, 47; E.133/1/36; E.133/3/399.

Chapter V

REGULATION BY LICENCE

I

The attempt to regulate the increasingly necessary wool-middleman trade by means of licences was an innovation of considerable importance, but it was not until the 1570's that it became a deliberate policy on the part of the government. In the meantime a step in this direction was taken in connection with the wool-export trade.

Licences to export wool were, of course, almost as old as the export trade itself, and had long provided a bone of contention between the Staplers and the Crown. At one time the granting of such licences had provided the Crown with an important supplementary source of revenue. But by the third quarter of the sixteenth century, conditions no longer favoured the levying of large fees or the extortion of handsome loans from alien merchants in return for the privilege of exporting wool. Not only had the foreign demand for English wool shrunk out of all proportion to what it had once been, but the potential demand for such licences had been reduced by the English government's pursuit of a policy of economic nationalism — the partial restraint on the purchase of wool by aliens was but one instance — which in all likelihood had driven many of the wealthier alien exporters to ply their trade elsewhere. The consequent drop in the value of wool-export licences rendered them unimportant as a possible source of Crown income and, at least from the mid-sixteenth century onwards, they were bestowed more with the intention of rewarding favourites and retainers than of increasing the revenues of State. Possibly some small nominal amounts were involved, for such licences were not valueless; but financially it would have been more advantageous to the Crown to have made these grants to the exporters themselves instead of, in the main, to favourites who, in disposing of them to alien merchants — as most of them did — had their own cuts to take from the business to make it worth while.

During the years immediately following the passing of the 1552 Act a number of wool-export licences was granted. But with the continued decline in the foreign demand for English wool it became increasingly difficult for exporters to find a profitable sale for the raw material abroad. The Crown endeavoured to meet the situation by authorizing the majority of licensees to ship wool that had been 'clacked, bearded and cleaned',[1] or by permitting export at a lower custom rate than was paid by the Staplers. Even so, the relatively high price of English wool and the uncertain international situation greatly reduced the possibilities of making large profits from the export of such wool abroad; and under these circumstances a more remunerative — and certainly a much surer — return was likely to be secured from its resale at home.

The number of export licences granted during this period was not large,[2] but, probably because of the uncertainty of the foreign market, the Crown authorized the three biggest patentees to market their wool at home should they so desire.[3] The first of these three grants was made in November, 1552, to John Stephens, gentleman and woolman of Bourton-on-the-Hill, Gloucestershire, and authorized the purchase of 500 sarplers[4] of wool for export or resale in the home market. In Mary's reign a similar grant for 400 sarplers was made to Matthew, Earl of Lennox, and Lady Margaret his wife. The third grant, which authorized the purchase of 1,000 sarplers was made by Elizabeth I to Robert Dudley, Earl of Leicester, in April, 1560.[5]

The licence system was always open to abuse, for there existed

---

[1] By the operations of 'clacking, bearding and cleaning' the impurities were removed from the wool, especially the tarry marks on the fleeces, and the inferior parts were clipped away; the wool could also be packed more closely together. A sack so clacked and bearded was estimated to be worth two to three times as much as a sack not so treated, and in proportion to its value paid lightly in custom. See Power and Postan, op. cit., p. 56; P.R.O. S.P. 15/9/56; B.M. Lansd. MS. 114, fol. 95.

[2] Between 1550 and 1563, ten patents were granted for the exportation of wool; of these, two were re-affirmations of grants previously made during these years (P.R.O. S.P. 15/7/59).

[3] In addition, two small grants were made for the specific purpose of allowing the purchase of wool for its resale at home (*Cal. Pat. 1553–4*, p. 80; *1560–3*, p. 167).

[4] 1 sarpler = 3 sacks of 26 stones each.

[5] *Cal. Pat. Edward VI*, iv, 266; *1553–4*, p. 102; *1558–60*, p. 321.

K

no effective method of ensuring that a licence holder did not buy above his authorized quota. Both the working of the system and the possibilities it gave for corruption are well illustrated by the activities of John Stephens and his associates.

Soon after obtaining his licence Stephens transferred shares in it of 100 sacks apiece to Anthony Ashefeld and John Croker, both gentlemen of Oxfordshire. Further, the grant made to the Earl of Lennox and his wife was sold by them to Stephens and Ashefeld, who in turn transferred to Croker a quarter share of the 400 sarplers. Once in possession of these licences Stephens and his associates embarked upon a great wool-buying campaign. Although customs entries provided a check on the amount of wool which alien merchants shipped under their authority, only rough estimates could be made as to the extent of the patentees' internal trade. By all accounts it was large enough, and following complaints by West Country clothiers that the licensees' activities were raising wool to unreasonable prices, Stephens, Ashefeld and Croker found themselves answering charges in Star Chamber. Prosecuted under the Act of 1552, they were accused of buying 4,000 sarplers of wool in and around the Cotswold country. Replying to the charge, the defendants claimed that they had bought only a small proportion of the wool authorized by the two licences and asked leave to purchase the remainder.[1] The verdict of the Court does not appear to have survived, but later developments suggest that the principal step taken as a result of the trial was the revocation of the authority to resell wool within the realm.[2]

The history of Leicester's licence was somewhat similar. Unlike Stephens, Leicester did not engage in wool-buying operations, and his patent, after finding its way into the hands of three Englishmen, passed to a group of alien merchants. An information on the 1552 Act in the Court of Exchequer against

---

[1] P.R.O. St. Ch. 4/3/63.
[2] Stephens and Ashefeld had later to stand trial to answer accusations made regarding excessive transportation of wool by alien merchants under their licence (*A.P.C. 1556–8*, p. 127; P.R.O. St. Ch. 4/8/14; B.M. Lansd. MS. 114, fols. 95–6). Nothing further is heard of the sale of wool within the realm. Despite the obvious case against them, the two men succeeded in obtaining permission to continue exporting wool in the months immediately preceding their trial (*A.P.C. 1556–8*, pp. 217–18). Not only that; they afterwards obtained the grant to Ashefeld of two further licences for the export of wool, though for smaller amounts and under less favourable conditions (*Cal. Pat. 1557–8*, p. 224; *1558–60*, p. 94).

two Midland wool dealers who pleaded that they had traded as factors of the aliens,[1] helped to bring the licence into disrepute, and when the grant was reaffirmed in May, 1562, the authority to resell wool in the home market was withdrawn.[2]

Informations upon the 1552 Act were fairly numerous in the 'fifties and 'sixties.[3] A few were brought against wool growers for holding back their wool from the market.[4] But the great majority of informations were against middlemen for illegally buying and selling wool. It is, however, impossible to argue that because dealers were frequently prosecuted, then the Act was being rigorously enforced. For if such informations as were brought show that the law made itself felt in some cases, they also show that in these instances, and in many others as well, judging from contemporary complaints, the legislation was being disregarded. The smaller dealers were often successful in avoiding the law. Petty transactions held little interest for the common informer. They were more difficult to keep track of than wholesale breakages of the law. But, apart from that, it was not always profitable to sue for small amounts; expenses entailed by legal proceedings could be disproportionately heavy in relation to the hoped-for gain. Thus it was that informations were seldom brought for dealings involving less than 100 tods of wool: a fact which tended to the concentration of prosecutions upon areas where conditions favoured buying by larger rather than smaller dealers. Such areas were those where the markets to be supplied were some distance away, and where the price of wool was high relative to that in the rest of the country, as, for example, in the Cotswolds, the Midlands, and in the counties of Hereford, Shropshire, Stafford and Lincoln.

If the activities of the smaller dealers were on the whole not worth prosecuting, those of the larger dealers were often more difficult to prove as being outside the law. The trial of Stephens and his associates and the later prosecution involving Leicester's licence suggest that there was some justification for the complaint made in 1560 that 'if informations have been given for

---

[1] P.R.O. E.133/1/36.
[2] *Cal. Pat. 1560–3*, p. 270. At this date only 110 sarplers, of the 1,000 authorized, had been exported.
[3] See M. W. Beresford, 'The Common Informer, The Penal Statutes and Economic Regulation', *Econ. Hist. Rev.* 2nd ser. x (1957), 223.
[4] e.g. P.R.O. E.159/7 Elizabeth I. Mich. 198.

buying wool contrary to statute, the offender pretends himself deputy to a licence holder, by an antedated authority, and so the Queen is defrauded of her fine'.[1] When licences were passing from one hand to another, and being divided out amongst dealers, the common informer could not be sure whether he was prosecuting a genuine licence holder or not; neither, for that matter, could he be certain that a defendant would not invent such a privilege specially for the occasion with the compliance of a genuine licensee. As those dealers who possessed, or feigned to possess, a licence were among the wealthiest in the country, their activities were an obvious subject for the attention of the informer. But alas, too often in these cases, informers found that incriminating evidence showing dealers guilty of buying and selling wool was not enough to secure their conviction, and that all the cost and trouble to which they had been put were wasted.

II

The authority given to the larger export licensees to deal in wool within the realm having proved open to abuse, the government refrained for a time from granting similar privileges. But eventually the growth in the production of the new draperies led to a revision of this attitude. Though the most spectacular expansion in the output of the new draperies came in the seventeenth century, by 1570 they were being produced on a large enough scale in Norwich to necessitate the employment of considerable quantities of wool grown outside the confines of Norfolk. The Act of 1552, following the 1547 Act, had permitted wool dealers to buy and sell wool only within that county.[2] A grant was accordingly made to four aldermen of Norwich[3] authorizing them or their factors to buy wool anywhere within the realm on condition that it should be sold to persons 'inhabitinge or resydant within our said citye of Norwiche or wythin the libertye or franchice thereof', and at no place elsewhere.[4]

The licence granted to the citizens of Norwich was unusual in that it was for an unspecified period of tenure and authorized

---

[1] *Cal. S.P. Dom. 1547–65*, p. 500.   [2] Supra, pp. 118–19.

[3] These were John Alderiche, 'nowe Maior of our sayed Citie of Norwyche', Robert Suckelynge, Thomas Layer and Simon Bowde.

[4] P.R.O. C.66/1062, mm. 31–2, 23 October, 12 Elizabeth I.

the purchase of an undefined quantity of wool. Later wool patents clearly defined both the amount of wool and the time within which it was to be purchased, and as a precaution against the grants being misused, their recipients were hopefully requested to endorse on 'the backsyde of these our Lettres Patentes' the quantity of wool which they bought. Such was the case with the licence granted to James Cottesford, a Cranbrook clothier, in January, 1574, for the purchase and sale of 500 tods of wool a year for twelve years,[1] the patent received by William Wilson of Market Rasen in December, 1575, to buy and sell 4,000 tods annually for four years,[2] the grant made to Richard Chapman of Hampton Court in August, 1576, authorizing a yearly trade in 500 tods for five years,[3] and the licence granted to Simon Bowyer, Gentleman Usher to the Queen, in October, 1576, to buy and sell 500 sarplers within the following ten years.[4] These grants authorized the purchase and sale of wool at any place within the realm, and it is noticeable that all were made at a time when trade was generally good. Sir Francis Walsingham received the only other important wool patent to be granted in the 1570's. This licensed the export, at the usual custom and subsidy, of 1,000 sarplers of clacked, cleaned and bearded wool, and permitted the resale of refuse wool in the home market. Originally the grant had been made in May, 1572, the wool to be exported within the following seven years, but Walsingham had been unable to take any immediate advantage of the patent, and in January, 1575, it was surrendered at his own request and replaced by a similar grant with a twelve-year tenure.[5] This gave him a practical monopoly of the licensed wool-export trade.[6]

The grants to trade in wool within the realm seem to have been prompted by a mixture of motives. The desire to foster industry and employment was a not unimportant factor, particularly in the case of the licence granted to the aldermen of

[1] P.R.O. C.66/1111, m. 21.
[2] B.M. Lansd. MS. 21, fols. 180–5.
[3] P.R.O. Cal. Pat. 17–30 Elizabeth I, fol. 6.
[4] B.M. Lansd. MS. 22, fols. 96–9.
[5] P.R.O. C.66/1131, mm. 24–5.
[6] Walsingham also had a very large interest in the cloth-export trade. He received a licence in September, 1574, to transport 8,000 cloths; a licence in April, 1577, to transport 30,000 cloths; and a licence in September, 1579, to transport 70,000 cloths (P.R.O. S.P. 12/175/19).

Norwich. But if the services of the wool dealer, both as a sorter of wool and as a link between distant markets, were becoming increasingly necessary, why was the 1552 Act not repealed? The answer seems to be partly that the clamour of vested interests had persuaded the government that unrestricted buying of wool was harmful, and partly that the Crown gained financially by the Act's remaining in force. Fines levied for infringements of the law were always welcome additions to the royal income. Nor was this the only way in which restrictive legislation could prove financially advantageous to the Crown. Dispensations could be granted in return for fees, or as pure privileges to favourites and retainers. In the latter case such grants served as an alternative to some other reward, and although Elizabeth was very sparing in making direct payment for services she was liberal with these.[1] Such an explanation could indeed apply to Simon Bowyer's licence and to the export licence granted to Walsingham. It also helps to explain why a grant should have been made to William Wilson, for Wilson's brother Thomas moved in the highest Court circles and was, among other things, a Master of the Court of Requests and the author of the celebrated *Discourse upon Usury*.[2]

Wool patentees were seldom active wool buyers, at least not on any considerable scale. James Cottesford engaged in wool-buying operations,[3] so too did William Wilson,[4] but for the most part they, and the other wool patentees, sub-let their licences piecemeal to dealers in return for the payment of an admittance fine and a yearly rent. The licence granted to the aldermen of Norwich was exceptional in that the patentees themselves participated in a very considerable wool trade: Simon Bowde and Thomas Layer buying large quantities of wool in the inland counties, particularly Northamptonshire, while their alien factors frequented the London wool market.[5]

As the business of leasing a share in a wool licence was one which not all dealers could afford, it was with men of 'very good creditt' that the patentees mostly dealt. The Staplers, many of whom had turned to the internal wool trade after the loss of

---

[1] E. F. Heckscher, *Mercantilism* (1934 edn.), i, 254.
[2] P.R.O. S.P. 12/255/45.
[3] P.R.O. Req. 2/109/3.
[4] P.R.O. S.P. 12/105/95.
[5] P.R.O. S.P. 12/114/40, 41; Req. 2/169/12.

Calais in 1558,[1] were foremost among the dealers to be licensed by Simon Bowyer and William Wilson, while yeomen, gentlemen, drapers, merchant tailors, leather sellers and wool winders were tenants of James Cottesford.[2] Though a considerable number of these dealers came from London and transacted much of their wool business in the capital, others dwelt and conducted the major part of their operations further afield. The dealers licensed by Cottesford included men from the counties of Huntingdon, Bedford, Hertford, Northampton and Derby, as well as from London. Roger Sedgewick, for instance, came from St. Ives, Huntingdonshire, and, if the information which was exhibited against him in the Court of Exchequer in 1567 is any guide, carried on a large trade in Lincolnshire as well as in Norfolk wool.[3] Similarly, Robert Blackstock, one of Bowyer's licensees, purchased wool at numerous fairs and markets in the country, and disposed of a large part of it to clothiers at Reading. Blackstock traded in partnership with William Jackson, a Buckinghamshire woolman.[4]

Licences were sub-let to dealers under various conditions of tenure. The admission fine and yearly rent which the patentee received depended primarily upon how much wool the dealer was licensed to buy and, to a lesser extent, upon the relative bargaining powers of the two parties. Cottesford usually let his licences on a six-yearly tenancy basis. Some of his tenants were licensed to deal in 200 tods of wool each year, others to trade in 60 or 100 tods. The fines which he charged, even for similar licences, varied considerably. A licence to buy 200 tods of wool each year for six years cost Roger Sedgewick a £10 fine, while it cost Robert Smith, a Bedfordshire yeoman, only £6. The annual rent charged in each case was £5. For a similar licence Andrew Milward, a Derbyshire draper, paid a £5 fine and a £6 rent.[5] If, in Sedgewick's case, for example, a dealer considered his fine as an overhead charge on his first year's trading only and added it to his first year's rent, he would find that the cost of his licence worked out at ninepence on every stone of wool licensed,

[1] Infra, pp. 159–60.
[2] B.M. Lansd. MS. 48, fol. 156; ibid., 114, fols. 94–5; P.R.O. S.P. 12/105/95; S.P. 12/114/42.
[3] P.R.O. E.134/9 Elizabeth I. Hil. 3; Req. 2/122/32.
[4] P.R.O. Req. 2/30/56.
[5] P.R.O. E.133/3/399; S.P. 12/114/42; Req. 2/109/3; Req. 2/243/53.

or approximately half of the normal profit margin of an unlicensed dealer. If, however, he thought of his fine as being spread over the whole of the six years of his tenancy, he would then conclude that the cost of his licence amounted to a charge of only fourpence on every stone. Though the different results thus obtained would have been due to nothing but arithmetical juggling, doubtless some dealers took the short view and some the long, and probably price policies were shaped accordingly. Apart from passing it on to buyers in the form of higher prices, there was only one way in which a dealer could materially lessen the burden of this overhead charge, and that was by purchasing wool in excess of his licence.

Though many wool dealers resorted to this practice, they did not do so only as a means of spreading their overhead costs. The amount of wool authorized to be purchased under patent was only a small proportion of that grown in the country. Consequently, licences frequently underrated the normal size of a dealer's business, and to exceed them was but to carry on an accustomed trade. The authority to buy a limited amount of wool which a licence conferred upon its holder could be used to protect him in his illegal traffic, and providing that he did not act foolishly, and did not mind making false returns to the patentee,[1] there was little likelihood of detection. When a patentee abused his authority, however, things could go badly for his tenants. Cottesford, who was found guilty of this misdemeanour in 1577,[2] was allowed to retain his grant, but many of the licences issued by him were made void. Instead of being compensated for their financial loss, the dealers whom he had illegally licensed were reprimanded by the Privy Council, informed against in the Court of Exchequer, and finally bound 'in great somes of money' that they would neither buy nor sell wool.[3]

---

[1] Cottesford required that his tenants should 'covenante in there deputacions to indorse yearelye at a certen daye' (P.R.O. E.133/3/399).

[2] It was stated that Cottesford 'hathe above xl assignes vnder hym . . . which doe by yerelie xx tymes more then his licence doth warrant' (P.R.O. S.P. 12/114/41). A more moderate estimate credited him with having licensed dealers to buy 'two thowsand todds of woll or ther aboutes more then he lawfully could graunt' (P.R.O. Req. 2/243/53).

[3] P.R.O. Req. 2/109/3; Req. 2/243/53; E.133/3/399. In spite of these restraints, Roger Sedgewick was soon trading again on a large scale. See P.R.O. Req. 2/122/32.

III

It was only to be expected that the activities of wool middlemen in general, and licensed dealers in particular, should be blamed for the increase in the price of wool which followed the resumption of commercial intercourse between England and the Netherlands in April, 1573, after more than four years' nominal interruption. As the ensuing expansion in cloth exports came to an end, the agitation against wool middlemen became more clamorous, and the government decided to take action. At the end of October, 1576, the Lords of the Privy Council ordered certain wool buyers from London, Northampton and other places to appear before them for questioning.[1] This was followed at the end of November by the issue of a proclamation prohibiting the purchase of wool by licence before All Saints next (i.e. 1st November, 1577) and forbidding the Merchants of the Staple to buy any wool before the end of the following February.[2] The proclamation had little lasting effect. Within a few months at least two wool patents — those of Cottesford and the Norwich aldermen — had been exempted from its terms,[3] while the Staplers continued their trade as before.

The sheep-shearing season was close at hand when, on the last day of May, 1577, the Lords of the Privy Council were moved by the agitation against wool middlemen to make a more determined attempt than hitherto to stamp out unauthorized buying and selling of wool. To achieve this end the Council decided that the proclamation of November, 1576, should be rigorously enforced, and that bonds of £100 should be taken from all broggers as security against their dealing in wool. Letters were accordingly sent to Justices of the Peace throughout the country informing them of this decision and demanding, in no uncertain terms, their co-operation in the matter.[4] Local administration lay mainly in the hands of the landed interests, and the Justices showed no enthusiasm over the task assigned to them. Indeed, they did the absolute minimum that was necessary, taking bonds only from those dealers whose names had

---

[1] *A.P.C. 1575–7*, p. 223.
[2] *Tudor and Stuart Proclamations*, 712. The proclamation also ordered that all licences should be returned into the Exchequer for revision within two months.
[3] P.R.O. Req. 2/243/53; S.P. 12/115/23; *A.P.C. 1575–7*, p. 281.
[4] P.R.O. S.P. 12/113/21, 22; Hist. MSS. Comm. *Townshend MSS*. pp. 3–4.

been forwarded by the Council, and were in no hurry to do even that. And 'as touchinge the proclamacion made for restraynynge of suche as had lycences to buye', they informed the Council several months later, 'we do not knowe sythence the makinge of the same that any persones here hath disobeyed yt'.[1]

The government considered the restraint of wool middlemen as fundamental to its policy for bringing down the price of wool, and the attitude of the local officials was not encouraging. It soon became apparent that the measures initiated by the government were not having the required effect; and the Council, at a loss as to the next practical step to take, instituted an inquiry into the causes of the high price of wool, and invited suggestions from cloth manufacturers, Merchant Adventurers and Staplers for the remedies to be applied.[2]

The clothiers whose opinions were asked were unanimous in attributing the high price of wool to the engrossing activities of middlemen, which, they stated, forced them to make their purchases at second or third hand at enhanced prices. Some dealers, it was alleged, sold wool at 'dyvers tymes of the yere' it 'never beinge removed from the shippe masters or growers howses'.[3] The Staplers and the licensees were named as the chief offenders; but the common broggers' activities were also severely criticized, and their business methods shown to be no better than those of the richer dealers.

Outwardly, at any rate, both clothiers and Merchant Adventurers were convinced that the engrossing of wool by middlemen was the chief reason for its increase in price, and only the Suffolk clothiers, prompted by their own private interests, attempted to offer any alternative solution.[4] The remedies were therefore obvious, and the manufacturers demanded that all licences should be revoked and stringent measures taken to prevent wool middlemen from trading in the future.[5] The Suffolk clothiers again showed an unnatural zeal

[1] P.R.O. S.P. 12/115/28, 29.   [2] *A.P.C. 1575-7*, p. 366.
[3] P.R.O. S.P. 12/114/32.
[4] The Suffolk clothiers resented the competition of the manufacturers of the new draperies, and they accused the bayes makers of reselling much of the wool which they purchased, and the alien manufacturers of smuggling yarn abroad and of increasing the demand for wool by converting it into 'many slight and vaine comodities wherein the common people delight and bestowe greate somes' (P.R.O. S.P. 12/114/33).
[5] P.R.O. S.P. 12/114/25-28, 32-34, 40.

for reformation, and they requested that manufacturers purchasing wool from dealers, as well as the dealers themselves,
should not only forfeit the wool which they purchased, but
should also suffer one year's imprisonment. 'This', they stated,
'we praie to haue laid on ourselves for our dulnes is suche that
we see no other waie to reforme it.'[1]

The urgency with which the clothiers put forward their case
against the wool middlemen leads one to look (not unsuccessfully) for ulterior motives behind their agitation. It is true that
the charges which they preferred, although exaggerated, were
not altogether unfounded. Without middlemen the price of
wool would, of course, have been lower: they added to the
number of buyers and so increased the effective demand for the
raw material. But whilst not ignoring this as a genuine motive
for their agitation, there were yet other important and un-
disclosed reasons why these manufacturers desired the middlemen to be eliminated.

The clothing interests represented in the 1577 Government
Inquiry were by no means fully representative of the industry as
a whole. The clothiers were broadcloth manufacturers — from
the West Country, Suffolk, Worcester City and Newbury — and
the views which they submitted for the consideration of the
Privy Council were those of the most important, the most
capitalistic, and the most vociferous, section of the English wool-
textile industry. The opinions of the small independent manufacturers, who made coarse cloth or worsted fabrics, had not
been asked for, but had they been given they would have been
very different from those which the wealthier clothiers expressed. Having neither the time nor the money to travel into
the country to buy their wool, the small manufacturers placed
an excessive reliance upon the middlemen to supply their
requirements. This reliance became greater as the production of
coarse woollens and worsted fabrics expanded, thus necessitat-
ing the tapping of an ever-widening source of raw material
supply. Without wool middlemen the small manufacturers were
without raw material. The wealthier clothiers were well aware
of this fact, and knew that with the middlemen expelled from
their trade, and with a practical monopoly of the country's wool
supply in their own hands, they would be able to destroy the

[1] P.R.O. S.P. 12/114/33.

small manufacturers as competitors and subjugate them to their own authority. In a number of instances such results had already followed from the working of the 1552 Act,[1] and it was not without reason that some of the poorer manufacturers later complained:

> If the Statute take effecte in this behalf the trade thereof wyll be dryven into a fewe ryche mens handes, soe that the poore shall not be paide for their worke but as it pleaseth the ryche, and the cloth shall reste in their handes to sell at their pleasure.[2]

A rigid enforcement of the 1552 Act, especially with such penalties as the Suffolk clothiers proposed, would have very much restricted the production of the new draperies by the rich, as well as by the poor manufacturers. The majority of the new drapers fell into the second category, but a small number of bayes makers were men of good substance. Whereas the poorer manufacturers normally bought their wool (ready-sorted) from middlemen, the wealthier bayes makers purchased long-woolled fleeces direct from the growers. In addition to long wool, such fleeces also contained much short and fine wool unsuitable for the manufacture of bayes. As this superfluous wool often made up a large proportion of the whole purchase,[3] it could not be wasted, and the bayes makers took the obvious course by reselling it (illegally) to clothiers. The rigorous enforcement of the 1552 Act would have put an effective end to this practice, and only by carrying on a subsidiary manufacture of cloth would the bayes makers have been able to make their own trade profitable.

While the wealthy clothiers were blaming the middlemen for the high price of wool, the Staplers, whom they had named among the chief offenders, were endeavouring to clear their characters at the expense of everyone else's. They agreed with the clothiers that the engrossing of wool by middlemen was the chief reason for its rise in price, but judiciously refrained from including themselves among the engrossers. 'The great nomber of Broggers that are increased of late yeares of all sortes of people . . . ys the cheiffeste cawse of the dearthe of woolles',

---

[1] P.R.O. S.P. 12/115/40.   [2] P.R.O. S.P. 12/117/38.
[3] According to the Suffolk clothiers, four-fifths of the wool which the bayes makers purchased was unsuitable for the manufacture of bayes (P.R.O. S.P. 12/114/33); but this seems to be an exaggeration.

stated the Staplers, and went on to name the glovers and the white tawyers as the principal offenders. The Company followed this charge by joining in the general chorus of accusation against the licensees; by pointing out, as the Suffolk clothiers had done,[1] that the manufacture of the new draperies increased the demand for English wool; and by alleging that the recently-made wool staple at New Woodstock in Oxfordshire[2] had led to much wool being forestalled and engrossed into a few rich men's hands. Then came the most pertinent observation of all:

> The greate nomber of brode whightes made in the Realme doth manye tymes rule the pryses of woolle by reason they are so spedelie and so easealye converted owt of woolles into clothes and brought to the markett and vented soe redelye in such great nombers.[3]

Having thus set down what they considered to be the causes of the high price of wool, the Staplers then proceeded to outline the remedies to be applied. The major part of the merchants' proposals dealt with the elimination of other middlemen, and they requested that the 1552 Act should be ratified by proclamation and the penalties mentioned in the Act imposed upon all offenders without favour or pardon. In order to make the legislation effective they suggested that no person except a licensee should be allowed to sell wool in a market town unless he first of all presented to the mayor or bailiff of the town a certificate, signed by the minister, constable and four householders of his parish, to the effect that the wool which he was putting to sale was the produce of his own sheep; any licensee selling wool was similarly to show his licence to the mayor or bailiff of the town, who were to notify the Lord Treasurer on its expiration.[4] As much wool was sold outside the public markets, these proposals, even if workable, supplied no real solution of how to keep the middlemen in check; and other suggestions which the Staplers made were equally open to objection.[5]

In addition to measures to be taken against middlemen, the

---

[1] Supra, p. 136, n. 4. [2] Supra, p. 121.
[3] P.R.O. S.P. 12/114/39. [4] Ibid.
[5] One impracticable proposal was that all patentees should be questioned on the licences which they had sub-let, and all known wool buyers and wool growers questioned on the wool which they had bought and sold, and the statements thus obtained correlated in order that unauthorized wool buying might be detected (P.R.O. S.P. 12/114/30).

Company also put forward proposals which aimed at restricting the manufacture of the new draperies and the production of broadcloth. These recommended that the new drapers should be compelled to make one piece of linen cloth for every four pieces of worsted, and the manufacturers of white broadcloth compelled to make one piece of linen cloth for every five broad whites, or alternatively to dye and dress every fifth cloth which they made. Directly related to the Staplers' export trade was the Company's request for the renewal of the proclamation which had been made in 1553 prohibiting the pulling or clipping of fells between Shrove Tuesday and shearing time.[1] The bayes makers used from 20 to 25 lbs. of fell wool in making the weft of their cloth; and by 1577, with the growth in the production of the new manufacture and the falling off in the continental demand for wool, the export trade in fells, as in fleece wool, had greatly diminished. Finally, the Staplers requested that clothiers should be forced to maintain a stable level of employment among their employees irrespective of fluctuations in the foreign market.[2]

On receiving the opinions of the merchants and clothiers on the causes of the high price of wool, the Lords of the Privy Council, reassured that their diagnosis was correct and supplied with the names of the chief offenders,[3] proceeded with their course of action against the middlemen. Letters were once again sent to Justices of the Peace throughout the country urging their co-operation in the matter.[4] But there was little assistance to be obtained from that quarter; and at the beginning of August the Privy Council appointed 91 Commissioners to 'have the special oversight for the restraint of unlawful buying and engrossing of wool' in 21 counties where the wool dealers were especially active.[5] The proceedings of the Commissioners remain a complete blank; and apart from a record to the effect that Sir Robert Doyly and George Davers were no longer

---

[1] *Tudor and Stuart Proclamations*, 438. In February, 1578, the merchants obtained the issue of the proclamation which they desired (ibid., 736); but in spite of this, and in spite of the fact that in September of the same year a request for the shipment of fells was received from Haarlem and Leiden in Holland (*A.P.C. 1577–8*, p. 322), the trade did not improve, and save for occasional shipments from Hull passed completely away (Rich, op. cit., p. 68).

[2] P.R.O. S.P. 12/114/39.

[3] See P.R.O. S.P. 12/110/8; S.P. 12/114/28, 31, 39, 40.

[4] *A.P.C. 1575–7*, p. 386.   [5] P.R.O. S.P. 12/115/14; *A.P.C. 1575–7*, p. 366.

available to act as Commissioners in Oxfordshire, having lately died of the plague,[1] no information whatsoever on the subject appears to have survived.

IV

During the next few years the regulation of the wool middleman trade was left very much in the hands of local officials, and the Lords of the Privy Council seldom interfered except in cases where gross breaches of the law were brought to their notice.[2] The restraint which the 1576 proclamation had placed upon the purchase of wool by licence was only temporary,[3] and before the end of the year licensed dealers were once again authorized to go about their business. 1578 was a comparatively quiet year; but a further increase in the price of wool, and a renewal of the agitation against middlemen during the early months of 1579,[4] led to the issue of another proclamation temporarily prohibiting the purchase of wool by licence.[5] The whole matter was very confusing; and in 1581, some time after the licensees had again been authorized to trade, an information was exhibited against Simon Bowde, one of the Norwich patentees, in the Court of Exchequer for illegally buying and selling wool. Having finally settled for a policy favourable to the wool licensees, the Privy Council decided to make the position quite clear. Accordingly, the withdrawal of the information was ordered, and local officials throughout the country were notified that in future genuine licensed dealers were not to be restrained.[6]

During the next five years the Council's attitude towards middlemen became, if anything, more tolerant. Dealers continued to buy wool very much as they had done previously. But apart from a desire to uphold the law, there was no compelling reason why the government should interfere with their trade: wool prices had temporarily ceased to rise, cloth exports were being maintained at a fairly high level, and the clothiers' agitation against middlemen was less violent than hitherto. Moreover, even had the government wished to attend to such matters, the task of bringing the country to a state of military preparedness left it little time to do so.

[1] *A.P.C. 1577–8*, pp. 8–9.   [2] *A.P.C. 1577–8*, pp. 24–5; *1580–1*, p. 193.
[3] See supra, p. 135.   [4] B.M. Lansd. MS. 27, fol. 179; ibid., 28, fols. 61–2.
[5] *Tudor and Stuart Proclamations*, 738.   [6] *A.P.C. 1581–2*, pp. 48, 72.

It was partly for military reasons that a request made by the wool growers of Cumberland and Westmorland to be allowed the services of wool dealers was granted by the Privy Council in 1585, even though a similar request from the small manufacturers of the northern counties had been ignored eight years earlier.[1] The wool growers had petitioned the Council on the grounds that their wools were very coarse and had for long been sold to middlemen; but recently common informers had been active, and as the wool growers were required to undertake military duties which prevented them from going to market, their wool was likely to be left upon their hands. In granting the growers' petition, the Privy Council ordered that all proceedings against the dealers concerned were to be stayed, and no further action taken against them.[2] Although the Council's order related only to Westmorland and Cumberland, and did not mention Northumberland, in practice, middlemen were allowed to trade in all three counties under its protection.[3]

The informations which had been exhibited against the wool dealers of the northern counties had apparently exercised a considerable restraining influence upon the middleman trade in that region. In the remainder of the country, however, the activities of common informers seem to have done little to impede the middlemen in their business. Comparatively few informations were brought during the period 1570–86,[4] and when they were brought, the defendants often had an answer to them. The fact that many dealers possessed, or feigned to possess, a licence, made the informers careful as to whom they prosecuted. But it was not only by becoming licensed that dealers were enabled to avoid the law. Sometimes they practised 'with the wolmaster to make them a letter of Attorney as their deputies to sell soche wolles which intrewthe they aforehand had bought of

---

[1] In October, 1577, the clothiers of Lancashire, Richmondshire, Westmorland, Cumberland and Durham had petitioned the Privy Council stating that their 'habylytye' would 'stretche, neyther to buye any substance of woolles to maynteyn upon worke and labor, nor yet to fetche the same, the growyth of woolles beinge foure and fyve skore myles at the leaste'; and they maintained that if the 1552 Act were rigorously enforced, the inhabitants of Halifax would use their liberty to buy wool to 'wynne the trade of euerye cuntrye into their owne handes' (P.R.O. S.P. 12/117/38).

[2] B.M. Add. MS. 34324, fols. 8–9.   [3] See infra, p. 168.

[4] M. W. Beresford, *Econ. Hist. Rev.* 2nd ser. x (1957), 223.

them'. At other times they kept informers quiet by paying them a yearly fee.[1]

Among the informations which were exhibited against middlemen for illegally buying and selling wool, those brought in 1580 against Martin de la Falia, an alien merchant, stand out above all others. Charged in the Court of Exchequer with buying 7,500 tods of wool, and in the Crown Office with buying 5,000 tods, de la Falia pleaded that he had traded as a licensee of Sir Francis Walsingham, and Walsingham confirmed his story. The matter caused considerable comment at the time, for, apart from the large amounts of wool involved, there were strong suggestions that de la Falia had never had any connections with Walsingham until the time when the informations were brought against him; and it was alleged that the Principal Secretary had only participated in the business because his alien licensees had put pressure upon him to do so.[2]

Although it is impossible to say whether or not this charge was true, there can be no doubt that Walsingham was entirely dependent upon alien merchants for the sale of his licence. The Staplers could produce a host of reasons against becoming his tenants.[3] By that time, few of them had any interest in the export trade. Neither, for that matter, had most of the alien merchants who were licensed by Walsingham, and the authority which the possession of Walsingham's licence gave them to resell refuse wool within the realm — a privilege which the Staplers also possessed — was greatly abused.[4] This was largely attributable to the very poor overseas market. The foreign demand for English wool was such that by 1587, when Walsingham's grant expired, only a little over one-half of the wool shipments which he had been authorized to make, had in fact been made. But in spite of this, between the years 1582 and 1587 his alien licensees, with shipments of never more than 300 sacks per year,

---

[1] P.R.O. S.P. 12/115/40. See also S.P. 12/114/33; B.M. Lansd. MS. 172, fol. 242.
[2] P.R.O. S.P. 12/146/54. This was not the only time when Walsingham intervened on behalf of his alien tenants. In June, 1581, he ordered Robert Woodrofe, Stapler, to postpone proceeding upon an action which he had brought against Jerome Benalio for non-payment of the price of wool (P.R.O. S.P. 12/154/77).
[3] P.R.O. S.P. 12/154/33.
[4] Walsingham's licensees were said in 1582 to buy the highest quality wools, and after 'piking owte of the heade and best of the same wulles', to sell the remainder within the realm as refuse. Martin de la Falia was stated to sell as refuse at least one-half of the wool which he bought (P.R.O. S.P. 12/154/30).

were exporting more wool than the entire Staple Company put together.[1]

V

As Secretary of the Privy Council and as an important wool patentee, Sir Francis Walsingham was the obvious person to whom schemes relating to the wool trade should be addressed; and it was to Walsingham that John Johnson, an ardent pamphleteer and one-time Stapler,[2] propounded his plans.

In 1577 he wrote to Walsingham informing him that the 'disorderly' buying of wools could not be reformed by laws alone 'seing that fewe or none in the countrey occupieng buying and selling but they dayly offende therin'. As a remedy he proposed that all dealers wishing to buy wool or fells should be licensed (or in Johnson's own words, 'provided yearly with a testimonial'). For this purpose Walsingham was to have a special office created for himself in the Exchequer, whilst Johnson and his friend, Lisle Cave,[3] were to issue the licences. The fees which were to be charged for these licences were to be divided among the three principals, Johnson estimating that the yearly profits would be great enough to allow Cave and himself 'twoo hondreth markes or more' for their share, and Walsingham at least one thousand pounds for his. Nobody in possession of this knowledge was likely to be fooled by Johnson's claim that the operation of his scheme would decrease the number of wool buyers and bring down the price of wool; and there was good reason for his 'remembraunce' to Walsingham:

> In the disclosing of this matter, there neadith not (except it please your honor) to make any mention of the fees of one half peny of a todde, or other fees, nether shall the same fees neade to be spoken of in the publicacion of the matter: for it is to be understandin that fees be insedentes to offices, and ther fore neade not be named in any open soirte but to be receaved of the parties whose dewtie it shalbe to paie them.[4]

---

[1] B.M. Lansd. MS. 113, fol. 65.

[2] John Johnson was the senior partner of a firm engaged in various branches of overseas commerce which went bankrupt in 1553. For an account of the firm's last years see Barbara Winchester, *Tudor Family Portrait* (1955).

[3] In James I's reign Lisle Cave seems to have shared a patent to import Spanish wool with Sir Michael Stanhope. See Hist. MSS. Comm. *Salisbury MSS.* xviii, 160, 161, 386.

[4] P.R.O. S.P. 12/109/37.

Johnson's plan was not adopted. Another of his proposals was that the Staplers should be authorized to supply wool to alien manufacturers at specially appointed staple towns in England. This suggestion, endorsed by the Staple Company,[1] was first addressed to the Privy Council in July, 1577. Nothing came of the matter, and it was let drop until 1582, when it was revived and was the subject of a considerable correspondence between Johnson and Walsingham.[2]

Johnson had worked out the business in detail. He proposed that three places should be appointed as staple towns, and selected London, Thetford and Winchester on the ground that their 'indifferent' geographical situations suited Staplers and new drapers alike. At these towns the Staplers were to sell assorted wool to alien manufacturers and English bayes makers, who were to be forbidden to purchase wool elsewhere. Wool sales were to be taxed at such rates as the Privy Council thought fit, and the proceeds sent to the Exchequer. The incidence of such taxes, ventured Johnson, could always be passed on to the buyers, and therefore the Staplers could raise little objection to them. He foresaw a possible difficulty with the merchants over the fixing of maximum prices,[3] but thought that this was necessary as a guarantee to the manufacturers that they would be treated fairly. It is doubtful whether this trade with alien manufacturers would have been sufficient to have kept the Staplers fully occupied; and Johnson's further proposals that English clothiers should be allowed to buy their wool at staple towns, and that all Spanish and other foreign wools imported for the manufacture of hats and felts should be put to sale only by a merchant in a staple town, suggest that the scheme was partly a blind to enable the Staplers to extend a legalized control over the larger part of the internal wool trade.

Walsingham's chief interest in the project was in the profit which it would bring both to himself and to the Crown, and Johnson endeavoured to enlighten him. He estimated that the Queen's revenues would be increased by at least twelve thousand

[1] P.R.O. S.P. 12/114/29; S.P. 12/154/34.
[2] P.R.O. S.P. 12/114/58; S.P. 12/154/22, 30; S.P. 12/155/80; S.P. 12/156/3, 3 (i), 9, 10.
[3] For the maximum prices which Johnson suggested for different types of wool, see P.R.O. S.P. 12/154/30.

pounds a year,[1] but was unable to say 'what the merchantes of the Staple will geve to hym that shall procure the same matter to be brought to passe'. Johnson continued:

> Neither know I how to move the merchantes of the Staple to departe from any money for the same considring their disagrement in soch thinges.[2]

Walsingham was not impressed; and Johnson's scheme went the same way as its predecessor.

VI

There were no further notable developments until 1586, when Simon Bowyer, whose patent was shortly due to expire, decided to press his claims for a further grant. Bowyer's suit was for a licence to trade annually in one thousand sarplers of wool and for a commission to be sole informer against all unauthorized wool dealers.[3] The commission, Bowyer claimed, was necessary in view of the excessive buying of wool by dealers and the corruption of the common informers. The suit, which was supported by a number of clothiers,[4] was rewarded by the drawing up of the necessary letters patent.[5]

Unfortunately for Bowyer, the licence to trade in one thousand sarplers of wool each year was itself a violation of an undertaking which the Crown had given to the Company of the Staple in September, 1584, to grant no further wool licences during the following seven years.[6] The Company and the wealthy clothing interests lost no time in pointing this out, and Bowyer's patent was revoked before he had an opportunity to use it.[7]

---

[1] A more detailed estimate shows that this figure was meant to include the amount of customs duty to be paid on the export of the new draperies. Johnson thought that 20,000 of these cloths could be made and exported each year, and calculated that 2,000 sarplers of wool would be used up in the process; customs duty paid at the rate of 6s. 8d. on a cloth would bring in £6,666 13s. 4d., and taxes on wool sales in staple towns levied at an average rate of £3 on a sarpler would add a further £6,000 (P.R.O. S.P. 12/156/10).

[2] P.R.O. S.P. 12/156/3.

[3] Bowyer first asked for these powers in 1577, but strenuous opposition from the Staple Company and other wool interests led to the suit's being temporarily shelved. See P.R.O. S.P. 12/114/41; S.P. 12/115/40; S.P. 12/146/77.

[4] B.M. Lansd. MS. 48, fols. 156–8, 163.

[5] Ibid., 48, fols. 160–1.   [6] Infra, p. 164.

[7] B.M. Lansd. MS. 48, fol. 159; ibid., 65, fol. 144; ibid., 114, fol. 95.

A licence to buy and sell wool being out of the question, Bowyer recommenced his suit for the commission which had been taken from him, but with no immediate success. A contraction in the foreign demand for English cloth, which had depressed the price of wool, had accompanied the outbreak of regular warfare with Spain, and Bowyer's suggested commission found no support among the wool growers who, with 'two or three yeeres wolles on theire handes' did not wish 'theise harde yeeres to be hindred of theire sales any manner of waye'. The wealthy clothiers, on the other hand, were against the commission on the ground that it would effect no reformation, and they argued:

> The suitor for the Bill, by havinge a licence heretofore to buy, and sell woll against the lawe, dothe now knowe thereby whoe will be his best Customers to be sued or compounded with by his former sales, made vnto theim, . . . and maye by waye of remitter vnderhande have his first suite to suffer vnlawful buyinge and sellinge of woll as before he was aucthorized to doe.[1]

For a time these arguments prevailed, but eventually, in July, 1590, fresh letters patent[2] were drawn up, conferring upon Bowyer the powers for which he asked.

By the patent, Bowyer was commissioned as sole informer to enforce the 1552 Act and the Act of 1532[3] which dealt with the true winding of wool. He was authorized to compound on behalf of himself and the Crown with any offenders and to give discharges for offences, the Crown's share of the penalties to be paid periodically into the Exchequer. An additional clause provided that should the grant be proved hurtful to the commonwealth before six members of the Privy Council, it was to be declared void. Subject to this stipulation, the patent, which was passed without fee, was to remain in force until September, 1596, but two years later the grant was ratified[4] and the tenure extended to June, 1599.

The grant to Bowyer of the office of sole informer did not put an automatic end to the activities of the common informers: it

---

[1] Ibid., 51, fol. 95.
[2] Ibid., 65, fols. 194–202; Signet Office Docquets, IND. 6800, July 1590.
[3] Supra, p. 123, n. 4.
[4] Signet Office Docquets, IND. 6800, June 1592.

was not meant to. When the patentee's claims had been disputed in 1587, it had been remarked:

> Every Courte of Recorde, maye and will take an Informacyon
> for wolle at any other persones handes then the Suitors in this bill.
> But in the ende all common informers, will put in informacyons
> vnder the Suitors Authoritie, to be well backed by him.[1]

And Bowyer had no intention of preventing the common
informers from exhibiting informations against wool dealers
providing that he himself received an ample cut from the proceeds. The informers, however, felt no inclination to share the
fruits of their labour with Bowyer, and in April, 1591, the Privy
Council ordered that the patentee should be allowed to have his
own attorney in the central courts to prevent informations
being exhibited and compositions being reached without his
knowledge and permission. At the same time the Council wrote
to the Council of the Marches of Wales requesting that bonds
which they had been ordered to take from wool dealers in May,
1590, as a safeguard against their trading in the future, should
be delivered to Bowyer for prosecution in the Exchequer.[2]

Without the none-too-willing assistance of local officials[3] it
proved impossible to pursue the commission rigorously in all
parts of the country — the offenders were too many, the area to
be covered too large, and Bowyer's agents too few. Far away
from London much wool brogging continued unrestrained; and
at the height of the wool-selling season in 1593, the Privy
Council saw fit to write to selected officials in Lancashire,
Shropshire and Staffordshire, requesting them to instruct all
wool dealers who had not already compounded with the patentee to 'resort unto Mr. Bowyer as well to take order with him
for the moyeteie accrewinge unto her Majestie as unto himselfe',
and asking for the names of those dealers who refused.[4]

This, the last recorded Privy Council reference to Bowyer's
commission, is of considerable interest. For it suggests, as indeed
the terms of the patent suggest, that the government considered
Bowyer's grant primarily, not as a means of preventing middlemen from trading, but as a fiscal expedient to raise revenue.
Action was to be taken against wool dealers, not because they

---

[1] B.M. Lansd. MS. 51, fol. 95.   [2] *A.P.C. 1591*, pp. 65–7.
[3] *A.P.C. 1592*, pp. 349–51.   [4] *A.P.C. 1592–3*, p. 371.

continued to buy and sell wool, but because they continued to do so without compounding for their offences. In practice, therefore, Bowyer's grant amounted to a wool licence to buy an unlimited quantity of wool, and gave him 'ij or iij Suites of advauntage besides'.[1] Those dealers who could afford to make the payments which Bowyer demanded, as well as those who managed to escape his attention, were able to continue their business; and though the period during which Bowyer's grant remained in force witnessed a rise in the number of informations brought for illegally buying and selling wool[2] it seems unlikely that the total volume of the middleman trade was significantly diminished as a result of the patentee's activities.

VII

The termination of Bowyer's patent was the signal for a number of would-be patentees to explore the possibilities of a further grant. Among the more notable figures of the day, both Sir Thomas Wilkes and the Earl of Cumberland petitioned for a licence to buy and sell wool,[3] but without success. Eventually, in March, 1602, a grant authorizing the purchase and sale of 500 sarplers of wool each year during the following ten years, was made to Sir Edward Hoby,[4] whose London residence in Canon Row was situated close to the old Westminster wool staple.[5]

As was to be expected, the wealthy clothing interests opposed the grant. But Hoby was an influential man; besides being a nephew of the late Lord Burghley, under whose auspices he had risen into high favour at Court, he was also a noted Member of Parliament and a keen theologian.[6] Also, by 1602 the government had come to recognize the validity of some of the arguments which were put forward in support of the middleman trade.[7] Nevertheless, the wishes of the wealthy clothing interests

---

[1] B.M. Lansd. MS. 51, fol. 95.

[2] See M. W. Beresford, *Econ. Hist. Rev.* 2nd ser. x (1957), 223–4.

[3] P.R.O. S.P. 12/255/45; S.P. 15/34/21.

[4] P.R.O. C.66/1570, m. 25. This was not the only grant which Hoby received. In October, 1597, he obtained a commission to search out and prosecute all offences against the statute prohibiting the exportation of iron from England, his reward being half of the penalties incurred (*Cal. S.P. Dom. 1595–7*, pp. 455, 523).

[5] J. Stow, *A Survey of London in 1603*, ed. C. L. Kingsford (1908), ii, 102.

[6] *Dictionary of National Biography* (1891), xxvii, 53.

[7] These were centred on the needs of the small manufacturers and wool growers. See P.R.O. S.P. 12/90/38; S.P. 12/261/63; B.M. Lansd. MS. 65, fol. 144.

had to be considered, and Hoby was authorized to buy wool only in certain specified counties where the manufacture of cloth was insignificant or was organized on non-capitalistic lines.[1]

The government did not have the same financial interest in Hoby's grant as it previously had in Bowyer's patent, and the Council's activity on Hoby's behalf did not go beyond an occasional instruction to local officials to proclaim the Act of 1552.[2] But the patentee had his own methods of dealing with offending middlemen, and the procedure which he used to license dealers is made clear by some of his surviving correspondence.[3]

Upon his wool business Hoby employed several agents in different parts of England, each covering a number of counties. In the North his agent, Francis Bayllye, compounded with dealers for licences and collected fines and rents in the counties of Nottingham, Derby, York and Lincoln. Bayllye's headquarters were at East Retford, and his business took him periodically into the surrounding region and sometimes to London.

An agent's task was not easy. Occasionally a dealer or potential dealer came to Bayllye of his own free will, but these were exceptions. Broggers who were engaged in a profitable, but unlawful trade generally endeavoured to avoid Bayllye and the expense which a meeting with him would entail. The unlicensed dealers were safe enough from Bayllye as long as their identities were unknown to him, and there was good reason for the agent to complain to Hoby:

> At my cominge forthe off Yorkshier I came through Lyncolneshier and makinge inquirie for the wolle buyers ther inhabitinge they concealed themselves from me.

Sooner or later, however, many of the dealers were faced with the immediate prospect of compounding for a licence, and in

---

[1] The counties were Warwick, Stafford, Shropshire, Northampton, Leicester, Nottingham, Derby, Lincoln, Rutland, Cambridge, Huntingdon, Lancashire, Hertford, Buckingham, Bedford, Hereford, Monmouth and any of the counties within Wales.

[2] *A.P.C. 1601–4*, pp. 489, 500.

[3] This correspondence is in the possession of the Advocates' Library, National Library of Scotland, Edinburgh, reference ADV. MSS. 34.2.15.

anticipation of such business we find Hoby's representative writing to his employer at the end of August 1602:

> May it please yow to send by this Bearer xx peace off Indentures with Blancks for the parties names and the place the[y] dwell in and for whatt quantitie. I hope betwixt this and Michaellmas to retorne them all to yow agayne with reasonable fynes and rents with securitie to yowr good likinge.

The quantity of wool that most dealers were licensed to buy varied between two and five sarplers a year, and Hoby examined his licensees' account books in order to satisfy himself that their trades were accurately assessed. A rent of threepence for every stone of wool licensed, or £1 for every sarpler, was the standard which the patentee instructed one of his agents to bear in mind when levying his charges. The admission fines were equivalent to the yearly rents, and their expense was particularly burdensome to the poorer dealers, who needed careful handling lest they gave up trading.

Through Hoby's position and local connections,[1] the Council in the North lent the weight of its authority to Bayllye's activities, and at his request issued directions for the attachment of John Metcalfe and William Lodge, two large wool dealers from Leeds who, despite Bayllye's efforts, would neither compound for licences nor desist from dealing. On another occasion the agent informed Hoby:

> It hath pleased her Maiestyes Counsell in the North to graunt there Commission to attach the bodies of fiftye persons, which are the greatest offendors within the Countye of Yorke upon my peticion made to them.

Support for Bayllye's activities came also from a number of Yorkshire clothiers, and these agreed to a meeting with the agent in order to 'devise some present cours for the supressinge of the great number of wooll drivers' within the county. But here, if previous experience was anything to go by, Bayllye was doomed to disappointment. Twelve years earlier Randolph Tench, a Leeds clothier and one of the West Riding's growing class of capitalist manufacturers, had endeavoured to persuade

---

[1] Hoby's brother, Sir Thomas Hoby, was a prominent local figure and a member of the Council in the North.

the Privy Council to interfere with the trade of wool dealers in the northern parts, but without success.[1]

In spite of local support from clothiers and officials, legal action was, in fact, often the only way in which a recalcitrant dealer could be brought to heel. We find Bayllye in November, 1602, forwarding a list of broggers' names to London, with a request for the direction of subpoenas from the Crown Office. In his next letter to Hoby, he writes:

> That it would please you the suppenes maye be sente down for those persons whom I wrote for hopinge by that meanes to compell the most of them to compounde for lycence.

Bayllye was not Hoby's only representative to invoke the assistance of the law in order to effect his employer's ends. William Patrick, hot on the chase of unlicensed dealers in Lincolnshire, Norfolk and Suffolk, writes concerning the offenders:

> Thay be common brokers not vsing any other trade but this, chardge every man with V^c Toddes.

The faith which Hoby's men rested in these means was probably not misplaced: an information for unlicensed dealing could prove costly, and would almost certainly make an offender view the alternative expense of a licence in a more favourable light. But none of the earlier wool patentees seems to have found it necessary to resort to coercive legal proceedings in order to persuade dealers to take out licences, and it is an indication of the general disregard into which the 1552 Act had fallen that such action had to be taken in 1602.

Though Hoby's patent limited his licensees' purchases of wool to certain specified counties, it placed no similar restriction upon their sales. Kent was one of those counties where Hoby had no authority to buy wool, and the fact that the manufacturing towns of Canterbury and Sandwich were served largely by Flemish wool dealers who bought their wool within the county,

---

[1] On receipt of Tench's complaint the Privy Council instructed the Lord President of York to take bonds from the wool dealers as security against their trading in future. But fortunately for Tench's numerous small competitors, the Earl of Derby wrote on their behalf to the Privy Council and the trade of the northern wool dealers was allowed to continue (*A.P.C. 1590*, pp. 168, 370–1). See also *A.P.C. 1590–1*, p. 163.

made the permission to sell wool there of little practical use. It was Hoby's opinion that the aliens should be prevented from buying wool except under his licence, and in October, 1602, he endeavoured to bring this about. But the Flemings were in a strong position to resist his demands. Only three years previously the Privy Council had stayed informations which had been exhibited against them in the Court of Exchequer for illegally buying and selling wool,[1] and the aliens claimed that they had neither the means nor the need to travel to the nearest counties to Kent where Hoby was authorized to buy wool, in order to make their purchases. The matter was considered by a committee of councillors, and the aliens seem to have been successful in maintaining their position.

Hoby's profit from his wool patent provided him with a very useful addition to his income. His licences yielded an average annual rent of £500,[2] but not all of this was clear profit. A deduction of £20 had to be made for the Crown's yearly rent,[3] and the wages and expenses of agents like Bayllye had to be met. Probably the expenses were not large, for in order to keep down these costs, Hoby employed men who could normally be accommodated in their own homes or in those of their relatives.

The patent was a cause of considerable annoyance to a number of wealthy clothiers, and in April, 1606, having unsuccessfully disputed the ratification of the grant on the succession of James I, they voiced their complaints before Parliament. The clothiers argued that the patent was a grievance: dealers bought wool in excess of their licences; purchased it by advance contracts; charged the clothiers high prices, especially at the end of the year when wool was scarce; added sand and water to their wool in order to increase its weight; and deceitfully mixed different sorts of wool together. Some of the complaints concerned legitimate business practices, as Hoby's counsel pointed out, and the others were doubtless exaggerated. The clothiers

---

[1] In 1591, 1599 and 1613 the Privy Council stayed proceedings upon informations for illegally buying and selling wool which were being prosecuted against alien manufacturers from Canterbury, and took similar action when informations were exhibited against aliens from Norwich and Colchester (F. W. Cross, *History of Walloon and Huguenot Church, Canterbury* [Huguenot Society Publications, XV], p. 191; *A.P.C. 1598–9*, pp. 646, 737; *1613–14*, pp. 8–10).

[2] *The Parliamentary Diary of Robert Bowyer, 1606–1607*, ed. D. H. Willson (1931), p. 142.

[3] P.R.O. C.66/1570, m. 25.

found it impossible to make out their case, and Parliament ruled that the patent was no grievance.[1]

James I had always felt a warm regard for Hoby,[2] and in August, 1607, he extended the tenure of his wool licence to 1622.[3] Hoby died in March, 1617, but his patent was surrendered two years before then. How this came about will be related in due course.[4]

[1] P.R.O. S.P. 38/7/20th July, 1604; *The Parliamentary Diary of Robert Bowyer*, pp. 131, 141–2; *H. of C. Journals*, i, 299, 303.
[2] *Dictionary of National Biography* (1891), xxvii, 53.
[3] *Tudor and Stuart Proclamations*, 1045.
[4] Infra, pp. 165–6.

Chapter VI

THE STAPLERS IN THE REGULATION
OF THE WOOL TRADE

I

The Act of 1552 had been passed largely at the instigation of the
Merchants of the Staple, with the object of bringing new life to
their sinking export trade.[1] Following this measure the Staplers'
fortunes did indeed revive somewhat. Shipments made by the
members of the Company rose from 2,300 pockets[2] in 1551, and
2,340 in 1552, to 6,300 pockets in 1553, 5,400 in 1554 and 4,700
in 1555.[3] To attempt to account for these figures solely in terms
of the anti-middleman legislation of 1552, would be to ignore
the effects of other more important influences. The large jump
in wool exports between 1552 and 1553 can be accounted for, in
the first place, by the temporary fall in the price of wool — a
fall partly resulting from the 1552 Act, but due mainly to the
contraction in cloth exports; secondly, by the continued rise in
the price of Spanish wool;[4] and thirdly, by another collapse in
sterling: factors which all made for the relative cheapening of
English wool in the continental market.

Neither was this revival in shipments limited only to wool.
The reaction of cloth exports to the changed situation was somewhat slower, but eventually, with costs painfully adjusted and
in response to the weakening of the exchange-rate, they once
more shot up to reach a new record in 1554.[5] Almost inevitably,
a rise in the price of wool accompanied the revival, and the

---

[1] Supra, pp. 112–15.
[2] A pocket of wool was normally 336 lbs., and so was 28 lbs. (1 tod) less than the
wool sack of 364 lbs. About 3 pockets of wool went to make a sarpler (Rich, op. cit.,
p. 20).
[3] Ibid., pp. 19–20.
[4] In 1552, in order to keep down wool and cloth prices in Spain, the regrating of
wool had been forbidden by statute (Hamilton, op. cit., p. 285).
[5] Fisher, *Econ. Hist. Rev.* x (1940), 103.

Staplers again felt the familiar pinch of shrinking markets. But even so, all was not well with the cloth trade. Soon the great boom in cloth exports began to overrun itself, and in 1556 all shipments of cloth to the Netherlands had to be stayed for four months in order to relieve the glut there.[1] The expansion was over; and by the opening of Elizabeth's reign cloth exports were back again at the level which had obtained before the boom years of the 1540's.[2]

It was a very shaky economic foundation upon which the wool-export trade had now come to rest. Succoured by the inflation in the Spanish economy, it could not hope to survive when this advantage was offset by the upward trend in English wool prices, and when the political instability of the times resulted in the closing of foreign markets and a contraction in the continental demand for wool.

The first great set-back came in 1558 when Calais, so long the staple town for English wool, was taken by the French. Inevitably, there followed a period of disorganization whilst negotiations as to the future of the Staplers' trade took place between the government and the Company. The immediate emergency was met by the grant of special licences to the merchants for the shipment of their wool to Bruges. The export of wool elsewhere than to Calais was an offence against the 1552 Act, and in return for this privilege, and perhaps also because Spanish wool at this time was being made subject to heavy export duties,[3] the Crown claimed an increment in the customs of 1 mark per sack in 1559 and 26s. 8d. in 1560.[4]

It was not until 1561 that a decision was reached as to which permanent staple town should succeed to the position vacated by Calais. Concerning this, there were two schools of thought. The Staplers themselves favoured a Staple overseas, and used all the stock arguments of mercantilism to back their case. In opposition to this view was the belief that a return to a series of

[1] Ibid., pp. 103–4.
[2] An annual average of 93,812 shortcloths were exported from London in 1559–1561 (ibid., p. 96).
[3] In 1559 Philip reacquired the seaport customs duties which in 1469 had been alienated from the control of the royal exchequer, and promptly undertook to exploit this new source of income by laying a series of heavy export duties on wool (J. Klein, *The Mesta, A Study in Spanish Economic History, 1273–1836* (Cambridge, Mass., 1920), p. 46.
[4] *Cal. Pat. 1557–8*, pp. 300, 460, 462; *1558–60*, pp. 245, 411–12.

English staple towns after the model of 1353 would be of most advantage to the kingdom.[1] Neither was the right of the Staplers to the wool-export trade allowed to pass unchallenged. Some merchants from outside the Company offered to submit to heavier wool-export duties if the trade were placed in their hands; while the Queen was urged how much more profitable it would be for her if she herself took over the export and sale of wool and fells.[2] But in spite of these arguments, the Staplers' financial services to the Crown were too useful, and their experience of the trade too great, for their position to be seriously undermined.

The Staplers, unsettled by the temporary arrangements made, continued to agitate for the establishment of their trade on a more regular footing, but it was not until the May of 1561 that the Company at last received its coveted charter.[3] From the deliberations of the committee to which the matter had been entrusted, there had emerged the conclusion that a Staple established in the Netherlands would stand a much better chance of meeting the competition of the Spaniards than a series of staple towns in England; and by the new patent the Staple was to be held at Bruges, Middleburgh or Bergen, but was removable to England at nine months' notice. But although the new charter enabled the Staplers to buy wool for export despite the terms of the 1552 Act, and ratified their privilege of selling refuse wool within the realm, it was not a matter for unqualified self-congratulation by the Company. A request to be allowed to sell wool in England to alien merchants for shipment to the Mediterranean, contrary to the statute of 1429, had been turned down by the committee.[4] But worse still, the export duty, so long until 1558 at 40s., was raised by the charter to £3 on each sack up to a total of 3,000 a year and 53s. 4d. for each sack above that total.

It was a feeble trade which the Company now carried on; the

[1] At first Cecil held this opinion and seems to have been prepared to defend it before Parliament in 1559. The argument was that the setting up of home staples would increase the customs revenue (since aliens paid a higher export duty than natives) and maintain the decaying outports (Hist. MSS. Comm. *Salisbury MSS.* i, 164). An abortive Bill 'to reduce the staple into England, Wales and Ireland from beyond the sea' was introduced into the Commons in February, 1562 (*H. of C. Journals*, i, 65).

[2] Hist. MSS. Comm. *Salisbury MSS.* xiii, 57; xiv, 55.

[3] *Cal. Pat. 1560–3*, pp. 30–1.   [4] Rich, op. cit., pp. 28–9.

shipments of wool and fells between 1559 and 1561 had barely reached the 3,000 sacks a year[1] mentioned in the charter, and the following decade saw no improvement in exports to Bruges, where the Company elected to hold their Staple. About 3,000 sacks a year was the maximum amount ever shipped there under the terms of the 1561 patent,[2] and even that deficient trade — but one-tenth of the Staplers' trade in its more prosperous days — was liable to be interrupted by religious troubles in the Netherlands and diplomatic disputes with Spain.

It was under the pretext of taking precaution against the plague raging in London that the Spanish government from 1562 to 1564 placed restrictions upon the entry of English woollen manufactures into the Netherlands. The prohibition had repercussions upon the Staplers' trade,[3] but its effect was much more severely felt by the cloth-exporting industry; an abnormally low average of 61,200 shortcloths was exported from London during these two years,[4] with widespread unemployment at home as its consequence. A provisional agreement for the resumption of free intercourse between the two countries being reached towards the end of 1564, there followed a year of excessive commercial activity as the Merchant Adventurers returned to Antwerp and the pent-up stocks of cloth swamped into the market. Thus, during the year ending Michaelmas, 1565, London exported 134,000 cloths:[5] a figure more than double the average of the previous two years, and well over one-third higher than the average for the succeeding decade.

This boom in cloth exports was accompanied by a considerable rise in the price of wool. Fears that a shortage of the raw material might lead to a recurrence of heavy industrial unemployment led the Privy Council in the spring of 1566 to forbid the Staplers to ship wool until further orders. In the meantime, in order to relieve the scarcity, the Staplers, despite the terms of the 1552 Act, were authorized to sell the wool then

---

[1] For figures of the Staplers' shipments 1559–61, see ibid., pp. 22–4, 31–2.

[2] Ibid., pp. 32–5.

[3] Ibid., p. 52; *A.P.C. 1558–70*, p. 147. Henry Boithe of Leicester, Stapler, 'fledde into partes vnknowen' on being unable to find a market for over £500 worth of 'almost rotten' wool, which he had purchased on credit from two large wool growers in 1562 and 1563 (P.R.O. Req. 2/176/45; Req. 2/179/46).

[4] Fisher, *Econ. Hist. Rev.* x (1940), 96.

[5] L. Stone, 'Elizabethan Overseas Trade', *Econ. Hist. Rev.* 2nd ser. ii (1949), 37.

upon their hands to cloth manufacturers within the realm. By taking this course the Crown sustained 'no small loss' in customs revenue;[1] but important as fiscal motives were during this period in determining governmental policy, in the final analysis they gave way to considerations for the maintenance of social order: the memories of 1536 and 1549 were too vivid in the official mind for it to be otherwise.

The first great reaction to the removal of trade barriers had spent itself by the end of 1565, and, as commercial activity slackened and the volume of cloth exports settled down at a lower and more normal level, so the demand for wool abated. Wool having become more abundant in the summer of 1566, a petition from the Staplers on 8th July requesting permission to continue shipment in their accustomed manner was received by the Crown and Privy Council with sympathetic consideration. In signifying agreement to the renewal of shipments, Elizabeth was at pains to point out that the grant recently made to the merchants for the selling of wool within the realm should be thereafter void.[2] It was not without reason that the Queen drew attention to this matter; for the temporary licence of 1566 had but legalized tendencies which for several years past had become increasingly apparent in the Staplers' trade.

II

The likelihood of such a wealthy body of merchants as the Staplers carrying on a wool trade at home was dependent upon two fundamental conditions. First, that the returns to be secured from dealing in wool within the realm should be greater than those obtainable by its export. Secondly, that the size of transactions which it was possible to conduct with English manufacturers should be large enough to allow the merchants the fullest and most effective use of their capital. Both these conditions were fulfilled in the sixteenth century: the first through the upward trend in English wool prices, and the second through the widening of the internal wool market.

Purely on a profit basis, the advantages of wool dealing at home had probably been plain to the Staplers at least as early as the 1530's, but do not appear to have evoked any great reaction

[1] P.R.O. S.P. 12/39/43; S.P. 12/40/33.   [2] P.R.O. S.P. 12/40/31, 33.

M

from them. In the following decades, however, the expansion of cloth output and the emergence of a more clearly defined geographical division of labour, created the need for a middleman of more substance than the common brogger, to span the increased distance between grower and manufacturer. The potentialities of such a situation were too apparent for them to be ignored for long. At the height of the mid-century boom in cloth exports, when their own foreign market was contracting upon them, it seems likely that some Staplers engaged in unlawful wool dealing within the realm.[1] In 1553 the revival of wool shipments brought some alleviation of the difficulties experienced by the merchants consequent upon the decline in their export trade. The recovery, however, was but short-lived; and as foreign wool sales once again fell off and fresh set-backs followed in rapid succession, more and more Staplers turned to conducting an illegal trade at home. This was not the official policy of the Company; indeed, it had passed ordinances against the 'brogging of woulles'.[2] But the cause of this antithesis between the Company's official policy and the activities of its members is easily resolved.

As a source of income, the wool-export trade was drying up. In 1560 it was claimed that the Company of the Staple was of 'the nombre at least of iij^c householdes besides c youngemen':[3] a number far too large to be sustained solely by the comparatively meagre wool shipments which prevailed throughout most of the sixteenth century. The merchants could, and did, obtain compensation for the decline in wool exports by engaging in other business activities supplementary to their main trade.

The most evident and attractive prospect was to participate in the profits to be gained by exporting cloth. This a few Staplers had been doing in the more prosperous wool-exporting days of the fifteenth century, and their number continued to increase despite the objections of the Adventurers, while some

[1] In 1549, the rise in the price of wool showing no sign of abating, a proclamation was issued ordering that offenders against the Act of 1546 should be punished by imprisonment. This penalty, it was stated, would be incurred not only by broggers but also by Merchants of the Staple who sold wool, other than refuse wool, within the realm. A similar penalty was laid down for those illegally buying yarn or plucking the wool from staple fells (B.M. Harl. MS. 4943, 18 May, 1549).

[2] See Rich, op. cit., pp. 162–4 for the 1565 'Ordinaunce againest brogging of woulles'.

[3] P.R.O. S.P. 15/9/56.

also became members of the rival Company.[1] But cloth exporting was not the only possibility. Apart from general merchanting, the export of lead had always been a privilege of the Staplers' Company, and there was the as yet small but growing trade of importing Spanish wool.

Although a clear-cut division cannot be drawn, those merchants whose interests had widened with time from the export of wool to the larger field of general foreign trade comprised the wealthiest, most authoritative and policy-making section of the Company.[2] Outside of this circle, the allegiance of most Staplers remained attached to wool rather than to foreign trade; and with the decline of wool exports and the growth of the internal wool market there was a general movement from about 1560 onwards in favour of wool brogging at home. Thus while the official voice of the Company was raised against the development of the home cloth manufacture and the illicit activities of broggers, many of its members were fostering that development by engaging in similar activities to those which were the subject of censure. By joining in the Company's general denouncement of wool broggers these Staplers could perhaps hope to eliminate some of the competition in their new-found line of business. But such a course held dangers if by it attention was focused upon the Staplers' own illegal proceedings. True, they could put up a better defence to accusations than could the common broggers; for their ancient trade enabled them to plead 'transportation' as a reason for buying wool and 'refuse' as a reason for selling it within the realm. But the larger volume of their business made them a more obvious and profitable target for the common informer, and they did not always escape the retribution of the law. Indeed, during the

---

[1] As cloth exports increased, the Merchant Adventurers strongly challenged the right of the Staplers to participate in the trade, and in 1505 took their case to Star Chamber. The verdict of the Court was ambiguous, but was interpreted by the Crown and the Staplers to mean that the latter could export cloth paying the necessary impositions on actual shipments, but could not be compelled to pay a hanse to the Company of Adventurers. Despite this, 'wise merchants became members of both Companies', there being 73 Staplers, of whom 14 had been Mayors, who joined the Adventurers' Company during the reign of Henry VIII (Rich, op. cit., pp. 71–2).

[2] When the Staple Courts were held overseas — as at Bruges in 1565 — it was natural that the views of the exporting merchants should dictate the official policy of the Company, even though such views may not have been representative of those held by the majority of its members.

1560's they figured prominently amongst the dealers who were prosecuted in the Court of Exchequer upon the Act of 1552.[1]

By 1570 the Staplers' export trade was of little significance. In 1569 the religious disputes in the Netherlands had forced the merchants to remove their Staple from Bruges to the Adventurers' refuge at Hamburg.[2] This was the final crushing blow to an already very much weakened trade. Even at Bruges the Staplers had experienced great difficulty in meeting the competition of Spanish wool; at Hamburg, with higher transport costs, they found it virtually impossible. The market for English wool was so bad that some merchants later claimed they had shipped back to England wools which had lain unsold for five years at Hamburg.[3] By 1574 the Staplers had re-established themselves in Bruges, but some shipments continued to be made to Hamburg, and in 1579 Middleburgh was also tried as a mart. The opening up of Bruges in 1574 brought London's shipments in that year to over 1,100 sacks. This was a small enough export, but the increase in the price of wool made it impossible to maintain shipments even of this size. They dropped to 700 sacks in 1575, then to 600, and so to between 100 and 200 sacks in the period 1580–5.[4]

There was little profit to be made by exporting wool, not even, the Staplers decided, as licensees of Sir Francis Walsingham.[5] It was only natural that the great majority of the Company should lose their interest in the trade, and should turn ever more persistently to broking wools within the realm as a means of livelihood. When questioned by the Privy Council at the end of 1576, the Mayor of the Company, Sir Thomas Offley, was unable to deny this. The increase in the price of wool, he claimed, 'by reason of the common brooginge and buyenge and sellinge of wooll' made it unprofitable to make shipments to the Staple. The merchants were unacquainted with any other trade, and therefore, he went on, 'I must spare the punishment of them according too our ordinaunces.'[6]

---

[1] See, for example, the preponderance of Staplers prosecuted for offences between 1560 and 1565 listed in P.R.O. E.133/1/36; E.134/7 Elizabeth I. Hil. 1.
[2] Rich, op. cit., pp. 64–5.   [3] P.R.O. S.P. 12/114/29.
[4] Rich, op. cit., pp. 67–8.
[5] Walsingham endeavoured to let his licence to the Staplers, but was unsuccessful (P.R.O. S.P. 12/154/3).
[6] P.R.O. S.P. 12/110/8.

The Company's ordinance against the brogging of wools was manifestly out-dated. Wool broking was now the chief support of most of its members. Deplorable as this might seem to some of the older exporting merchants, the time had clearly come for the Company to revise its official attitude towards wool dealing at home. The first step was taken in May, 1577, when a new ordinance was passed permitting Staplers to engage in licensed wool dealing within the realm.[1] The same year saw the Company appealing to the Privy Council for a special licence to sell wool in England to alien manufacturers, on the ground that 'moest of those straungers that clothe now in England, did clothe English wulles in the Lowe Countreys'.[2] The request failed, as did a similar petition in 1582.[3]

Unable to gain a privileged legal footing in the internal wool trade, the Staple Company also failed to maintain its right to export cloth. Following the Star Chamber verdict of 1505,[4] the Staplers had continued to make shipments of cloth to the continent, although not on any large scale. But as the sixteenth century progressed, the control of the Merchant Adventurers over the trade became more efficient and authoritative; and in the Adventurers' charter of 1579 the clause, reserving to the Staplers the right to share in the monopoly of the trade to the Netherlands by shipping wools and fells to the Adventurers' marts, was cancelled. Making negligible shipments of wool, the Staplers were greatly tempted to encroach upon the Adventurers' trade; and in an attempt to force all cloth-exports to their marts the Adventurers demanded that only those Staplers who were also members of the Adventurers' Company should be allowed to transport cloth. The quarrel between the two Companies dragged on before the Privy Council until 1586, and meantime the Staplers were forbidden to make shipments of cloth abroad. In the following year the 'stand' of clothing led the Council to authorize any merchant, native or alien, to buy and ship cloths, subject to certain conditions. But this merely placed the Staplers on a par with other merchants: they had failed to vindicate their claims for special treatment.[5]

The wool-export trade was not sufficient to maintain more

[1] P.R.O. S.P. 12/113/19.   [2] P.R.O. S.P. 12/114/29.
[3] P.R.O. S.P. 12/154/34.   [4] See supra, p. 161, n. 1.
[5] Rich, op. cit., pp. 71–7.

than a very small fraction of the two hundred householders and hundred young men who now constituted the Staple Company;[1] and the merchants could have obtained but scant consolation for their failure to retain a strong footing in the cloth-export trade from the fact that in 1584 they had been granted a ratification of their privileges to export wool. But however small it was, there was some consolation to be gained from the grant. True, the custom and subsidy on the export of wool had not been re-assessed at 40s. per sack as the Company had requested in 1577.[2] But there was a confirmation of the merchants' privilege to sell refuse wool in England; an undertaking by the Queen that she would grant no further licences, either to buy and sell wool within the realm or to transport wool, during the term of the next seven years; and permission to the Staplers to ship wool to 'any place beyonde the seas being in amytye' with England.[3] The merchants subsequently made shipments to Rouen, Amsterdam, Leghorn, Middleburgh and Venice;[4] but the competition of Spanish wool was too strong for such shipments to be other than trifling.[5]

It was in the internal wool trade that the Staplers' future lay; and whether selling wool under the protection of a licence or under colour of refuse wool, it was to serving the needs of the home market that the Company as a whole now turned.

III

In 1614 the exportation of English wool abroad was forbidden.[6] Although the Company of the Staple endeavoured, without success, to obtain exemption for its members, at first sight the great majority of Staplers might seem to have been little affected by the prohibition. But in actual fact the matter went much deeper. For over half a century most of the Company had pursued a profitable business at home. When shipment abroad was forbidden, the Staplers' nominal reason for buying wool was deprived them, and they could no longer plead 'transportation' as the motive for a suspect trade. Following the prohibition, and

---

[1] Ibid., p. 75.   [2] P.R.O. S.P. 12/114/29.
[3] P.R.O. S.P. 12/173/20.   [4] Rich, op. cit., p. 77.
[5] See Hist. MSS. Comm. *Salisbury MSS*. iii, 132. The Staplers' position was not made any easier by the fact that in 1586 the Estates decided to impose a new and heavy tariff upon the import of English wool and fells (*A.P.C. 1586–7*, pp. 206–7).
[6] Infra, p. 188.

with the law as it then stood, the merchants' position from thenceforth — unless they held a licence from Hoby — was on a level with that of the despised wool brogger.

The Staplers' vulnerable position soon invited attack, and in the following Hilary term informations against a number of them were exhibited in the Court of Exchequer.[1] A request by the merchants to the Lord Exchequer for permission to sell the wool then upon their hands within the realm, met with a favourable response, and the informations were accordingly stayed.[2] By their actions the Staplers liberally interpreted this concession, and they continued the buying and selling of wool as they had done for so many years previously. But not for long was the enjoyment of this illegal traffic to be left in peace.

From 1612 to 1614 there had been a considerable agitation against the 'abuses of wool broggers' by the manufacturing interests, and throughout the following year, with the cloth trade remaining sluggish, the complaints of the clothiers continued. As usual, the middlemen were blamed for the 'high' price of wool (which the manufacturers always found to exist whenever there was a fall in the demand for cloth), while emphasis was also laid upon the brogger's falsifications and mixtures of wools which, it was claimed, disabled a clothier from making his cloth 'of that true and perfect making which he ought'.[3] In his endeavours to give the Cockayne cloth venture[4] every chance of success, James was willing to listen to such an argument, and in May, 1615, it was rewarded by the issue of a proclamation[5] commanding that the Act of 1429,[6] which forbade the middleman trade in woollen yarn, and the Act of 1552 should be strictly observed.

It was obvious, however, that the law could not be rigorously enforced whilst licensed dealers continued to trade and whilst prosecutions were left in the hands of the too-often-corrupted common informer. Thus there existed in the wealthier clothiers' view, a strong and evident case for the calling in of these licences and for the appointment of a commission to prosecute offenders

[1] P.R.O. E.159/447/12 James I. Hil. fol. 123 etc.
[2] P.R.O. S.P. 14/84/36, 37.
[3] P.R.O. S.P. 14/187/43; B.M. Lansd. MS. 152, fols. 223–4, 228. There was also a growing agitation against the activities of yarn middlemen. See ibid., 152, fols. 223–4; *A.P.C. 1613–14*, p. 12.
[4] See infra, pp. 187–8.   [5] *Tudor and Stuart Proclamations*, I 165.
[6] *Statutes of the Realm*, 8 Henry VI, c. 5.

according to the strict letter of the law.[1] The latter suggestion was received with considerable interest in certain court circles, where the possibilities of exploiting a patent similar in nature to the grant previously held by Simon Bowyer recommended themselves to a group of undertakers and would-be patentees. Of these, Viscount Fenton,[2] who had the King's ear on many matters of importance, was the chief. After much negotiation, and at considerable cost to Fenton and his associates, Hoby was persuaded to surrender his licence, and this was followed on 22nd July, 1615, by the granting of a fresh patent.

The new grant, which was for thirty-one years, gave to Fenton, Roger Gwynn, John Gwynn, Matthew Gwynn and Christopher Nicholl the right to all penalties (including those taken to the use of the King) incurred for offences against the 1429[3] and 1552 Acts. The King, who was to receive a rent of £1,500 a year for the duration of the grant, undertook that pardons or dispensations would not be given. A rider was added to the effect that the patent was not to be prejudicial to Halifax.[4]

Every assistance was forthcoming from those manufacturers who hoped to benefit from the drive against wool middlemen. The clothiers of the Worcester Company, for instance, paid £10 to John Gwynn 'for his efforts to suppress all Brogers and Staplers'.[5] However it was that John Gwynn (who seems to have been the most active of the patentees) obtained his intelligence, it was sufficient for him to lay an overwhelming mass of informations against wool dealers in the Exchequer during the following Michaelmas term.[6] As to be expected, the Staplers, who offered the most obvious and profitable targets for prosecution, were the chief subjects of the proceedings. Scarcely a member of the Company could have escaped from Gwynn's net, which had been spread to cover the majority of the wool-growing counties in the land. And the number of informations laid was more than matched by the over-generous amounts sued for: each defendant being accused of buying 1,000 tods of wool or more, valued at

[1] P.R.O. C.66/2069, m. 7; *A.P.C. 1615–16*, p. 624.
[2] Formerly Thomas Erskine and later the Earl of Kellie.
[3] *Statutes of the Realm*, 8 Henry VI, c. 5.
[4] P.R.O. C.66/2069, mm. 7–9.
[5] Society of Antiquaries Library, Prattinton MSS, v (Worcester City), fol. 175.
[6] P.R.O. E.159/449/13 James I, Mich. fols. 57–219^d.

thirty shillings per tod.[1] The Court, uncertain what to do, adjourned the proceedings until the following Hilary term, and ordered that in the meantime the Staplers should attend the Privy Council for further instructions.

Never before had the Staplers' fortunes sunk so low, and never before had they been so glad of the breathing-space allowed them to make out their case. In the necessity of the moment the merchants were forced to state the plain facts of their own trade without that taint of hypocrisy which had coloured many of their utterances on previous occasions. Petitioning the Privy Council on 24th December, 1615, the Staplers humbly reviewed their position, and asked that 'if theyr trade appeare to bee vsefull for the Comonweale they desire to continew it. If otherwise they humbly desire that they may bee freed from any farther charge or hazard of theyr estate'. They admitted, with refreshing candour, that ever since the loss of Calais they had 'ymployed the greatest parte of theire stocke in drivinge theire trade at home', and sought to justify this by emphasizing the utility of their services to wool growers and to small manufacturers. Their restraint, they said, was 'desired but for the profitt of a fewe rich clothiers who desire to exercise the trade wee lived by'.[2]

Annexed to the suit was a paper[3] setting out in greater detail the reasons why it was impossible to dispense with the wool chapman. In this and in other papers[4] particular emphasis was laid upon the services rendered by the middlemen to the manufacturers of the new draperies. The encouragement of this type of manufacture at the expense of the production of woollen cloth, it was argued, was to be desired, as it would afford the poor a greater amount of employment as well as increasing the customs revenue.

In putting forward their strongest possible case the Staplers had no option but to defend wool dealers in general. To eliminate the middleman, they claimed, would entirely disrupt

---

[1] At this price, a dealer buying 1,000 tods of wool was liable to a penalty of £3,000.

[2] P.R.O. S.P. 14/84/36, 37.

[3] P.R.O. S.P. 14/80/13. This is the well-known document printed as Appendix A, ii, in G. Unwin, *Industrial Organization in the Sixteenth and Seventeenth Centuries* (1904). The date should be December, 1615, and not January, 1615, as assigned.

[4] P.R.O. S.P. 14/80/15, 16.

the trade of the smaller manufacturers. They even went so far as to argue that it was doubtful whether 'there be a number sufficient of ye Company of Staplers to serve the market beinge that the broggers and loose dealers in wooll intended to be cut of are above a thousand in number'. For once, the arguments of the Staplers had much to recommend them, and the Privy Council decided to adjourn proceedings until the legality of the position had been more fully investigated. There followed a series of meetings in the Council Chamber with the different interests concerned at which the matter was thrashed out. Supported by the large wool growers and by the Mayor and Aldermen of London, who had some interest in the outcome,[1] the Staplers developed their arguments and in June, 1616, after much controversy, a compromise solution was eventually reached.

By order of the Council it was laid down that for a probationary period of one year manufacturers should be given the pre-emption of buying wool between shearing time and Michaelmas. During the remaining months of the year, wool dealing was to be permitted. There were two important exceptions to the order. The first exempted Wales and the counties of Northumberland, Westmorland and Cumberland: a privilege which the northern counties had enjoyed since 1585.[2] The second proposed the licensing of middlemen for the express purpose of carrying wool from the inland counties to specified markets in the outlying regions engaged upon the manufacture of the new draperies — in Kent and Devon, as well as Norfolk.[3]

In practice, the pre-emption order proved extremely difficult to enforce, and before summer was past the activities of middlemen were being cited by manufacturers and cloth exporters as causing wool to rise to an unreasonable price to the detriment of cloth exports. Greatly concerned about the condition of the English woollen industry, the Privy Council determined that growers as well as dealers who illicitly entered into advance contracts for the delivery of wool after Michaelmas should be

[1] Leaden Hall was leased by the City of London to the Company of the Staple (see supra, p. 92). Apart from this, the Staplers endeavoured to have at least one Alderman of London as a member of their Company. See B.M. Add. MSS. 43849, fol. 10.
[2] Supra, p. 142.
[3] *A.P.C. 1615–16*, pp. 356, 385, 512–13, 536, 564–5, 578, 624–6, 669–71; B.M. Lansd. MS. 152, fols. 225–8; B.M. Add. MS. 34324, fols. 10–14.

punished, and warrants were directed to a number of alleged offenders.[1]

IV

The turn of events satisfied neither Fenton and his associates nor the Company of the Staple, and much quiet negotiation took place behind the scenes. A solution which could be acceptable to both parties had been suggested by the Staplers at the end of December, 1615, when the Company had stated its readiness, if given the monopoly of the middleman trade, to expand its size to meet the needs of the market by admitting dealers on the payment of £100 apiece.[2] Such a course held a twofold attraction for the wool merchants. First, it would establish them legitimately and exclusively in their business; and secondly, it would supply them with substantial sums of money with which they could free themselves from the informations of the patentees. To Fenton, John Gwynn and the others, the proposition seemed equally attractive. Through it, they could not only hope to benefit, from the admittance fines of the new Staplers which would be paid over to them, but also, by the very fact of the Staplers' monopoly, they would be in a position to employ their patent fully throughout the year against those dealers trading outside the authority of the Company. As things stood, with pre-emption, the patentees were unable to make use of their grant during the greater part of the year.

With such advantages to be gained by both sides it was not long before common agreement on objectives was reached. There was some difference with regard to terms; but ultimately it was agreed that Gwynn's informations and the assistance of Fenton and his associates in the project should be valued at double the amount originally suggested by the Company. This sum was to be obtained from the fines of 200 men, each paying £100 for his admission to the freedom of the Company. The outlay necessary to the obtaining of a new charter was to be made by a group of undertakers, some of whom were members of the Company. This expense, however, was to be recovered

---

[1] *A.P.C. 1615–16*, pp. 624–5; *1616–17*, pp. 6, 16, 24–6, 35; B.M. Lansd. 152, fols. 225, 257–8, 271–2; P.R.O. S.P. 14/88/76.
[2] P.R.O. S.P. 14/80/15.

from additional entrance fees of £10 apiece imposed by the Company upon those redemptioners who became Staplers through the coercive offices of Lord Fenton. Supplementary to this, the new recruits were to be squeezed by the Company for further yearly payments of twenty shillings each.[1] Thus, the cost to each redemptioner was £111 on his admittance to the Company, to be followed in future years by additional levies of twenty shillings. This compared very unfavourably with the usual hanse which Staplers who received their freedom through apprenticeship or patrimony had to pay.[2]

Towards the end of February, 1617, the ground having been prepared, the Staple Company accordingly petitioned the Privy Council, requesting that the wool-middleman trade should be placed in the hands of its members and limited to a number of specified staple towns in England. On 24th March, a proclamation was drawn along the lines suggested. Twenty-three staple towns were appointed,[3] these being selected on the ground of their nearness to the cloth-manufacturing centres or, because of the fear of illicit transportation, of their remoteness from the sea.[4] After well over two hundred years England was again possessed of staple towns: this time for the purpose of serving the home textile manufacture.[5]

The great majority of staple towns possessed no form of staple government, or only its merest vestiges, but this did not prevent

---

[1] *Commons Debates, 1621*, ed. W. Notestein, F. H. Relf and H. Simpson (1935), iv, 66, 96–7; ibid., v, 487, 504, 506–7; B.M. Add. MS. 43849, passim.

[2] In 1623 the hanses for apprentices and sons of members were laid down at 6s. 5d.; in addition, other small levies were sometimes made (B.M. Add. MS. 43849, fols. 22–22ᵇ). This heavy discrimination against redemptioners was not new. The Ordinances of 1565 had laid down that the hanses for admission by apprenticeship or patrimony should normally be 3s. 4d.; but by redemption a 'mere merchaunt' was to pay 50 ounces of fine gold or its equivalent in ready money, and an artificer or brogger was to pay 100 ounces of fine gold or its equivalent. At the current price of gold in 1565, the brogger's hanse of 100 ounces would have been equal to £300 (Rich, op. cit., pp. 132–3).

[3] These were London, Canterbury, Exeter, Norwich, Worcester, Shrewsbury, Winchester, Reading, Cirencester, Kendal, Sherborne, Devizes, Rochdale, Taunton, Richmond, Wakefield, Halifax, Coggeshall, Oswestry, Northampton, Lincoln, Woodstock (Oxfordshire) and Brackley (Northamptonshire). Leicester was added early in 1618, at the request of the Mayor and Aldermen of the town. See P.R.O. S.P. 14/92/28(i); *Records of the Borough of Leicester, 1603–1688*, ed. H. Stocks (1923), pp. 170, 172.

[4] *A.P.C. 1616–17*, pp. 158–9, 179–81; *Tudor and Stuart Proclamations*, 1197.

[5] The medieval English staple towns had been established in order to facilitate the collection of customs upon wool exports. As late as 1561, when the Staplers received their new charter, home staples were still thought of as serving this function (see supra, pp. 156–7).

Fenton and the Company from forcing many dealers to give up their trade altogether, if they were unable or unwilling to pay the heavy admission fines for the freedom of the Company. Very soon complaints were being voiced by growers and small manufacturers in different parts of the country about the lack of buyers and sellers of wool and the general inconvenience of the staple system.[1]

The greatest outcry against the Company came from the wool growers of Northumberland, Cumberland and Westmorland, whose recently affirmed privileges for the free buying and selling of wool[2] had been taken from them on the establishment of the home staples. Petitions to the Privy Council pointed out that Kendal, being the only staple town to be appointed for the three northern counties, was too far distant for most of the many poor wool growers to take their wool to for sale. Some of the northern wool was grown at a distance of over a hundred miles from the chief manufacturing centres, and few clothiers came to buy. Following the restraint upon local middlemen much wool had been left upon the growers' hands. As for the Staplers, it was stated that they seldom traded in those counties, and that when they did 'beinge in nomber a fewe combine together and buy onelie at their owne rates and make one purse'.[3] The wool growers' case was too strong for the Staplers to argue the question other than moderately before the Council; and to placate the Northerners they offered to buy all the wools of the three counties at reasonable prices, and to admit as members of their Company any dealers who wished to join. To this suggestion the wool growers agreed; but in order to safeguard their interests, they proposed that commissioners should be appointed from the northern counties to fix an 'indifferent' price for their wool according to current market conditions. The Council agreed to this proposal and in June, 1619, commissioners were accordingly nominated. At the same time it was ordered that, until the Staplers had fulfilled their promises, local dealers should be permitted to purchase wool, and informations against

[1] P.R.O. S.P. 14/80/14; S.P. 14/105/147; S.P. 14/108/34; S.P. 14/109/29, 40; S.P. 14/121/169; B.M. Harl. MS. 6846, fol. 128; B.M. Add. MS. 34324, fols. 14-22; *A.P.C. Jan. 1618-June 1619*, pp. 148, 374-5, 445, 461, 468-9.
[2] Supra, p.168.
[3] B.M. Add. MS. 34324, fols. 14-16; *A.P.C. Jan. 1618-June 1619*, pp. 468-9.

either middlemen for buying wool or growers for keeping it longer than one year should be stayed.[1]

The tide of Council opinion had now definitely begun to turn. In November, Richard Ayre, a common informer, was committed to the Marshalsea until he withdrew informations which were being exhibited by him against wool dealers of Halifax.[2] The justification for this action was based upon the Act of 1555, whereby Halifax was exempted from the terms of the anti-middleman legislation.[3] No such exemption, however, had been given to Cornwall. Yet, following complaints by the inhabitants of Cornwall, the Council, in June, 1620, directed that informations against local wool dealers should be withdrawn and forbade any similar prosecutions to be instituted in the future.[4] It was not to be long before the application of these measures was made general.

The slump in overseas demand for English cloth, even more than the restriction on the number of wool buyers, had resulted by May, 1620, in a substantial fall in the price of English wool; and there was every likelihood that the fall would continue when the summer wool clip was thrown on to the market. Alarmed by this possibility, Lord Spencer and other wool-growing J.P.'s of the Midlands protested in strong terms to the Privy Council about the harmful effects of the Staplers' monopoly and requested that the restraint on wool dealers should be relaxed. In their report to the Council, the committee to whom the wool growers' petition had been referred, argued that the low price of wool — and therefore, some contemporaries were inclined to believe, the low price of cloth — was due to a shortage of wool buyers; and this opinion was later reinforced by the Justices of Assize in a report based on the interrogation of clothiers living within their circuits. In the light of these considerations, the Council decided towards the end of October that all proceedings against wool broggers should be stayed, and also forbade, until further orders, the future prosecution of informations against dealers for buying and selling wool.[5]

No further action was taken until the beginning of 1621, when

---

[1] B.M. Add. MS. 34324, fols. 21–2; *A.P.C. Jan. 1618–June 1619*, pp. 469–70.
[2] *A.P.C. July 1619–June 1621*, p. 65.   [3] Supra, p. 120.
[4] *A.P.C. July 1619–June 1621*, pp. 227–8.
[5] *A.P.C. July 1619–June 1621*, pp. 207–8, 246–7, 288–9, 293–4.

Parliament, highly critical of the many patents of monopoly which had recently been granted, and deeply concerned over the serious depression which had by then become general throughout trade, met again after a dissolution lasting seven years. Fenton's 'broggers' grant', although not yet condemned, was under debate when the June adjournment led to an abrupt interruption of parliamentary business.[1] The Commons agitation against matters of grievance continued in the Council Chamber, and on 10th July was rewarded by the issue of a proclamation revoking Fenton's patent and many of the other privileges which had been the subject of censure.[2] This, however, did not end Parliament's interest in the matter. The wool grant (in return for which James had received not a penny of his promised £1,500 a year rent)[3] had brought into the pockets of the patentees sums totalling more than £16,000, and the Commons determined upon the repayment to wool dealers of all money which had been obtained from them by coercive means.[4]

The Staplers fared no better than Fenton. Hardly had Parliament sat when the reasons for the fall in the price of wool were debated in committee. The Company's patent and proclamation were condemned and confiscated,[5] while a Bill for the 'free liberty for buying and selling wools' was one of the first measures to come before the Lower House.[6] This advocated the repeal of the 1552 Act, and authorized all persons, except those growers whose yearly clip exceeded twenty tods,[7] to engage in wool-dealing activities. The main purpose of the Bill was to raise the price of wool, a proposition which a few years earlier would have been acceptable only to the wool growers themselves. Now, however, it was generally recognized as a starting point for discussion.[8] By the end of May, the measure had been

---

[1] *H. of C. Journals*, i, 621.

[2] *Tudor and Stuart Proclamations*, 1314.

[3] *Commons Debates, 1621*, v, 468–9. See also P.R.O. S.P. 38/12, 14th August, 1622.

[4] *H. of C. Journals*, i, 630, 643, 651, 669, 712, 715, 758, 796.

[5] *Commons Debates, 1621*, v, 468–9, 486–8, 503–7; B.M. Add. MS. 43849, fol. 86.

[6] *H. of C. Journals*, i, 520.

[7] By making this exception it was hoped that the engrossing of wool would be prevented; but as the idea had been originally suggested by the large wool growers themselves (*A.P.C. July 1619–June 1621*, pp. 207–8) it could have been of no great practical importance.

[8] *Commons Debates, 1621*, iii, 319; ibid., v, 26, 177, 468, 505; ibid., vi, 6, 431.

passed by both Houses,[1] but before it could be brought to shape, Parliament was adjourned. While the Privy Council's order for the stay of informations upon the 1552 Act still stood, the fact that the Bill had not passed through its final stages was of little practical importance. Other and more urgent business therefore occupied the 1621 Parliament when it reassembled after the summer recess, and it was not until 1624 that the 1552 Act was eventually repealed.[2] The restrictionist policy embarked upon during the trade slump of the mid-sixteenth century was thus reversed; but it had taken seventy years and a more serious depression in trade to bring it about.

v

The repeal of the anti-middleman legislation in 1624 was made against the wishes of the wealthy clothing interests, and during the next few years they argued unsuccessfully for some restriction to be placed upon the activities of wool dealers.[3] Attempts to obtain the total suppression of the wool-middleman trade were made in the later decades of the century, but during the 'thirties it was the comparatively newly-evolved middleman trade in yarn, rather than in wool, which attracted the hostile attention of the capitalistic clothiers. This at least was true of the West of England broadcloth region, where the yarn middlemen had emerged since the beginning of the century as a strong and independent force.[4] From other parts of the country the government continued to receive occasional complaints about the engrossing activities of wool dealers. In 1636, the J.P.s of Suffolk petitioned the Privy Council on behalf of the clothiers of the county asking that, if wool middlemen could not be entirely restrained, for their numbers to be 'abridged' and their trade restricted to certain months of the year.[5] In 1640, a report from a commission appointed to consider the woollen industry of the kingdom, recommended the suppression of all dealers in wool and yarn except in Devon and Yorkshire.[6] In the same year clothiers from Leeds and Halifax petitioned the Council de-

---

[1] *H. of C. Journals*, i, 627–8; *Commons Debates, 1621*, ii, 392, 414; ibid., iii, 359.
[2] *Statutes of the Realm*, 21 James I, c. 28. No new Act was made at this time for the buying and selling of wool.
[3] P.R.O. S.P. 14/135/52; B.M. Stowe MS. 554, fol. 45; B.M. Add. MS. 34324, fols. 25–6.
[4] Ramsay, op. cit., pp. 88–99.
[5] P.R.O. S.P. 16/319/42.   [6] Ramsay, op. cit., p. 98.

nouncing the engrossing and forestalling of wool by middlemen at their local markets, and requesting that dealers should be restrained from buying at the market towns of Leeds, Wakefield, Ripon, Doncaster and Pontefract.[1] It is doubtful whether the petitioners were as poor as they represented. Halifax manufacturers had welcomed the wool dealers' services in 1555, but the parish had become more prosperous since then, and it now contained a fair number of substantial clothiers who could hope to benefit from a curtailment of the wool middlemen's activities. But in 1640 the government had little time to deal with petitions of this nature; it was deeply involved in political difficulties, and the middleman trade was allowed to continue unrestrained.

The war which ensued between Crown and Parliament lasted for five years. In the end it was won by the parliamentarians who, having behind them the capital, the eastern counties and the clothing towns, possessed the greater financial strength. The wealthy manufacturers, some of whom had financed the parliamentary cause,[2] determined to benefit whilst the memory of their services was still fresh, and in November, 1646, they presented a petition to the House of Commons asking for the redress of their grievances. The petition listed four main complaints. These concerned the illicit transportation of wool; the corruption and abuses practised in the winding of wool; the engrossing of wool by middlemen; and the manufacture of cloth by clothiers who had not served an apprenticeship.[3] Laws remained in force against the first two[4] and

---

[1] P.R.O. S.P. 16/460/64.

[2] In 1642 the clothiers of Coggeshall, Essex, 'in their ardent affection to the Parliament . . . lent great sums of money upon the public faith', and £6,000 was still owing to them in 1652 (*Cal. S.P. Dom. 1651–2*, p. 481). The Coggeshall clothiers took a leading part in the agitation which is described in the text following. See ibid., pp. 479–80; P.R.O. S.P. 18/25/51.

[3] *Cal. S.P. Dom. 1645–7*, p. 586.

[4] Statute 23 Henry VIII, c. 17, for the true winding of wools, had been made perpetual in 1571 (see supra, p. 123, n. 4). Bills to amend this legislation were introduced into Parliament in 1628, 1641 and 1675 (*H. of C. Journals*, i, 882; ibid., ii, 95; ibid., ix, 318–19), but none of them ever reached the Statute Book. The wool winders' operations were still nominally controlled by the Staple Company. In 1620 the Mayor of the Staple had authorized Philip Boulton, a sworn wool winder, to apprehend 'such persons as should winde fold and lapp wooll contrary to the Statute'; but he was later 'ymprisoned and disgraced for executing the same' (B.M. Add. MS. 43849, fols. 6, 13). In 1636 Sir John Mildram, acting on behalf of Charles I, proposed to the Company that a tax of twelve pence should be levied on every pack of wool sold in the kingdom, part of the proceeds to be used 'in maintayning of fitt persons to serch for the preventing of . . . deceipts'. In their reply the

N

last[1] of these offences, and the manufacturers pressed for their effective enforcement. But the middleman trade was unrestrained, and the manufacturers demanded that it should be once more made illegal. The Staplers, who had successfully resisted an attempt to license the trade in 1630,[2] and who had been unsuccessfully approached by Charles I as a possible source of revenue in 1635,[3] took up the challenge; and during the next six years a stream of pamphlets, broadsheets and petitions testified to the fierceness of the controversy.

In defence of their trade the Staplers brought forward a host of arguments, most of which had been advanced before. But though the merchants' arguments were substantially the same as those used in earlier years, there was a significant change of emphasis. In the sixteenth and early seventeenth centuries the wool middlemen had been declared to be necessary on two main grounds: they supplied credit to wool growers and manufacturers, and they linked up distant markets. Though these considerations were now urged by the Staplers, they were no longer put forward as the principal justification for their trade. Times had changed, and the change was reflected in the great emphasis which the merchants now placed upon their wool-sorting functions and in their contention that they always gave the growers a good price for their wool. To forbid their trade, the Staplers continued, would be to take away the independence of the smaller manufacturers: the richer clothiers would engross the wools of the kingdom into their hands, 'and then as the greater fishes devour the lesse, so will the rich clothiers devour the poor'.[4]

The wealthy manufacturers completely contradicted the Staplers' arguments or modified them to their own advantage.

Staplers informed the Attorney-General that they could not 'discerne that they shall have any ease of reformacion therof in the way now proposed vnto them' (B.M. Add. MS. 43849, fols. 83–84b).

[1] For laws relating to apprenticeship in the woollen industry see Lipson, op. cit., ii, 37–44, 72–6.

[2] B.M. Add. MS. 43849, fol. 55b.

[3] In May, 1635, Sir Richard Lydall informed the Staple Company: 'his Majesty hath now cast his eye vppon them and for 20,000 li. per ann. is content to graunt the sole trade of exporting woollen clothes vnto them for that the Merchant Adventurers patent is now att the Kings mercie' (ibid., fol. 76b). The King's proposition followed an unsuccessful attempt by the Staplers in the previous year to assert their right to export cloth. See Rich, op. cit., p. 82, n. 2.

[4] *B.M. Pamphlets*, 712. g. 16/3; P.R.O. S.P. 16/515/139.

The poorer growers, they stated, were just as able to obtain credit or ready payment for their wool from the richer clothiers as from the Staplers, but too often the manufacturers were fore-stalled by the middlemen's practice of laying earnest. And as for dealers being necessary to carry wool between the growers and the manufacturers — 'between the bark and the Tree' — it was not unusual for clothiers to travel fifty or a hundred miles in order to obtain their raw material at first hand.

The Staplers' claim that their wool-sorting operations were of great value brought forth the most derisive comments from the manufacturing interests. Many Staplers, alleged the clothiers, sold wool in the fleece without making any attempt to sort it. Their sorting of wool was the 'greatest mischief'; for they used deceit and mixed several counties' wool together, and this caused 'much false and bad cloth to be made in England' and lowered its reputation abroad. Neither, continued the clothiers, was it necessary to have middlemen to sort wool. Manufacturers were the most competent to do their own sorting, and they were able to use up all the wool which they bought from the growers by making it into different varieties of cloth and worsted. This practice may have been well suited to the business of the capitalist manufacturer, but it could hardly be adopted by the small independent clothier with his trifling output of one type of cloth. The wealthy manufacturers were well aware of this, and they argued: 'the poor clothier had better be a journeyman to him that buys his wool of the growers than trade for himself by buying of the pretended sorters of wool'.[1]

If the middleman trade were forbidden, the manufacturers declared, there would be no danger of the richer clothiers engrossing the country's wool, for the manufacturers were many and widely dispersed; but, they argued, this could not be said of the Staplers who, 'by their corporation, are the better enabled to ingross the greatest part of the wool of this nation, for they can agree together in a joint stock'.[2]

Finally, the manufacturers endeavoured to answer the Staplers' assertion that the middlemen paid the growers the best price for their wool. At first the clothiers denied the merchants' contention; but later they abandoned their ground expressing

---

[1] *Cal. S.P. Dom. 1650*, p. 407.   [2] Ibid., p. 408.

the hope that 'the Growers, though many and great, do not so desire their own profits, as thereby to prejudice the generall trade of this Nation'.[1] But the growers saw no reason why they should lose in order that the wealthy manufacturers might gain; and petitions were sent to the Council of State for Trade from the Earl of Westmorland and other landowners in Northampton-shire and from landlords and wool growers in Warwickshire and Romney Marsh asking that the middleman trade should be allowed to continue.[2]

If the manufacturers had hoped that their requests would be speedily granted they were destined to be disappointed. The committee of the House of Commons to whom their petition was referred sat for over a year before drawing up a report, and even then this did not recommend the complete restraint of the middleman trade for which the manufacturers had asked.[3] It advocated that the resale of wool in the fleece should be made illegal, but suggested that the resale of wool in a sorted con-dition within three months of its purchase and the resale of skin wool by fellmongers should be permitted.[4]

The report was never submitted, however, and for the next few years the dispute dragged on before the Council of State and the Council of Trade appointed by Parliament.[5] Eventually, in May, 1651, the Council of State made a determined effort to get the business settled, and it invited the clothiers, Staplers, fellmongers and wool growers to meet together to consider the expedients necessary for regulating the wool trade. The growers declined to attend the meeting, but the other three parties sent representatives, and in June their resolutions were forwarded to the Council of Trade.

On some of the issues which had been raised in the clothiers' petition there was considerable agreement. All were agreed that the exportation of wool should be made a felony; that abuses in

---

[1] E. Rozer, *Reasons shewing the desires of the Cloathiers and Woollen Manufacturers of England . . . Against Ingrossing and Transporting of Wooll and Fullers Earth* (1648); *Cal. S.P. Dom. 1650*, pp. 406–9; *B.M. Pamphlets*, 712. g. 16/3.

[2] *B.M. Pamphlets*, 712. g. 16/3, p. 22; P.R.O. S.P. 18/25/38–41.

[3] The report, however, advocated that the laws regulating the apprenticeship of clothiers and the exportation of wool should be strictly enforced. It further recommended that the statutory penalty of 6d. per fleece on deceitfully wound wool should be doubled, and suggested that a penalty of 6d. per sheep or 6d. per fleece should be imposed upon those persons who washed sheep or wool in salt water in places where fresh water was available (P.R.O. S.P. 16/515/128).

[4] Ibid.   [5] P.R.O. S.P. 18/25/33.

the winding of wool should be punished; that fellmongers should
be permitted to buy and sell fell wool; and that no person should
be allowed to deal in wool without having first served a seven
years' apprenticeship in the trade. On other points there was a
conflict of interests.

The fellmongers claimed that from 'time out of memory' they
had dealt in fleece wool as well as in fell wool, and they now
urged their 'undoubted right' to do so. In addition, they proposed that clothiers and other manufacturers should be given
the pre-emption of buying fleece wool until 1st August and of
fell wool until 30th September; and to this they added a suggestion that no person should be allowed to buy and sell fleece
wool without sorting it.[1]

The Staplers were not willing to compromise over their own
trade, and they naturally opposed the fellmongers' proposals.
Neither were the merchants content to stay merely on the
defensive. They saw that the clothiers' agitation could be turned
to good account: that it could help the Staple Company to
regain the legal monopoly of the middleman trade in fleece
wool which it had lost in 1620. The case which the Staplers put
forward for the consideration of the Council of Trade was therefore less a defence of their own trade than an attack upon that of
their rivals. They recommended that the fellmongers' wool-
buying activities should be limited, and that some 'fit penalty'
should be laid down to prevent men of 'other professions' from
dealing in wool in the future. Of their own claims to the trade
the merchants said little, save to point out that it had always
been 'the proper and ancient right' of Staplers to buy and sell
wool, they 'having no other means of livelihood'.[2]

The Committee for Trade appointed by the Common Council of the City of London to whom the matter was referred,
thought otherwise; and at the end of June they reported to the
Council of Trade: 'We are of opinion that, though the Staplers
formerly had a legal being, it is now expired, at least as to the
commodity of wool, . . . and we do not now conceive them at all
necessary, but in many respects disadvantageous as being the
principal cause . . . of discouragement and destruction to
clothing.'[3]

[1] *Cal. S.P. Dom. 1651*, pp. 198–9, 247–8.
[2] Ibid., pp. 248–9.   [3] Ibid., p. 270.

This championing of their cause encouraged the wealthy manufacturers to intensify their efforts to obtain the suppression of the wool middlemen; and petitions from clothiers and counter-petitions from Staplers, fellmongers and wool growers continued to keep the issue very much alive until well into 1653.[1] Finally, disillusioned by their lack of success, the manufacturers allowed the matter to rest.

VI

The slackening of the agitation against the wool middlemen marked a definite stage in the decline of the Company of the Staple. Under Lord Fenton's patent many dealers had become Staplers in order to avoid prosecution;[2] in the early 1620's, as the result of the grant of special privileges,[3] the Company had received an influx of merchants anxious to export cloth; and during the recent agitation some wool dealers had thought to play safe and had joined the Company.[4] But now that wool middlemen were not being seriously called in question, the Staple Company had little to offer in return for the large admission fines which it demanded for membership by redemption. It had no special privileges for trading in wool nor for exporting cloth.[5] Consequently, after the mid-seventeenth century, redemptioners were few and new recruits were drawn very largely from merchants who were made free by apprenticeship or patrimony.[6] But though its membership slowly declined, the Company still had many years of active existence before it.[7] The great wool-stapling days of the Middle Ages could never be completely forgotten, but the Company was now only interested in the wool trade at home. Although the charter which the Staplers had received from James I in 1617 had long outlived its purpose, it was confirmed in 1669;[8] and far from wanting to export wool, the Company was actively concerned that the

---

[1] P.R.O. S.P. 18/25/33–43, 48–51; S.P. 18/35/116.
[2] Supra, pp. 169–71, 173.   [3] Infra, p. 193.
[4] B.M. Add. MS. 43849, fols. 9, 96[b] et seq.   [5] Supra, p. 176, n. 3.
[6] See B.M. Add. MSS. 43849–43852.
[7] The Staple Company continued to survive until modern times: in its later years as an exclusive family affair. By 1928 the membership was very limited indeed, and the remaining members agreed to terminate the Company (Rich, op. cit., p. 2).
[8] B.M. Add. Charter 70834. Following the Restoration all companies were obliged to renew their charters, and the Staple Company deferred from doing so until a warrant was issued against it. The confirmation cost the Staplers £83 (B.M. Add. MS. 43849, fols. 131–2).

prohibition on its export should be effectively enforced and maintained.[1]

Of the last declining years of the other great wool company of former times — the Company of Woolmen, Wool packers or Wool winders — little is known. Even before the end of the sixteenth century it had been well on the road to extinction — so much so that Stow, the contemporary historian of London, could write: 'The Company of Wooll-packers, I know not what to say of them.'[2] Yet the Company was in existence when Stow wrote, and it continued to survive until at least 1672 and possibly for another hundred years after that.[3] But by 1658 the Company had long ceased to exercise any effective control over the wool trade; and even one of its few remaining members could go over its head to petition the Protector for a commission and proclamation to reform the deceits used by 'inexpert and unsworn persons' in the folding and winding of wools.[4] The draft of a proclamation was drawn up but the Company was 'not so much as named therein'.[5] In 1664 the Company was more fortunate; and in reply to a petition from its officials asking that the proclamation of James I for the true winding of wools should be reviewed, it was proclaimed that no person should wind or pack wool 'unless admitted thereto by the Company of Woolmen of London, on oath to use no fraud therein'.[6] But nothing could revive the Company's fortunes; its days were numbered, and it passed quietly into oblivion.

The decline of the old wool companies was to some extent paralleled in the cloth trade. Here, as a result of changes in the pattern of English overseas commerce during the seventeenth century, the Merchant Adventurers lost steadily in prestige and importance to the Levant and East India Companies. At the same time as they were becoming less important as exporters of cloth, the Merchant Adventurers — along with the drapers — were also becoming less important as buyers in the home market. But as buyers, their place was taken not so much by merchants

---

[1] In 1676 the Company paid William Carter £5 for the 'trouble and charges hee hath been at in prosecuting of those that doe transport wool into foreigne parts' (ibid., fol. 146). See also *H. of C. Journals*, xiii, 784; Rich, op.cit., p. 85.

[2] Quoted in W. C. Hazlitt, *The Livery Companies of the City of London* (1892), p. 153.

[3] Ibid., pp. 671–2.

[4] *Cal. S.P. Dom. 1658–9*, p. 45.

[5] Ibid., p. 105. No proclamation appears to have been made at this time, however.

[6] *Cal. S.P. Dom. 1663–4*, p. 469; *Tudor and Stuart Proclamations*, 3392.

of other established companies, as by a new class of middlemen: the factors of Blackwell Hall, the greatest cloth market in the kingdom.

The factors served the same purpose in the late stages of the cloth industry as the wool dealers did in the early stages. They were the middlemen who linked up the manufacturers of cloth, on the one hand, with their customers, the drapers and exporting merchants, on the other. But from being at the beginning of the seventeenth century merely the agents of West Country clothiers and Yorkshire merchants, whose cloth they sold in London on commission, they succeeded within the course of two or three generations in cutting off the country manufacturers from all direct contact with their customers, and in raising themselves to be 'the chief masters of the clothing trade'. Having secured possession of the stalls in Blackwell Hall during the period of the Plague and Fire of London,[1] the factors were in a strong position to control their client clothiers' trade; and they found that by selling their clients' cloth on long credit they could frequently oblige manufacturers with small reserves of capital to accept from them advances of money at interest and supplies of raw material, particularly of Spanish wool, with which to carry on their business.[2]

As suppliers of Spanish wool the Blackwell Hall factors stood in the same sort of relation to the small manufacturers as did the middlemen who dealt in English wool. The large manufacturers of medley cloth, who doubtless purchased the greater part of their Spanish wool supplies direct from the merchant importers, naturally resented the factors' activities; and in 1692, 'intending to Ruine all the middling and small clothiers', they introduced a Bill into Parliament to prohibit the factors from trading at all. But small manufacturers from Wiltshire, Somerset and Devonshire presented petitions against the Bill, and it was thrown out; and the following year a Bill to prohibit the factors from dealing in wool was also rejected.[3]

The Blackwell Hall factors' principal by-trade was the buying

---

[1] Lipson, op. cit., ii, 26–7; Ramsay, op. cit., pp. 135–6.

[2] *Reasons for Restraining the Factors of Blackwell-Hall from Dealing in Spanish and English Wooll; The Languishing State of our Woollen Manufacture, Humbly Represented to the Parliament.*

[3] *The Blackwell-Hall Factors Case.* A further unsuccessful attempt was made in 1698 to persuade Parliament to prohibit the factors from dealing in wool (*H. of C. Journals*, xii, 207).

and selling of Spanish wool. But the agents also dealt in English wool and had done so for a number of years.[1] During the clothiers' agitation this side of the factors' business was inevitably the subject of destructive criticism; and as the factors were said to conduct their trade in English wool in association with the wool broggers, the latter were also selected as a target for the clothiers' attacks.[2] There had been no outcry against the wool middlemen since the early years of the Commonwealth, but petitions now reached the Commons from clothiers in different parts of the country asking that the wool broggers should be restrained.[3] The dealers were said to engross wool; to retail it 'at excessive rates to the impoverishing of the Clothing-Trade and the ruin of many poor labourers therein';[4] and to make a profit of 10 per cent. on the wool which they bought — 'which is an hardship upon the manufacturer, and forces him to sell his goods at a proportionable Rate'.[5] In 1698, following petitions from clothiers of Worcester, Cirencester and Kidderminster, the matter was referred to a committee of the Lower House. But Parliament declined to intervene; and it was resolved that 'the Proprietor or Grower of Wool be not restrained from selling his wool to any Chapman he shall think fit to deal with'.[6]

The position of the wool middleman was thus finally secured. In the eighteenth century the continued change in the character of the English wool supply, and the more sharply defined division of labour, both geographically and within the wool-textile industry itself, served to make the wool middleman, or the wool stapler as the more substantial dealer was then called, one of the most respectable members of society. No longer denounced as a parasite upon the industry, he was described in 1747 as 'the sheet anchor of Great Britain'.[7]

[1] See B.M. Add. MS. 43849, fols. 46–46ᵇ.
[2] *Reasons for Restraining the Factors of Blackwell-Hall from Dealing in Spanish and English Wooll; The Clothiers Complaint, or, Reasons for Passing the Bill against the Blackwell Hall Factors. Humbly offer'd to the Parliament* (1692), pp. 5–6, 26.
[3] *H. of C. Journals*, x, 590 (1691); ibid., xi, 424, 717 (1696); ibid., xii, 91, 122, 150 (1698).
[4] Ibid., xii, 91.   [5] Ibid., xii, 277.   [6] Ibid.
[7] R. Campbell, *The London Tradesman* (1747), p. 199.

Chapter VII

THE ENGLISH AND IRISH WOOL TRADE
AND THE EXPORT BAN

I

By the end of the sixteenth century England's transition from raw wool exporter to cloth exporter had been virtually completed. Inevitably, this change in the nature of English exports increased the dependence of the native wool grower upon the home manufacturer and brought a great and growing government concern for the welfare of the wool-textile industry. In 1614 the export of wool was prohibited,[1] but long before this English government policy had been directed towards the subordination of the wool growing and merchanting interests to those of the increasingly important manufacturing class.

A step in this direction had been taken in 1465, with the passing of transitory legislation against wool dealers;[2] and several times during the reigns of the first two Tudors similar measures were enacted in an attempt to meet slumps in the cloth trade or as an antidote to high wool prices. It was not, however, until the 1552 Act that the policy of bolstering the clothing interests at the expense of the other groups became explicit, and it remained so throughout the late sixteenth and seventeenth centuries. Having enacted that the manufacturer should be the sole buyer of wool for English looms, the government could go only the one stage further, and prohibit its sale for foreign manufacture, in order to make industrial interests supreme. That this step was not taken in the mid-sixteenth century was probably due to several causes. It was directly precluded from consideration by the Staplers' political position at the time, and by the fact that the taxes levied upon wool exports, although very much diminished from what they had

[1] Infra, p. 188.　　　　[2] Supra, p. 114.

been in the fourteenth and fifteenth centuries, were still a substantial item of Crown revenue. More important, but less
apparent, must have been the fact that the industrial development of the country, although too rapid for the government's
liking, had not proceeded far enough for a permanent[1] step of
such a radical nature to be taken; in particular, the manufacture of the new draperies, and therefore the most effective
utilization of English long-wool supplies, was at that time in the
early stages of evolution.

By the end of Elizabeth's reign such considerations were
inapplicable or had lost much of their previous significance. At
one and the same time the abysmal decline in the wool-export
trade rendered the revenue to be obtained from the export of
the raw material unimportant as a source of Crown income and
stripped the Staplers of much of the prestige which had been
accorded them as a wealthy exporting Company. During the
second half of the sixteenth century cloth exports were on the
whole well below the high level of 1550–1.[2] But in all likelihood,
the output of cloth did not decline to the same extent. It is true
that during these years the tastes of the upper classes turned
more to silks and other luxury fabrics,[3] while 'new made stuffs'
diverted part of the old demand for broadcloths and kersies to
themselves.[4] But the traditional products may have gained some
compensation for these losses by a greater home demand for
clothing due to population growth, despite a fall in the wage-
earner's level of real income. In any case the probable absolute
— and certainly the relative — decline in the production of
English short wool points to the conclusion that, by the beginning of the seventeenth century, the capacity of the cloth industry
was large enough to absorb, without any great strain to itself, all
the short wool which English growers were capable of producing. Moreover, by this time the development of the manufacture of the new draperies had become substantial enough to
allow the growing supplies of English long wool to be turned to
a full and good account at home. Indeed, by about 1590 the

---

[1] In order to put pressure upon foreign countries or upon exporting merchants,
the government had a number of times in the past temporarily prohibited exportation.
[2] Supra, p. 43.
[3] L. Stone, 'Elizabethan Overseas Trade', *Econ. Hist. Rev.* 2nd ser. ii (1949), 49.
[4] Infra, p. 186.

progress of the new draperies had been such that it was being put forward as a reason for the promotion of a Bill in Parliament forbidding the exportation of wool and yarn.[1] Nothing came of the suggestion, however; indeed, at the time there was little point in it, for wool exports were negligible enough. Although during the next two decades the unlawful practices of wool smugglers were occasionally condemned[2] there was in reality no necessity for an agitation against the exportation of wool.

English wool was relatively dear, and it was only by evading the customs or by shipping under privilege that an exporter could hope to be adequately remunerated for his trouble, and even that was not certain. Had the price of home-grown wool continued to rise during the early years of the seventeenth century as it had done throughout the previous century, and had foreign wool prices remained comparatively stable, the demand for a policy of export prohibition and its endorsement by James I would have been meaningless. But in fact the great rise in the price of English wool was over by 1603,[3] and by 1610 the reason for its fall had become a matter for considerable conjecture. It was generally agreed that the increase in the production of wool was one of the dominant causes. But perhaps there was even greater justification in imputing the fall in wool prices, as some did, to the lack of cloth sales: an argument which the Lord Treasurer, in his defence of the new imposition upon cloth, vigorously refuted.[4]

It was not an unqualified benefit that the end of the Anglo-Spanish war brought to the English cloth trade. With the re-opening of foreign markets the immediate result was good. But the coming of peace in 1604 also meant increased competition from continental manufacturers. By 1610 many contemporaries were well aware of the changed situation. They complained of the growing habit at home and abroad of wearing silks and 'new made stuffs', and of the increase in the production of textiles upon the continent: in the Netherlands, Italy, Spain and France — where Spanish wools were used — and in Germany.

---

[1] P.R.O. S.P. 15/24/100.
[2] *Tudor Economic Documents*, i, 193–8. See also P.R.O. S.P. 12/114/29.
[3] Infra, p. 220.
[4] B.M. Lansd. MS. 152, fol. 229; Hist. MSS. Comm. *Downshire MSS.* ii, 336–7. See also P.R.O. S.P. 14/57/37.

The religious strife upon the continent during the last half of the sixteenth century had done much to disorganize the manufacture of textiles there, and to that extent advance the sale of English products. When, therefore, at the beginning of the seventeenth century, these countries (in particular the Low Countries and France) sought to promote and rehabilitate their textile manufactures, the effect upon English cloth sales and English wool prices was inevitably a depressing one. But this was not the only result. The increased production of textiles upon the continent raised the price of Spanish wool[1] at the same time as that of English wool was falling, so levelling out that disparity in prices which during the latter half of the sixteenth century had given the continental market in wool almost entirely to the Spaniards.

Despite the fact that English wool was again selling at competitive prices abroad and could be used as an obvious weapon of retaliation, the Flemish States in April, 1612, in their endeavour to re-establish the manufacture of woollens and other textiles, decided upon prohibiting the importation of English cloth.[2] The stage was therefore well set for the events which followed the inauguration of Alderman Cockayne's disastrous project.[3]

Despite enactments to the contrary,[4] the great bulk of English cloth was exported in an undressed and undyed condition to be finished abroad, notably in the Netherlands. With personal profit in view, Alderman Cockayne, a leading member of the Eastland Company, and other promoters urged that only dyed and dressed English cloths should be exported. Partly as a fiscal expedient, and partly in an endeavour to foster the native cloth-finishing industry, James I gave his support to the scheme; and in July, 1614, it was proclaimed that after 2nd November the

[1] The prices of some types of Spanish wool more than doubled between 1601 and 1612 (E. J. Hamilton, *American Treasure and the Price Revolution in Spain, 1501–1650* (Cambridge, Mass., 1934), pp. 358, 361).

[2] Hist. MSS. Comm. *Downshire MSS.* iii, 236, 273, 280.

[3] For a full account of this see A. Friis, *Alderman Cockayne's Project and the Cloth Trade* (Copenhagen and London, 1927).

[4] Acts against the export of unfinished cloth had been passed in 1467, 1487, 1512, 1523, 1536 and 1566. These were evaded by the grant of licences. The grant to the Merchant Adventurers in 1564, for instance, authorized them to ship 30,000 cloths a year 'not wrought or dressed'. Similar grants were made to individuals, including Walsingham, Raleigh and the Earl of Cumberland. See Lipson, op. cit., iii, 376 et seq.

exportation of undyed and undressed broadcloth would be prohibited. The privileges of the Merchant Adventurers were suspended, and a new company, incorporated as the King's Merchant Adventurers, took their place. The old Company had predicted that the United Provinces would close their doors to dyed and dressed English cloth, and before the end of 1614 the prediction was proved correct. Holland prohibited the importation of these cloths in November, and shortly afterwards the States General followed suit by issuing a prohibition comprising all the United Provinces.[1] The likelihood that this would happen had been allowed for in advance; and in an endeavour to persuade the Dutch from this course, and to reduce the competition from their manufacturers, it was decided to prohibit the export of English wool which, in view of the further rise in Spanish wool prices,[2] was in greater demand abroad. Previous to June, 1614, the Staplers had been deprived of their privileges of transportation,[3] and this was followed in the September by a proclamation enforcing a general prohibition of exportation. Not only were the wools and woolfells of England, Wales and Ireland forbidden, upon pain of forfeiture, to be transported by any persons to foreign parts but, in order to prevent smuggling, their export to Scotland and their carriage from port to port was also prohibited. It was further ordered that the Act of 8 Elizabeth forbidding the carriage abroad of rams, sheep and lambs — which was allegedly responsible for the fineness of Spanish wool — should be put into execution, upon pain of one year's imprisonment and the loss of the left hand for the first offence and felony for the second. Finally, the exportation of fuller's earth was also forbidden, and the following month the prohibition was extended to include woollen yarn.[4]

The effects of the order that wool was not to be shipped from port to port were forcibly felt at the ensuing sheep-shearing time, when wool shipments along the coast were apt to be heaviest. The coastal trade had become of considerable importance between Ireland and the English mainland, and between South Wales and the South West of England; and follow-

---

[1] Ibid., iii, 381; Friis, op. cit., p. 277.
[2] Hamilton, op. cit., p. 361.
[3] Hist. MSS. Comm. 2. *Third Report*, p. 15.
[4] *Tudor and Stuart Proclamations*, 1150, 1153; P.R.O. S.P. 14/187/31.

ing complaints from these places the Attorney-General ruled that it had never been intended to restrain the transportation of wool from port to port within England and Wales. The coastal traffic in wool was therefore permitted to continue, providing that each shipper entered into good bond for the destination and returned a certificate upon its performance.[1] Similar conditions were laid down respecting the transport of Irish wool, the Farmers of the Customs being asked to consider the most convenient ports in Ireland and in England between which shipments of wool could be directed.[2]

II

The attempt to export only dyed and dressed English cloth proved an immediate failure, and it was not long before permission had to be given to the King's Merchant Adventurers to export it in an unfinished state. In spite of this, the foreign market for English woollen cloth continued to shrink.[3] The restoration of the old Company of Merchant Adventurers to its former status in August, 1617, brought no permanent improvement, and by 1621 the country was in the throes of the worst trade depression in its history.

The Bill to free the middleman trade in wool was but one measure to be debated by members of the 1621 Parliament in their attempts to legislate a cure for the depression. The exportation of wool, woolfells and fuller's earth had already been forbidden by proclamation, but a Bill to this effect was introduced into the Commons on 19th April.[4] Although most members were agreed that some such measure was necessary in view of the great distress in the cloth industry, differences of opinion existed on particular issues.[5] These had still not been

[1] But in 1621, the fear of illicit transportation led the Privy Council to instruct the port officers of Milford that shipments of wool should be permitted only to the ports of Bristol, Barnstaple and Minehead, and then only after adequate measures had been taken for their landing at one of these three ports (*A.P.C. July 1621–May 1623*, pp. 72–3). See also P.R.O. S.P. 14/122/130; S.P. 14/123/28, 54.

[2] *A.P.C. 1616–15*, pp. 183, 185, 241, 243, 639.

[3] Friis, op. cit., pp. 333–4.   [4] *H. of C. Journals*, i, 582.

[5] A number of members were against the penalty of felony which the Bill imposed; others wished for the measure to be made probationary, 'because two knaves may else question a man of great estate for his estate and life'. Various provisoes were suggested: to provide against the carriage of wool into Scotland; to forbid the transportation of sheep from England into Ireland; to allow Berwick to export the wool growing in its vicinity; to permit Spanish wool which could find no sale in England to be re-exported; to provide for patents for the transportation of wool into Jersey and Guernsey (see infra, p. 212); and to permit the exportation of

resolved by 4th December when the Bill was withdrawn in favour of another measure.[1] This also proved abortive. In subsequent Parliaments, Bills to prohibit the exportation of wool were introduced with monotonous regularity,[2] but many years were to pass before one succeeded in completing all the necessary stages in both Houses. In the meantime the prohibition continued to be enforced by proclamation.[3]

Parliament had every reason to express its concern over the depression. The seriousness of the state of affairs in the cloth trade was shown by the fact that whereas in 1618 (which had been only a moderate year), 102,300 shortcloths had been exported from London, in 1622 this total had fallen to 75,600 cloths,[4] and in 1623 was probably less.[5] The condition of the sheep-farming industry was also depressed. Consequent upon the reduction in the consumption of wool, the adverse effects of the fall in its market price were felt by large numbers of the rural population. Many farmers experienced difficulty in meeting their rent demands, and some were obliged to surrender their leases.[6] The possibility of eviction probably led the poorer wool-growing tenants to accept whatever price was offered for their wool. But many larger growers, it was alleged, held back their clips in the hope that prices would rise.[7] From such stockpiling tactics, two results were likely to follow: the market for wool would continue to be glutted for some time, irrespective of an increase in demand; and a definite recovery in the price of wool would be made more remote.[8]

northern woolfells from Newcastle — an authority which had been obtained in 1618, and which was subsequently withdrawn by proclamation in 1621 (*A.P.C. Jan. 1618–June 1619*, pp. 122, 136–7). For the debates on this Bill see *H. of C. Journals*, i, 582, 628, 653–4; *Commons Debates 1621*, ii, 396; ibid., iv, 275, 378–80; ibid., vi, 213.

[1] *H. of C. Journals*, i, 658; *Commons Debates, 1621*, ii, 499. This Bill contained the provision that 'the Lords of Parliament to be tried by their peers'.

[2] Between 1624 and 1629 four Bills to prohibit the exportation of wool and woolfells etc., were introduced into the Commons (*H. of C. Journals*, i, 676, 678, 769, 772, 812, 818, 820, 824, 835, 838, 927, 929, 931). Two of these were passed by the Lower House: one on the 26th April, 1624, and the other on the 18th March, 1626.

[3] Proclamations were issued in 1621, 1622, 1632 and 1656 (*Tudor and Stuart Proclamations*, 1314, 1334, 1651, 3075), and an Ordinance against the export of wool was made on the 19th January, 1648 (*Acts and Ordinances of the Interregnum*, i, 1059).

[4] Fisher, *Econ. Hist. Rev.* 2nd ser. iii (1950), 153.

[5] See B.M. Add. MS. 34324, fol. 26.

[6] W. R. Scott, *Joint Stock Companies to 1720* (Cambridge, 1910), i, 170; P.R.O. S.P. 14/131/29.

[7] P.R.O. Sackville MS. Old No. 4881; S.P. 14/127/103; S.P. 16/21/66.

[8] See B.M. Add. MS. 34324, fol. 26; ibid., 34217, fol. 14.

The policy of withholding wool from the market was condemned by the Lords of the Privy Council. In February, 1622, the Justices of the Peace of the ten chief cloth-manufacturing counties were informed by the Council:

> . . . and for the incouragement of the cloathier wee lett you knowe that wee will by no meanes indure that the wooll growers shall ingrosse their woolls and keepe them in their hands, two, three or more years togither to increase the price thereof . . . but that they moderate their demands according to the changes of the markett.[1]

There was, however, another side to the picture as the J.P.'s of Oxfordshire pointed out:

> . . . wee have likewise inquyred of the clothiers and by other the best meanes we could of such as ingrosse woolles of which sorte we knowe none. But wee rather heare that many who have wooll at this present to sell would very willingly parte with the same, could they have chapmen at reasonable prises.[2]

This, indeed, was the crux of the matter, as the Lords of the Privy Council were themselves aware; and their command that wool growers should moderate their demands, was shortly afterwards followed by the issue of instructions to a newly appointed Commission for Trade that some means should be found to raise wools 'to their former price and estimation'.[3]

Previous to this, however, the Council had appointed a Committee to investigate the reasons for the decay in the cloth trade.[4] The clothiers who were called before the Committee, ventured many opinions as to the causes of the depression and suggested numerous remedies.[5] Perhaps, inevitably, they made adverse comments upon the subject of the wool-middlemen's activities; but these were made without great emphasis.[6] Ranked much higher by the clothiers as a cause of the depression was the increase in the manufacture of textiles abroad, which, they claimed, was much facilitated by the illicit transportation of wool and other raw materials from Britain. The only way of preventing this, they argued, was to prohibit the exportation of wool and other cloth-manufacturing materials

[1] P.R.O. S.P. 14/127/76; *A.P.C. July 1621–May 1623*, pp. 131–3.
[2] P.R.O. S.P. 14/128/20.　　　[3] P.R.O. S.P. 14/133/29.
[4] *A.P.C. July 1621–May 1623*, pp. 201–2.
[5] B.M. Stowe MS. 354, fols. 63–5.　　　[6] B.M. Galba MS. E. I. fol. 390.

o

under the severest penalties; to take steps so that the wools of Scotland as well as of Ireland and Wales would be exported only to England; and to prohibit the port-to-port trade in wool, except from the Isle of Wight and the Isle of Man to the English mainland.

Another grievance voiced by the clothiers concerned the limitation to privileged Companies of the export trade in English cloth. As a cure, they suggested that liberty to export cloth should be allowed to all English merchants, or, failing that, to the Merchants of the Staple.[1] A Bill for this purpose had already been introduced into the Commons,[2] but had not succeeded in completing all the necessary stages when Parliament had been dissolved.

The substance of most of the proposals made by the clothiers was subscribed to by the Committee in their report to the Council. The depression, they declared, had been brought about by many causes: the false and deceitful making, dyeing and dressing of English cloth; the impositions upon cloth which raised its price to the foreign buyer; the wars in Germany; the mingling of wools and the enhancing of their prices by wool middlemen; the restrictive policies of merchants who were privileged to export cloth; the scarcity of coin; and the increased home consumption of foreign manufactured silks and stuffs. All these reasons were produced, but, stated the Committee, 'the chiefe cause that lesse quantity of our cloth is vented . . . is the making of cloth and other draperies in forreigne partes in more aboundaunce then in former times, beinge therevnto chiefly inhabled by the woolles' and other materials 'transported from England, Scotland and Ireland'. It was therefore urged that severe penalties should be imposed upon any persons who transported wool or connived in its transportation, and that orders should be issued forbidding Spanish or Turkish wool to be shipped to the Low Countries or to Germany either in English bottoms or by Englishmen serving in foreign bottoms.[3]

The Committee's report was followed at the end of July by

---

[1] B.M. Stowe MS. 354, fols. 63–5.

[2] The Bill was introduced on 26th April, 1621. For the debates on it, see *H. of C. Journals*, i, 592, 612, 630; *Commons Debates, 1621*, ii, 443; ibid., iv, 316; ibid., v, 221; ibid., vi, 195. See also ibid., vii, 226–38; B.M. Harl. MS. 7617, fol. 87.

[3] B.M. Galba MS. E. I. fols. 390–1; B.M. Stowe MS. 554, fol. 45 et seq.

the issue of a proclamation. This prohibited the export of wool, woolfells, yarn, fuller's earth and wood ashes upon pain of Star Chamber, and forbade any customs officer to certify wool as being landed without making adequate verification of the fact.[1] The proclamation made no mention of the port-to-port trade in wool, however; and although demands continued to be made that wool should be conveyed only by land carriage,[2] these, too, were unsuccessful.

Further investigation of the matters which had been complained of was entrusted into the hands of a Commission for Trade. The proceedings of this body were prolonged over a considerable period. But eventually, as a result of the Commissioners' recommendations, the Staple Company gained a precarious footing in the cloth export trade.[3] Not that the majority of Staplers took advantage of this opportunity, most of the merchants still preferring to conduct their home trade in wool.[4]

Of more interest than this, however, are the first few articles of inquiry which were supplied to the Commissioners. These set out the government's policy for the wool trade: wool was to be raised to its former price; the prohibition placed upon its export was to be rigorously enforced; all unmanufactured Irish and Scottish wools were to be brought into England and sold there at 'reasonable' prices; and a glut of wool was to be prevented. These were to be the means whereby, it was hoped, prosperity would return to the English cloth industry and a favourable balance of trade would be secured.[5]

These conclusions rested mainly upon the assumption that continental manufacturers found it difficult to dispense with British wool. The argument was that in order to achieve a

---

[1] *Tudor and Stuart Proclamations*, 1334. The proclamation also ordered that blacks and mournings at funerals should be made of English cloth.

[2] P.R.O. S.P. 14/135/26; B.M. Add. MS. 34324, fol. 25; B.M. Harl. MS. 7617, fol. 88.

[3] The Staplers were given authority by the Privy Council to export dyed and dressed cloths, kersies, dozens and new draperies (*A.P.C. June 1623–March 1625*, pp. 268–9). The white cloth trade, however, was still reserved to the Merchant Adventurers. A resolution to this effect was passed in the 1624 Parliament (*H. of C. Journals*, i, 780); and several Bills on the matter were introduced into the Commons in 1624 and 1625 (ibid., i, 698, 728, 836). The Staplers' exports of textiles were soon interfered with, and the merchants enlisted the aid of the Council (*A.P.C. March 1625–May 1626*, p. 32).

[4] B.M. Add. MS. 43849, fol. 9.

[5] P.R.O. S.P. 14/133/29; S.P. 14/135/52, 53.

favourable balance of trade, a significant increase should be made in the value of exports or, what was much the same thing, in the value of cloth exports; that an increase in exports, however, was largely dependent upon the extent and nature of foreign competition; but that as British wool supposedly possessed unique and valuable properties,[1] this competition could be considerably reduced by prohibiting the exportation of the raw material. Thus, providing that the prohibition was effective — and to be effective, all surplus Scottish and Irish wool would have to be imported — the way would lie open for an expansion in English cloth exports. From this last assumption, and from the platitude that the value of wool was increased by its manufacture into cloth, it was further argued that the greater the amount of wool which was imported from Scotland and Ireland, the greater would be the volume of English exports and the more favourable the balance of trade. But, the argument continued, the extent of this balance would vary with the price of cloth; therefore, as high wool prices would enhance the value of each cloth exported, whereas low wool prices and a glut of wool would make cloth cheap — besides giving a motive for transportation and lowering the value of land — it was better that the price of wool should be high rather than low.[2]

The central issue in the wool trade had thus changed. From the depression of the mid-sixteenth century to the depths of the more serious depression of the 1620's, the government had acted upon the view that the price of wool should be low; but now, having discarded this view, its chief endeavours in the future were to be directed at preventing its export.

III

The belief that English wool was indispensable abroad was responsible for the long series of government measures against

[1] It was said: 'in Spaine ther woll is fyne and will not make Cloth it doth thicken so fast. They with spending on[e] todd of theirs do spend three todds of ours. France, ther wooll is exceeding hungrye and will not clothe, but with one Todd of our wooll they spend three Todds of ther owne. . . . In like manner all the East Countryes, ther wooll is a hungry course woll not fitt to make any fine or good Cloth' (B.M. Harl. MS. 6806, fols. 243–4). For an examination of this view, see infra, pp. 212–14.

[2] B.M. Add. MS. 34217, fol. 14; ibid., 34324, fol. 25; B.M. Harl. MS. 6806, fols. 243–4; ibid., 7617, fol. 87; P.R.O. S.P. 14/127/19(i); S.P. 14/133/29, 35; S.P. 14/135/52, 53.

its export.[1] It was treated as axiomatic by the English manufacturing classes that foreign competition could be extinguished
by refusing to supply other countries with raw material; and for
over 200 years the clamour that they raised succeeded in denying the native wool growers a legal market for their produce
abroad. But despite the extravagant precautions that were
taken to prevent the exportation of wool to the continent, the
English cloth trade continued to remain generally depressed
and foreign competition showed no sign of abating. To the
English clothing interests the obvious explanation was that there
was a large-scale and illegal traffic in wool between Britain and
the continent; and this belief was propagated by a continuous
stream of pamphlet literature which described the owlers'[2]
trade in vivid and imaginative detail.

According to contemporary accounts, most English wool was
smuggled to the continent via two main channels: from the
south-east coast and from Scotland.[3] The former, in particular,
was shown by pamphleteers to be a smugglers' paradise:

> First in Romney Marsh in Kent, where the greatest part of
> rough wool is exported from England, put aboard French
> shallops by night, ten or twenty men well armed to guard it: some
> other parts there are, as in Sussex, Hampshire and Essex, the same
> methods may be used but not so conveniently. The same for
> combed wool from Canterbury: they will carry it ten or fifteen
> miles at night towards the sea with the like guard as before.[4]

The well-armed men were an indispensable part of the picture;
and they were featured in a proclamation of James II which
stated that 'this trade is carried on with armed companies of men,

---

[1] See infra, pp. 212–13.   [2] Wool smugglers were known as owlers.
[3] P.R.O. P.C. 2/54, fol. 155; *Cal. S.P. Dom. 1663–4*, p. 531; *1699–1700*, pp. 25,
62–3; *H. of C. Journals*, xii, 434; Hist. MSS. Comm. *House of Lords MSS.* N.S. v,
333; *England's Glory, by the Benefit of Wool Manufactured therein* (1669), p. 17. Until
the Union of 1707, England and Scotland pursued their own economic policies.
Scottish policy relating to wool was irresolute, the export being sometimes prohibited and sometimes allowed. But the prohibitions were usually little more than
nominal; and throughout the seventeenth century wool featured as one of the main
Scots exports (I. F. Grant, *The Economic History of Scotland* (1934), pp. 69, 75–6, 80–1,
177, 183–6, 189). Consequently, as large quantities of English wool were thought to
be smuggled across the border into Scotland and from thence exported to the
continent, the Scots were more than once urged that 'some course may be taken,
that no wools nor woolfells may be transported out of Scotland beyond the seas'
(*H. of C. Journals*, ii, 456). See also *A.P.C. 1616–17*, pp. 16, 25; P.R.O. S.P.
14/88/76; Friis, op. cit., p. 322.
[4] *England's Glory . . .* , p. 17.

who convey wool out of the kingdom, beat off customs officers and rescue goods seized by them'.[1]

It was alleged that, as a measure of precaution whilst the wool was afloat, it was sometimes pressed into packs with screws in order to give weight; after being covered over with white cloth these might then be passed for packs of cloth.[2] Another device was to press the wool into barrels, which were then washed over with brine-water in order that they might be taken for beef or herrings. 'These barrels are not put on board in ports where they are liable to be examined, but conveyed into creeks from whence they are shipped off.'[3] The suspected excessive transportation of wool was thought to be largely due to the use of such ingenious methods by the smugglers, as also to their desperate character. But negligence and corruption amongst customs officials and loopholes provided by the law were also held responsible.[4]

It would be of great interest to know the real extent of the leakage of British wool to the continent; but smuggled trade always defies any attempt at accurate analysis, and to accept the exaggerated estimates put forward by contemporaries would only be to beg the question. Although the trade may have been considerable, certain factors suggest that it was of proportions very much smaller than those generally supposed. The relatively low price of British wool throughout the greater part of the seventeenth century, for instance, may have provided an economic incentive to transport wool abroad, but it is also an indication of a glutted market at home: a state of affairs difficult to reconcile with the contemporary view that there was an excessive amount of wool exported. Furthermore, even though British wool may have been lower in price than that of Spain or France, it is doubtful whether the difference in price was often such as to allow exporters a very wide margin of profit on their enterprise once the costs and hazards of transportation had been taken into account. Long-staple wool may have been in great demand overseas where it was comparatively scarce, but no continental manufacturer was going to pay such an exorbitant

---

[1] *Tudor and Stuart Proclamations*, 3863 (1688).
[2] *Cal. S.P. Dom. 1671*, p. 421; *Statutes of the Realm*, 14 Charles II, c. 18.
[3] Lipson, op. cit., iii, 24.
[4] *Cal. S.P. Dom. 1677–8*, p. 71; *Tudor and Stuart Proclamations*, 1651 (1632); *H. of C. Journals*, xiii, 783; Hist. MSS. Comm. *Ormonde MSS.* ii, 268.

price for the raw material that it left him unable to compete on reasonable terms with his rival across the channel. Perhaps, most significant of all, was the apparent lack of success which attended the government's endeavours to catch the smugglers about their business. In 1664 the customs officers of Dover proudly boasted that, in pursuance of the proclamation of September, 1660,[1] they had 'prosecuted more offences in export of wool than the whole nation besides, the forfeitures being above £1800':[2] a truly trifling amount, were the export of wool as great as was commonly supposed. Even the appointment of ships in 1698, 'constantly to cruise on the coasts of England and Ireland' failed to achieve any spectacular results. Two years later the Admiralty reported that they had not taken a single vessel, while the cost involved amounted to £2,400 a month.[3]

IV

Whatever the truth of the matter, however, contemporaries were firmly convinced that huge quantities of British wool were used to feed the continental industry; and a ceaseless agitation was carried on by the clothing interests for the government to provide some effective remedy. The proclamations against the exportation of wool issued by James I[4] were repeated by Charles I and Cromwell[5] and embodied in an Act of Parliament at the Restoration.[6] But the matter did not rest there, and during the next forty years both Government and Parliament were kept busy devising fresh measures to prevent British wool from finding its way abroad.[7]

In the immediate post-Restoration years the apparent inability of the law to exercise any effective restraint upon the activities of illicit transporters led Parliament to review the penalties that were laid down for exporting wool. As early as 1621 these penalties had been criticized in the Commons as

---

[1] *Tudor and Stuart Proclamations*, 3256. [2] *Cal. S.P. Dom. 1664–5*, p. 153.
[3] *H. of L. Journals*, xvi, 569. See also *H. of C. Journals*, xiii, 426, 464.
[4] Supra, pp. 188, 190; *Tudor and Stuart Proclamations*, 1197 (1617).
[5] Supra, p. 190, n. 3. [6] *Statutes of the Realm*, 12 Charles II, c. 32.
[7] *Statutes of the Realm*, 14 Charles II, c. 18; 1 William and Mary, c. 32; 4 & 5 William and Mary, c. 24; 7 & 8 William III, c. 28; 9 & 10 William III, c. 40; 10 William III, c. 16; 11 William III, c. 13; *Tudor and Stuart Proclamations*, 3256 (1660), 3847 (1687), 3863 (1688), 3870 (1688), 4252 (1698).

being too mild, and it had then been proposed that wool smuggling should be made a felony.[1] It was not until 1662, however, that this suggestion was embodied in an Act of Parliament; and as a condition it was laid down that 'every Baron and other Peer of this Realm which shall be indicted or accused as principall or accessary in or to any offence made Felany by this Act shall have his . . . tryal by his . . . peeres as in cases of Felony att Common law'.[2] The sternness of the penalty seemed to make no great difference to the smugglers' trade, and in 1670 it was stated that only by making the exportation of wool a 'hanging' matter would the offence be effectively discouraged.[3] But the Parliament of 1696 took a different view, and in an Act of that year the severity of the penalty was modified in order to encourage the prosecution of offenders.[4]

Another clause of the 1662 Act forbade the carrying of wool by night, upon pain of forfeiture of the wool and horse. There was little to be said in favour of this Act, and much to be said against it; for its enforcement so hampered the legitimate carrying-trade that by the end of the century some manufacturers were wishing that it had never been passed.[5] Despite the 1662 Act, however, reports that large quantities of English wool were being exported to France from the Kentish coast continued to reach the government; and in 1669, in an endeavour to put an end to this alleged trade, two double shallops were sent to ply upon the south-east coast with orders to search all suspected vessels, and a troop of horse-guards was quartered in the vicinity of Canterbury.[6] Thereafter, naval and military support became a regular feature of the drive against the illicit transporter, some manufacturers and private persons fitting out sloops at their own expense for the purpose.[7]

Throughout the greater part of the seventeenth century the duty of preventing the exportation of wool was laid on the Commissioners of the Customs. But the ability and integrity of

---

[1] Supra, p. 189, n. 5.   [2] *Statutes of the Realm*, 14 Charles II, c. 18.
[3] *Cal. S.P. Dom. 1670*, p. 601.
[4] *Statutes of the Realm*, 7 & 8 William III, c. 28.
[5] J. Haynes, *A View of the Present State of the Clothing Trade in England* (1706), pp. 90–1; *H. of C. Journals*, xiii, 501.
[6] *Cal. S.P. Dom. 1668–9*, p. 556.
[7] Supra, p. 197; *Statutes of the Realm*, 7 & 8 William III, c. 28; 10 William III, c. 16; *H. of C. Journals*, xi, 594; ibid., xiii, 135, 165, 166, 857; *Cal. S.P. Dom. 1660–85*, p. 312; *1697*, p. 471.

these officials were widely questioned,[1] and even early in the century it had been proposed that special Commissioners for Wool should be appointed.[2] In 1628, Parliament had opposed the appointment of new officials on the ground that it might 'open a way for robbers and house breakers pretending the like power'.[3] The issue continued to be raised in the years that followed,[4] but it was not until June, 1688, that the Commission was granted; two months later a proclamation issued by James II made a request for voluntary contributions to assist the project.[5] After the Revolution fresh legislation was enacted, and the Commissioners' position was ratified.[6]

However good the scheme might have seemed in theory, in practice it failed to achieve all that was desired of it. Perhaps that was only to be expected. For the government made no provision for the salaries and expenses of the deputies whom the Commissioners appointed; and any hopes which there might have been that these agents would be able to maintain themselves solely out of their share of the fines imposed upon offenders were soon disillusioned. When wool officers were settled in all the maritime and northern counties in 1698 it was at the Commissioners' own expense: the agents engaging 'themselves in the said Service, without any Salaries, in hopes their good works would recommend them to future consideration'.[7] Some payment was made to the wool officers appointed along the coasts of Kent and Sussex;[8] but as for the remainder, it was reported in 1702 that 'they have withdrawn themselves having no allowance for such their Service'.[9] Petitions to the Commons from the clothing interests urged that wool officers should be given adequate financial encouragement:[10] the merchants and manufacturers of Wakefield suggesting that 'such agents and officers may have Salaries settled on them, out of a small tax to

[1] Supra, p. 196.
[2] *Commons Debates, 1621*, vii, 253.
[3] *Cal. S.P. Dom. 1625–49*, p. 309.
[4] Ibid., *1664–5*, pp. 64, 69; *1665–6*, p. 150; *1677–8*, pp. 241, 245; *1683*, p. 92.
[5] *Tudor and Stuart Proclamations*, 3870.
[6] *Statutes of the Realm*, 1 William and Mary, c. 32. The Commissioners appointed are named in the Act.
[7] *H. of C. Journals*, xiii, 41.
[8] Ibid., xiii, 847; ibid., xiv, 117. See also Hist. MSS. Comm. *House of Lords MSS.* N.S. v, 333.
[9] *H. of C. Journals*, xiii, 857.
[10] Ibid., xii, 512–13; ibid., xiii, 777, 857; ibid., xiv, 117.

be raised on wool'.[1] But the actions of wool agents were not popular, even among manufacturers. From many parts of the country came complaints, made by Staplers, fellmongers, manufacturers and wool growers, of agents misusing their authority. Much wool was stated to be seized by them, often under the pretence of being carried at unlawful hours, and large sums of money extorted for its continued passage;[2] and in March, 1702, a Committee of the Commons after investigating these charges found that 'several of the officers employed have been guilty of many corrupt and indirect practices to the great oppression and discouragement of the manufacturers of wool'.[3]

In its endeavours to prevent the transportation of wool abroad the government apparently received little assistance from the municipal authorities most directly concerned, and an attempt to awaken local officials to their national responsibilities was made by legislation enacted in 1696.[4] The clause in the Act of 1662 which had made the exportation of wool a felony was repealed. In its place a penalty was laid down of forfeiture of wool and ship, plus their treble value and treble the costs of prosecution. The 1696 Act continued:

> And the Inhabitantes of the respective Hundred Port or Place exempt next adjoyning to the . . . Kingdom of Scotland or to the Sea Coastes out of or through which any wooll shall be so carried or exported shall forfeit £20 if the said wooll exported shall be under £10 in value, but if it shall be of greater value then Treble the value thereof as also Treble Costs of Suit.[5]

These forfeitures were to be received by the informers, it being further laid down that the first three 'aiders' in the export of

[1] Ibid., xiii, 777. It had already been suggested in 1677 that one-quarter of the money received by the Governor of Ireland for licences to export Irish wool to England (see infra, pp. 205–6) should be used to pay officers to prevent the illicit exportation of English and Irish wool (*Cal. S.P. Dom. 1677–8*, pp. 241, 245). Proposals to lay a permanent tax upon wool were not new. For example, in 1588 it had been suggested to Lord Burghley that a yearly impost of 6d. per tod should be levied by Act of Parliament: the receipts to be used to buy corn for the relief of the poor and to increase the revenues of State (B.M. Lansd. MS. 58, fol. 99). For other tax proposals, see B.M. Stowe MS. 354, fol. 159; *Cal. S.P. Dom. 1702–3*, p. 518.

[2] *H. of C. Journals*, xiii, 246, 501, 570, 703, 720, 783–4; *Cal. S.P. 1702–3*, p. 520.

[3] *H. of C. Journals*, xiii, 783.

[4] *Statutes of the Realm*, 7 & 8 William III, c. 28.

[5] Ibid. Two years later it was enacted that 'the Hundred of Winchelsea in the Cinque Ports being divided by a Navigable Arm of the Sea so that the Inhabitants on the one side thereof cannot be privy to or prevent what is done by those on the other side . . . shall be deemed and taken in respect to the said Act as Two distinct Hundreds' (*Statutes of the Realm*, 9 & 10 William III, c. 40).

wool to prosecute informations against hundreds would themselves be exempted from prosecution.

Legislation passed in 1698[1] aimed at finding a solution to the difficulty of proving the intent to transport wool seized within near distance of the south-east coast and the borders of Scotland. It had already been suggested in 1669 that the owners of such wool should have the onus of proving that it was not being conveyed or intended for exportation;[2] but as much wool was grown in these areas and a legitimate wool trade carried on there, this proposal by itself had little to recommend it. The Act of 1698 therefore made allowance for these circumstances and ordered owners of wool shorn or housed within ten miles of the sea in Kent and Sussex to give an exact account of it in writing to the nearest port officer. Such wool was not to be moved towards the sea nor less than 15 miles inland, nor moved without notice being given of its removal. In each case the penalty laid down was the forfeiture of the wool and a fine of 3s. for every pound of its weight. A similar penalty was to be imposed upon owners of wool shorn and laid up within 15 miles of the borders of Scotland who failed to give an exact account of it to persons to be appointed in neighbouring ports and market towns for that purpose 'pursuant to the direction or true meaning' of the Act of 1688,[3] or who removed their wool without having obtained authority from these officials to do so. One-third of the penalty for offences was to go to the Crown and two-thirds to the informer. Finally, the 1698 Act extended the period in which prosecutions could be brought against illicit transporters from one year, as laid down by the Act of 1660, to three years after the offence.

The law forbidding the exportation of wool to Scotland became outdated by the Act of Union. The local registry of wool instituted in Kent and Sussex continued to operate, the

---

[1] Ibid.   [2] Hist. MSS. Comm. 7. *Eighth Report*, part i, p. 127.

[3] *Statutes of the Realm*, 1 William and Mary, c. 32. One clause of this Act laid down that wool carried to the sea-coast for shipment from port to port within the kingdom should be entered at the port of departure before being transported to within five miles of the coast. Owners of wool shorn within five miles of the coast were ordered to supply customs officers of the nearest port, not later than ten days after the shearing, with a written certificate of the number of fleeces shorn and where they were housed; they were further ordered not to remove their wool without certifying port officers at least three days in advance. Port officers were instructed to keep these certificates and to make a register of them.

Commissioners for Trade and Plantations claiming in 1702 that by the active enforcement of the law 'this unlawful trade is almost destroyed in those counties'.[1] A proposal that there should be 'a true and perfect register kept of all mens wools yearly growen within ye kingdome, to whom they are sould and what becomes of them', had been made early in the seventeenth century;[2] and following the institution of the local scheme in Kent and Sussex many demands were made for the establishment of a national system of official registers.[3] But no machinery was ever instituted for the purpose, it being held that the scheme would be very expensive to operate and would involve a 'multiplicity of accounts'.[4]

Besides those expedients actually adopted, there were numerous other proposals put forward for preventing the exportation of wool abroad.[5] Of these, perhaps the most interesting was a suggestion made in 1734 'for the Parliament to buy all the wool and yarn' of England and Ireland, and to 'sell it again at a proper price'.[6] The measure most persistently advocated, however, was the prohibition of the carriage of wool from port to port and down navigable rivers near the sea. It was urged that the greater part of the country's wool supply was conveyed by land carriage, which, though somewhat dearer than water carriage, afforded much less opportunity for illicit transportation.[7] Nevertheless, the coastal trade in wool was very considerable and, as had been demonstrated during the reign of James I,[8] not all manufacturers were in favour of its prohibition. Thus, while the government was prepared to interfere ill-advisedly with the port-to-port trade in fuller's earth,[9] the trade in wool was allowed to continue providing that

[1] Lipson, op. cit., iii, 27, n. 1. See also Hist. MSS. Comm. *House of Lords MSS.* N.S. v, 333–4.
[2] P.R.O. S.P. 16/44/38.
[3] *H. of C. Journals*, xii, 516, 518; ibid., xiii, 784; *Cal. S.P. Dom. 1702–3*, p. 518; J. Haynes, *A View of the Present State of the Clothing Trade in England*, p. 68; Lipson, op. cit., iii, 26–7.
[4] This was the opinion expressed by the Commissioners for Trade and Plantations in 1732. The registry in Kent and Sussex alone was said to cost the government £6,000 a year to maintain (Lipson, op. cit., iii, 27).
[5] See, for example, *Cal. S.P. Dom. 1668–9*, p. 5; *1670*, p. 8, *1671–2*, p. 155.
[6] Hist. MSS. Comm. *Egmont MSS.* iii, part ii, 28.
[7] Supra, pp. 191–2; *H. of C. Journals*, xiii, 784; ibid., xiv, 117; J. Haynes, *A View of the Present State of the Clothing Trade in England*, pp. 65–6.
[8] Supra, pp. 188–9.
[9] *Tudor and Stuart Proclamations*, 1802; *Cal. S.P. Dom. 1639*, p. 379.

ample security was taken for the safe delivery of the wool at a
port within the kingdom.[1]

v

While measures were being taken to prevent the exportation of
wool from England, attempts continued to be made to regulate
the trade in wool from Ireland. Having decided in the summer
of 1616 that a series of staple towns in Ireland and England
would best serve to prevent the transportation of Irish wool to
the continent, the Privy Council had proceeded to the appointment of Commissioners to investigate the matter.[2] By March,
1617, staple towns had been nominated and the project had
assumed definite shape.

The English ports chosen were London, Bristol, Chester,
Barnstaple, Liverpool and Milford.[3] These were to be the
receiving centres from the staple towns of Ireland 'without any
other novelty'. For Ireland, a selection was finally made of
Dublin, Drogheda, Cork, Limerick, Galway, Carrickfergus,
Londonderry and Youghal.[4] From these ports and no other was
wool to be shipped. Several of the Irish towns had been the
possessors of staple rights since medieval times, and they
objected to the conditions which the Privy Council wished to
impose as part of the new system. In particular, they refused at
first to acquiesce in the proposal that they should relinquish all
their rights to customs and forfeitures to which they were
entitled by the statutes of Elizabeth dealing with the exportation
of Irish wool.[5]

The Council's order that new charters should be obtained
before staple privileges could be exercised was another feature
to which the majority of the selected Irish towns objected; and
they refused to conform with the order on the ground that the
cost of going to London was too great. In consequence, they
were unable to export wool to England, and some merchant
exporters were put to the unnecessary expense of having to
carry their wool to Youghal — the only town apparently

---

[1] Supra, pp. 188–9; T. S. Willan, *The English Coasting Trade, 1600–1750*, pp.
4–7.
[2] G. O'Brien, 'The Irish Staple Organisation in the Reign of James I', *Economic
History* (1926), 46–8.
[3] *A.P.C. 1616–17*, p. 211.   [4] O'Brien, op. cit., p. 51.
[5] Ibid., p. 48; *A.P.C. 1616–17*, p. 195.

possessed of a charter.[1] The Lords of the Privy Council were consequently forced to climb down for a time on this issue; and at the beginning of December, 1617, they wrote to the Lord Deputy of Ireland giving permission for Irish wool to be provisionally exported from any of those ports which had been nominated as staple towns.[2]

As in England at this time, the conduct of the Irish wool trade was entrusted into the hands of a number of select merchants. Although known as staplers, the Irish merchants were neither members of the English Staplers' Company nor subject to the government of a single corporation as were their English counterparts. In Ireland, each staple town had an organization which was a distinct corporation with an individuality of its own.[3] On payment of the necessary fine for admission to one of these corporations, the merchants of a staple town were permitted to buy wool for export, but no one else was allowed to participate in the trade.[4]

By 1619 this restriction had become a cause of general complaint. The Irish landlords and wool growers, in particular, felt aggrieved by the new system. Their views were shared by the Lord President and members of the Council of Munster — themselves prominent landowners — and were addressed in the summer of 1619 to the government in Dublin. The case put forward was that the new regulations were making it impossible for the tenantry to pay their rents; that the market for wool was not as free or as convenient for sellers and native manufacturers as formerly; that the Irish staplers and their factors engrossed wool and transported it to England and foreign parts; that the wool growers were forced to sell it at unreasonable prices; and that because of these low prices, men either transported their wool abroad or 'let theire pastures for plowing and arable at easie rates and bring their English shepe back againe into England'. These and other complaints were forwarded by the Lord Deputy and Council to London. With them went a covering letter wherein the Irish Council expressed the opinion that the staple system had been 'discovered to be full of fraud and inconvenience', and they therefore recommended that some

---

[1] O'Brien, op. cit., p. 51; *A.P.C. July 1619–June 1621*, p. 158.
[2] *A.P.C. 1616–17*, p. 398.
[3] O'Brien, op. cit., p. 56. This had been the case in the Middle Ages.
[4] *A.P.C. 1616–17*, p. 211; *July 1619–June 1621*, p. 116.

different course should be pursued.[1] On receipt of this communication, the Privy Council proceeded to the appointment of Commissioners with powers of investigation.[2]

As the instructions to the Commissioners suggest, the Privy Council viewed the Irish wool trade as raising two distinct problems. First, and most important, was the need to ensure that Irish wool did not find its way to the continent. Second, there was the need for the trade to be organized in such a way that the Irish wool interests suffered a minimum of damage. After numerous hearings of the matter, the Council remained convinced that the most effective method of achieving the former end was by maintaining the machinery of the staple towns; and in order that this should work smoothly it was again decided to urge that the selected Irish towns should sue for their charters. The Council hoped that the second objective would be achieved if admission to the Irish staplers' organizations were thrown open, free of charge, to any trader who wished to join. In March, 1620, these decisions were accordingly communicated to the Lord Deputy and Council of Ireland with instructions that other staple towns should be appointed if those nominated still proved recalcitrant over obtaining their charters.[3] Apparently some of the selected Irish towns still remained obstinate, for shortly afterwards patents conferring staple privileges were granted to New Ross, Kinsale and Clare Ennis.[4]

VI

By 1620 the Irish staple system was showing signs of breaking down and by 1633 it had become obsolete.[5] In the latter year Strafford, newly appointed Lord Deputy of Ireland, wrote to the King stating:

> to entrust the exportation in the hands of the merchant staplers is a remedy worse than the disease . . . ; their charter is forfeited by non-usance, and shall never be renewed unto them again by my advice, it being a corporation newly set up by the device of my Lord Grandison, only, as they say here, to put some crowns in his purse.[6]

[1] B.M. Add. MS. 34324, fols. 23–4; O'Brien, op. cit., pp. 49–50.
[2] *A.P.C. July 1619–June 1621*, pp. 115–16. See also ibid., pp. 252–3, 265.
[3] *A.P.C. July 1619–June 1621*, pp. 157–8.   [4] O'Brien, op. cit., p. 51.
[5] Ibid., pp. 51–2.   [6] Ibid., p. 52.

In place of the staple system Strafford advocated that licences should be granted for the transportation of Irish wool to England. This, he argued, was to be desired for three reasons: first, it would benefit the customs, as the wool would pay duty four times if transported raw to England and brought back in the form of cloth; second, it would increase the exportation of wool, there being no means of working it up in Ireland; and third, it would assist the English clothing manufacture. King Charles's answer to the request was a grant of the right 'to give licences for transportation of wools out of Ireland into England only, with restraint of the staplers'.[1]

Thus in 1633 the licence system took the place of the staple system in regulating the exportation of Irish wool to England. And for the Chief Governors of Ireland a very profitable system it turned out to be. Strafford had estimated the profit to be gained from the sale of licences at some three or four hundred pounds a year.[2] This may have been a reasonable estimate at the time it was made; but as the export of Irish wool to England increased, so the receipts for licences rose. Between Michaelmas, 1678, and Michaelmas, 1681, these averaged over £3,500 a year;[3] and this figure must have shown a substantial increase by the end of the century when, it seems, the system was discontinued in favour of duty-free export.[4] In view of the profit to be made from such licences it was perhaps not surprising that some Englishmen were willing to believe the Chief Governor of Ireland guilty of giving licences collusively for the illicit transportation of Irish wool.[5]

Licences to export Irish wool to England were easy enough to obtain. They cost 4d. for every stone of wool licensed, plus an additional charge of between 10 and 20 per cent. of the prime cost. The former sum was received by the Chief Governor, the latter by his secretary. In 1678, the Duke of Ormonde estimated that for every £1,000 which he received for wool licences, his secretary received £100, and his secretary's clerk £5.[6] At this date a licence to export 1,000 stones of Irish wool cost £20, while a licence to export 200 stones cost £4.[7]

[1] Ibid.   [2] Ibid.
[3] Hist. MSS. Comm. *Ormonde MSS.* N.S. iv, 676.
[4] See *H. of C. Journals*, xiii, 159.   [5] Hist. MSS. Comm. *Ormonde MSS.* ii, 269.
[6] Ibid. See also ibid., N.S. v, 161; *Cal. S.P. Dom. 1673–5*, p. 172; *1677–8*, pp. 241, 245.
[7] Hist. MSS. Comm. *Ormonde MSS.* N.S. iv, 665 et seq.

Both Irish and English merchants transported the wool to England. The small exporters, who took freight for only four or five bags of wool at a time, frequently saved themselves the cost and trouble of taking out a separate licence for the small amounts which they exported, by endorsing licences taken out in the names of the more important exporters or in the name of the Clerk of the Custom House. As part-owners of vessels the larger merchants found the practice to be a profitable one, and they readily gave security for the true landing of the wool in England.[1]

Licences to export Irish wool amounted in effect to an export duty; and during the first half of the seventeenth century an import duty of 6d. per stone was also levied.[2] But in 1652, clothiers from the five northern English counties, where much Irish and some Scottish wool was used, petitioned the House of Commons asking that 'all wools whatsoever, which shall be brought into England, be Excise-free', and their request was granted.[3]

Though the licence system replaced the staple system in regulating the exportation of wool from Ireland, the trade was not allowed to continue after 1633 without some restriction as to the ports of departure and import. But between 1641 and 1678 the number of ports selected was so large that this limitation was of little practical consequence. By a proclamation issued in the former year,[4] twenty-five Irish ports were authorized to transport wool to England, while the English ports named were London, Bristol, Chester, Barnstaple, Liverpool, Milford, Exeter, Southampton, Plymouth and Minehead: an addition of the last four.[5] Between 1678 and 1688 only eleven or twelve of the chief ports in Ireland were allowed to export wool,[6] and by the Act of 1688[7] their number was further reduced to six. These were Dublin, Waterford, Youghal, Kinsale, Cork and Drogheda. At the same time the number of English ports was reduced to seven — Liverpool, Chester, Bristol, Minehead, Barnstaple, Bideford and Exeter — which, with the exception of Exeter,

---

[1] Ibid., N.S. v, 161–3. [2] *Tudor and Stuart Proclamations*, Ire. 338.
[3] *H. of C. Journals*, vii, 123. Spanish wool had formerly paid a duty of 12d. in the pound (*Cal. S.P. Dom. 1652–3*, p. 90).
[4] *Tudor and Stuart Proclamations*, Ire. 338. [5] See supra, p. 203.
[6] *Tudor and Stuart Proclamations*, Ire. 882 (1678), Ire. 932 (1684).
[7] *Statutes of the Realm*, 1 William and Mary, c. 32.

P

were all situated on the west coast away from the English Channel and a straight passage to the continent. Exeter's position was precarious, and in 1693 the fear that Irish wool would be run across to France once Land's End had been rounded led Parliament to close the port to this import.[1] The move was not at all popular with the merchants of Exeter, and for many years they agitated strongly against it.[2] But despite their numerous petitions, it was not until 1753 that the port was again opened to receive Irish wool, and even then none ever came in.[3] Before the end of the seventeenth century further alterations were made to the list of importing centres. In 1696, Bridgwater was authorized to import Irish wool 'for the furnishing of the clothiers in those parts of Somerset'[4] and the same Act of Parliament[5] conferred a similar privilege upon Whitehaven. Two years later Whitehaven's name was deleted from the list and replaced by that of Milford Haven.[6] But the latter port was not well situated to take part in the trade, and no advantage appears to have been taken of the permission to ship there.

Besides directing the trade in Irish wool to ports specially selected so as to minimize the chances of illicit transportation, the English government took other measures to prevent the smuggling of wool from Ireland. The procedure instituted early in the century,[7] of taking security of double the value of the wool exported and of returning certificates of landing, continued to be used;[8] and as the official machinery appeared to be incapable of dealing with offenders, the prosecution of forfeited bonds was sometimes placed in the hands of private individuals.[9] Towards the end of the century licensed exporters came under strong suspicion of shipping their wool elsewhere than to England; and in 1678 and 1684 the customs officers in Ireland were instructed to furnish reports on wool exported, and remaining to be exported, under recently granted licences.[10] The Act of 1696[11]

---

[1] Ibid., 4 & 5 William and Mary, c. 24.
[2] Hist. MSS. Comm. *House of Lords MSS.* N.S. ii, 247; *H. of C. Journals*, xii, 68.
[3] Hoskins, *Industry, Trade and People in Exeter*, p. 32.
[4] Hist. MSS. Comm. *House of Lords MSS.* N.S. ii, 194–5.
[5] *Statutes of the Realm*, 7 & 8 William III, c. 28.
[6] Ibid., 10 William III, c. 16.   [7] Supra, p. 189.
[8] *Tudor and Stuart Proclamations*, Ire. 599 (1658), Ire. 932 (1684), Ire. 1177 (1690).
[9] *A.P.C. July 1619–June 1621*, pp. 252–3, 265; *Cal. S.P. Dom. 1661–2*, p. 58; *1676–7*, p. 272.
[10] *Tudor and Stuart Proclamations*, Ire. 882, Ire. 932.
[11] *Statutes of the Realm*, 7 & 8 William III, c. 28.

went much further. By it, the Commissioners of the Customs in Ireland were instructed to transmit every six months to their counterparts in England a true and very full account of 'all such Wooll as shall be from time to time exported from any of the Places within the said Kingdome of Ireland from whence the same may be exported . . . in order that the same may be compared with the Account by the said Act appointed to be kept by the Commissioners of the Customs of this Kingdome'.

Finally, the government endeavoured to apprehend the illicit transporter of Irish wool by appointing ships to cruise round the coasts of Ireland and by offering substantial rewards to informers. The customary division of the forfeitures gave half to the informer and half to the Crown.[1] In 1688 the informer's share of the penalties was raised to three-quarters of the fine.[2] By an Act passed in 1698[3] the informer's share was again laid down as one-half of the forfeitures. This was evidently considered to be insufficient, for two months later a proclamation[4] announced that 'besides the reward of half-forfeiture, 5s. a stone will be paid on all unlawfully exported wool, flocks or woollen yarn': a considerable reward, though perhaps somewhat less than that offered in 1688.

VII

Every effort was thus made to ensure that Irish wool was shipped only to England. In 1615 it had been understood that this export should continue only until such time as 'the manufacture of clothe be better setled' in Ireland.[5] But by 1698, with the Irish textile industry beginning to show signs of rivalling that of England, particularly in the manufacture of serges, this well-meant intention had been forgotten; and in an Act[6] which Arthur Young later described as 'one of the most infamous Statutes that ever disgraced a legislature',[7] the export of Irish wool textiles to any places beyond the sea excepting England and Wales was forbidden.

---

[1] *Tudor and Stuart Proclamations*, Ire. 882 (1678), Ire. 932 (1684).
[2] Ibid., Ire. 995.
[3] *Statutes of the Realm*, 10 William III, c. 16.
[4] *Tudor and Stuart Proclamations*, Ire. 1374.
[5] *A.P.C. 1615–16*, p. 243.
[6] *Statutes of the Realm*, 10 William III, c. 16.
[7] A. Young, *The Question of Wool Truly Stated* (1788), p. 21.

This Act was mainly the work of the merchants and manufacturers of the serge region in the south-west of England. Since the Restoration these classes had watched with increasing alarm the growth of the Irish manufacture, seeing in its development a serious threat to their foreign markets[1] and to their supplies of Irish raw material. But they were not alone in agitating for the suppression of the Irish manufacture; and they obtained considerable support from the manufacturers of East Anglia[2] and the gentlemen and freeholders of Devonshire.[3] In opposition were the Irish gentry and the merchants of London;[4] but against numerous opponents in Parliament and one of the fundamental economic principles of the day — that the purpose of the colonies was to supply the mother country with raw materials and not to emulate her in manufactures — they could not hope to succeed. The Bill for the 'Incouragement of the Woollen Manufactures in the Kingdom of England' became law, and thereafter the export of Irish wool textiles became subjected to the same sort of regulation as her export trade in wool.[5] But whereas woollen manufactures imported into England paid duties which amounted almost to a prohibition,[6] wool in its raw state was admitted duty-free.

If Ireland could not export her woollen manufactures she would have to export her wool instead; and despite the gloomy forebodings of the opponents of the 1698 Act[7] there was little doubt that most of that wool would be exported to England and

---

[1] It was said that with cheaper wool and cheaper spinning the Irish could produce serges of the same quality as Devonshire for 25 to 40 per cent. less and sell them readily in Germany and Holland (Hoskins, op. cit., pp. 33–4). See also Hist. MSS. Comm. *House of Lords MSS.* N.S. iii, 108–11; *H. of C. Journals*, x, 611; ibid., xii, 64, 79.

[2] Hist. MSS. Comm. *House of Lords MSS.* N.S. iii, 130–3, 367–8. At the same time as they were taking part in this agitation the Colchester manufacturers were also petitioning that Colchester should be made an importing centre for Irish wool (*H. of C. Journals*, xii, 79), but without success.

[3] Hist. MSS. Comm. *House of Lords MSS.* N.S. iii, 131–3.

[4] Ibid., N.S. iii, 107.

[5] The ports selected to ship and import Irish wool textiles were the same as those used for Irish wool. The penalties for smuggling in each case were laid down by the Act as: 'Goods and ships forfeited. And that every of the offenders therein shall likewise forfeit £500. . . . And the Masters and Mariners thereof and other persons knowing and assisting shall forfeit £40 of which one Moyety shall be to him that shall sue for the same . . . and the other Moyety thereof to the Encouragement of setting up the Linnen Manufactures in Ireland to be disposed of by the Court of Exchequer there for that Use only.'

[6] Hoskins, *Industry, Trade and People in Exeter*, p. 34.

[7] Ibid., Hist. MSS. Comm. *House of Lords MSS.* N.S. iii, 108.

not to Scotland or the continent. Other things being equal, an increase in the import of Irish wool into England would lead to a fall in English wool prices and rents; yet an Act which was likely to bring this very situation about was passed by a Parliament dominated by landed interests. Why? The answer seems to be that in the opinion of contemporaries other things were not equal. As they saw it, competition from Irish manufactures was reducing the demand for English cloth abroad: a process which, if allowed to continue, would 'inevitably sink the Value of Lands and tend to the ruine of the Trade and the Woollen Manufactures of this Realme';[1] English wool prices would fall and the 'poor increase beyond the power of maintaining them'.[2] Thus the retaining of Ireland simply as a source of raw material supply for the English industry, was thought to be in the interests of England's manufacturing and landed classes alike. Whether the latter did in fact gain more through the anticipated increase in the demand for English cloth abroad than they lost through the increase in the supply of Irish wool at home seems very doubtful.[3]

The motives which prompted English landlords to vote for the suppression of the Irish wool-textile industry are of particular interest because of their great similarity to the motives which led them to pass the long series of measures against the exportation of English and Irish wool. Here, too, the fear was of foreign competition creating trade depression. Advocates of a stricter prohibition of the export of wool told Parliament:

> ... such Exportation is a great prejudice to the Farmers of this Kingdom, not so much wool being wrought here, the price thereof is much fallen and kept under by reason Forreign Markets are supplied by manufactures made abroad;[4] ... the low price of ... Wool ... makes your Rents come in so slow, and some perhaps not at all, and brings all the Lands and Estates of the Kingdom concern'd therein to a far less value.[5]

[1] *Statutes of the Realm*, 10 William III, c. 16.
[2] Hist. MSS. Comm. *House of Lords MSS.* N.S. iii, 131–2.
[3] In 1702 it was stated in the House of Lords that 'the great additions that have been made to our stock of wool by importations from Ireland' was one of the major factors responsible for the fall in the price of English wool and woollen manufactures (Hist. MSS. Comm. *House of Lords MSS.* N.S. v, 70). See also *H. of C. Journals*, xiv, 466; ibid., xv, 503.
[4] *Reasons Presented to the Parliament for a more Strict Prohibition of the Transportation of Wool, on Behalf of the Traders and Manufacturers in Wool.*
[5] *The Present Case of Our English Wool and the Manufacture of it.*

Such arguments as these could be calculated to carry weight, not only with Parliament but with the country at large. That they were generally accepted, if at times reluctantly, is shown by the fact that at no time during the seventeenth century was there an agitation for the total repeal of the laws prohibiting the exportation of wool; and only during the second half of the century, when wool prices and rents were frequently depressed, was there any sort of agitation for a limited export.[1] Even then, no Bill was ever introduced into Parliament for the purpose. The only export that was allowed was for trifling amounts of wool for the benefit of manufacturers in the Channel Islands.[2]

VIII

The argument for prohibiting the exportation of wool rested on one fundamental proposition: that British wool was indispensable for the continental textile industries. It was frequently asserted that 'by means of one pack of English or Irish wool exported' our competitors were able to improve 'a double if not treble proportion of their own'.[3] Spanish wool was said to be fine, but so short that it would 'hardly hold working': it was unsuited for worsted stuffs, but when used with English or Irish wool it made 'excellent fine thin cloth'.[4] French, Flemish and East Country wools were variously described as coarse, hungry and hairy: without a mixture of British wool they could not be

[1] *Reasons for a Limited Exportation of Wool* (1677); *Cal. S.P. Dom. 1663–4*, p. 11; *1675*, pp. 375–6; *1677–8*, p. 37; P.R.O. S.P. 29/251/95(i). Substantial export duties were offered, but to no avail.

[2] Licences to export wool to the Channel Islands were granted throughout most of the seventeenth century. The first licence was granted in 1619 and was for the export of wool to Jersey only (*Cal. S.P. Dom. 1580–1625*, p. 667). Later licences authorized shipment to Guernsey, Alderney and Sark. The amounts of wool involved were small. For instance, an Act passed in Charles II's reign authorized a maximum yearly export to Jersey of 2,000 tods, to Guernsey of 1,000 tods, to Alderney of 200 tods, and to Sark of 100 tods (*Statutes of the Realm*, 21 Charles II, c. 32). These quantities were doubled in the reign of James II by a grant to Sir Edward Cartwright (*H. of C. Journals*, xii, 516). The export of combed wool was sometimes allowed; and all wool was sent under bond that it would not be transported abroad. The only other exception to the laws prohibiting the exportation of wool was made in 1642, when the House of Lords ordered 'that there shall be Liberty of Transportation of One Hundred and Fifty Pounds worth of White Wool, for the Use of The French King' (*H. of L. Journals*, v, 249).

[3] *Cal. S.P. Dom. 1677–8*, p. 69; *1675*, pp. 374–5; *H. of C. Journals*, i, 552; *Commons Debates 1621*, vii, 251; *England's Glory, by the Benefit of Wool Manufactured therein* (1669), p. 4.

[4] *Reasons Presented to the Parliament for a more Strict Prohibition of the Transportation of Wool, on Behalf of the Traders and Manufacturers in Wool; Cal. S.P. Dom. 1675*, p. 374.

manufactured into a good 'vendible cloth or stuff'.[1] It therefore followed that foreign competition could be extinguished by refusing to supply other countries with raw material. The export of wool was forbidden; and when this failed to put an end to the woollen manufacture abroad the only explanation found acceptable was that an extensive smuggling trade was being carried on. It was unthinkable that continental industry could flourish independently of supplies of British raw material; yet this was indeed the case.

During the sixteenth century, far from finding English wool indispensable, continental manufacturers had replaced it with Spanish wool. The latter was cheaper and, by the end of the sixteenth century, finer[2] than that produced in England. The continental cloth industry found so little need for English wool in 1610 that it could be stated:

> The woolles of Spayne serve their owne contry all France and Italy and the Netherlandes, and our woolles not once asked after, except wee would suffer our sortes of woolles to passe, which maketh our bayes, sayes, and other stuffes of that nature.[3]

This, indeed, was the situation throughout the seventeenth century. As far as woollens were concerned, the continental manufacturers were perfectly capable of managing without British wool. Spanish wool had no superior for fineness, and to say that it needed a mixture of English wool to improve it was to contradict the evidence of industrial practice; for not only on the continent, but in England also, super-fine cloth was manufactured from Spanish wool alone.[4] Neither did continental manufacturers find it necessary to use English or Irish wool in the production of their inferior-quality woollens. Continental wools were mostly coarse, but not so coarse as to be incapable of manufacture into a saleable cloth;[5] moreover, if a mixture of some other wool were desired, there was no reason why low-grade Spanish wool should not serve the purpose. There was

---

[1] B.M. Harl. MS. 6806, fols. 243–4; Hist. MSS. Comm. *Egmont MSS.* iii, part i, 128; *Cal. S.P. Dom. 1675*, p. 374; *Reasons Presented to the Parliament.* . . .
[2] P. J. Bowden, *Econ. Hist. Rev.* 2nd ser. ix (1956), 48.
[3] B.M. Lansd. MS. 152, fol. 229.
[4] Hist. MSS. Comm. *House of Lords MSS.* N.S. v, 70; *Cal. S.P. Dom. 1650*, p. 21; J. Haynes, *A View of the Present State of the Clothing Trade in England* (1706), pp. 14–15.
[5] *Cal. S.P. Dom. 1650*, p. 21; E. Misselden, *The Circle of Commerce* (1623), p. 51.

more truth in the assertion that continental industry was unable
to dispense with British wool for the manufacture of worsted. In
the seventeenth century England and Ireland together accounted for the bulk of the world's supply of long-staple wool. A
limited amount of combing wool (*kamwool*) was also grown on
the continent, notably in North and South Holland, Brabant,
Friesland and Pomerania.[1] But English writers were seldom
prepared to admit that this was so, and when they did, it made
no difference to their basic argument: such wool was coarse, and
unless mixed with English or Irish wool it was 'fit only for the
coarsest sorts of goods'.

The view that British wool possessed unique and indispensable
qualities was not seriously challenged until the middle of the
eighteenth century,[2] and even then the export continued to be
prohibited until 1825. That Englishmen should have deluded
themselves for so long about the universal need for their wool
may be taken as a tribute to the great wool-stapling trade of the
Middle Ages and as an indication of the widespread ignorance
in England of the capabilities of continental wools. From such
ignorance many manufacturers were possibly not exempt: large
numbers of them may never have even seen foreign wools, let
alone worked with them. But manufacturers of Spanish cloth
and merchants with experience of continental industry were in
a position to dispel the myth about British wool, but wisely, they
refrained from doing so.

IX

The laws against the export of wool were designed for the
purpose of destroying foreign competition; in this they failed.
But they were not without effect in other directions. Through
them the price of wool in England was kept low and home
manufacturers abundantly supplied with cheap raw material.
Low wool prices were contrary to the declared policy of both
Government and Parliament, and several times during the
course of the seventeenth century measures were considered for
raising them.[3] But the conclusion which emerged was always

[1] C. Wilson, *Econ. Hist. Rev.* 2nd ser. xiii (1960), 214.
[2] By John Smith in his book, *Chronicon Rusticum-Commerciale or Memoirs of Wool* (1747).
[3] Supra, pp. 193–4; *Cal. S.P. Dom. 1629–31*, p. 147; *1635–6*, p. 302; *H. of C. Journals*, ii, 296; ibid., ix, 730, 733, 734.

the same: wool prices were low, not because of the laws prohibiting export, but because those laws were being continually broken. The official attitude had been clearly stated in 1621:

> Every M [i.e. thousand] todds of wooll sent thither [abroad] doth lose our kingdom of 4M Todds clothing, and the woll grewers the sale of 3M Todds, . . . and doth lose the maintenance of Five hundred people belonging unto the clothing of this one Thousand todds.[1]

It therefore followed that the prohibition of the export of wool was in the interests of landed and manufacturing classes alike; and from this assumption Parliament could not be moved, not even in the 1670's and 1680's when the price of wool — and of land[2] — became so low that some growers were led to agitate for a limited exportation.[3]

It was this alleged identity of interests between agriculture and industry that was largely responsible for the placidity with which the native wool growers accepted their confinement to the home market. Indeed, such agitation as they did raise during the seventeenth century was directed as much against the importation of wool from abroad as against the laws prohibiting its export.

As early as 1604 an abortive Bill to prohibit the import of all foreign wools was introduced into the Commons.[4] Though the native wool growers may have foreseen that Spanish wool would eventually replace the English raw material in the home manufacture of super-fine cloth, there is no evidence that this development was already in progress by 1604.[5] But by 1636 the Sheriff of Herefordshire had found cause to complain to the

---

[1] *Commons Debates, 1621*, vii, 250–1.

[2] In the 1670's complaints were made about 'the great abatements of rents and low value of lands' (*Treatise of Wool and Cattel*, p. 6; *Cal. S.P. Dom. 1675*, p. 376; *1677–8*, p. 37; B.M. Stowe MS. 210, fols. 43–6); and in 1685 it was alleged that the selling price of land had fallen by one-third during the preceding thirty or forty years (*A Treatise of Wool and the Manufacture of it*, p. 7).

[3] The request for a limited exportation of wool brought forth a number of replies from the clothing interests. See *The Proverb Crossed; A Discourse shewing That the Exportation of Wooll is destructive to this Kingdom; Reasons Presented to the Parliament . . .* ; *Cal. S.P. Dom. 1675*, pp. 373, 374; *1677–8*, pp. 69–70. These set out to show that the illicit transportation of wool 'is a principal cause of the growers vending it at so low a rate'; that 'its great cheapness does not arise from its being more than can be manufactured here but from want of a sufficient vent of it when manufactured'; and that a limited export 'though it may be for the profit of a few would unavoidably tend to take away the employment and maintenance of the poor'.

[4] *H. of C. Journals*, i, 181, 206.   [5] *Supra*, p. 47.

Privy Council that the importation of Spanish wool had impoverished the county, thus making the raising of 'ship money' very difficult;[1] and in 1642 the inhabitants of the county petitioned the House of Commons asking that the import should be restrained.[2] Nothing came of the petition however; and as the production of super-fine cloth increased, so the need for Spanish wool became greater. Before the end of the century wool growers in other parts of England found cause to complain. In 1675 the import of Spanish and other foreign wools was said to have reduced the amount of English wool used in the production of fine thin cloth to one-third of what it had been thirty years previously;[3] and in 1684 the Grand Jury of Somerset at their General Quarter Sessions submitted that the duty-free import of Spanish and other foreign wools 'is a very great prejudice to the price of English wool and so consequently contributes much to the Abatements of Rents and Profits issuing from Lands'.[4] But Spanish wool was essential to the English fine woollen industry, and despite the complaints of the native wool growers the import continued to grow.[5]

In the last few decades of the century the importation of Irish wool was another subject of complaint by the English wool growers.[6] But if the import of wool from Ireland increased, and the price of wool in England fell, the English landed interests were themselves partly to blame. Since early in the century they had argued that the importation of cattle from Ireland 'decayed' the breed of English cattle and depressed the value of land; and in 1667 an Act was passed forbidding the importation of cattle from Ireland or 'any other place beyond the seas'.[7] As a consequence, the production of wool in Ireland was stimulated, the Irish stocking 'their Pasture-grounde with sheep instead of great-Cattel, and those of the best breed of England'.[8] More and more Irish wool was thrown on the English market, and the situation was further aggravated at the end of the century by the suppression of the wool-textile industry in Ireland.[9] The import

---

[1] P.R.O. S.P. 16/346/6.   [2] *Tudor and Stuart Proclamations*, 2104.
[3] *Cal. S.P. Dom. 1675*, p. 376; *1677–8*, p. 37; *Treatise of Wool and Cattel*, p. 7.
[4] *A Treatise of Wool and the Manufacture of it*, p. 24.
[5] Hist. MSS. Comm. *House of Lords MSS.* N.S. v, 70.
[6] Supra, p. 211, n. 3; *Cal. S.P. Dom. 1677–8*, p. 37.
[7] Lipson, op. cit., iii, 198.
[8] *The Proverb Crossed*, pp. 23–4; *Cal. S.P. Dom. 1673–5*, pp. 168, 170.
[9] Supra, pp. 209–11.

of Irish wool into England was all the more resented by the English wool growers because of its low price. As early as 1674 it was pointed out that 'the Irish wool buyers . . . may gainfully undersell the English wool-sellers, whereby both the freeholders and tenants of England and Ireland, who are sheepmasters, visibly decay';[1] and a proposal was made for the formation of a company to buy up all the surplus wool of Ireland 'that comes to the ports [there] at honest and equal rates between buyer and seller'. Despite the contention that this would raise the price of wool in England, prevent its illicit transportation from Ireland, and discourage the woollen manufacture there, the scheme was not adopted.[2]

The English wool grower's position during the greater part of the seventeenth century was therefore far from being an enviable one. Confined to serving the needs of a frequently depressed home market, which turned more and more to using cheaper and finer wools imported from abroad, the grower could find consolation only in the fact that the middleman trade was unrestrained; and even this benefit was not allowed to go unchallenged. Of less importance than the agricultural classes in both numbers and wealth, the clothing interests were yet able to secure the adoption of a policy detrimental to the prosperity of those in whose hands the control of government lay. Their success provides a lesson in the way in which a vociferous section of the community, by dint of sustained and organized propaganda, can obtain general acceptance of its own selfish aims in the name of public necessity.

[1] *Cal. S.P. Dom. 1673–5*, p. 171.
[2] For a full account of this scheme, see *An Account of the Late Design of Buying up the Wool of Ireland in Company* (1674); *Cal. S.P. Dom. 1673–5*, pp. 170–3.

GLOSSARY

TYPES OF SHEEP

Crone : old ewe, unfit to bear any more lambs.

Ewe : female after the third shearing time, i.e. after it has been shorn twice.

Hogg : sheep of either sex from the first until the second shearing time. Hoggs are either *wether hoggs* (i.e. castrated males) or *gimmer hoggs* — sometimes *theaves* — (i.e. females).

Lamb : young sheep from birth until weaning or until the first shearing time (when it is not then normally shorn).

Puck : poor quality lamb, unfit to be kept for fresh stock and fetching a very low price.

Shearling : sheep of either sex from the second until the third shearing time, i.e. after it has been shorn once. Shearlings are either *shearling gimmers* or *wethers.*

Tup or *Ram :* ungelded male.

Wether : gelded male sheep.

WEIGHTS OF WOOL

Pocket : normally 336 lbs., i.e. 28 lbs. less than the wool sack.

Sack : usually 364 lbs.

Sarpler : 3 sacks or pockets of wool.

Tod : the most common measure of weight in the internal wool trade, equivalent to 28 lbs., or 2 stones.

APPENDIX

MOVEMENTS IN ENGLISH WOOL PRICES, 1450–1699

1450–99 = 100

Year	Index Number	Year	Index Number	Year	Index Number	Year	Index Number
1450	91	1484	132	1518	113	1552	192
1451	70	1485	117	1519	126	1553	124
1452	71	1486	116	1520	117	1554	166
1453	71	1487	104	1521	103	1555	160
1454	80	1488	101	1522	122	1556	262
1455	80	1489	112	1523	94	1557	272
1456	95	1490	88	1524	96	1558	143
1457	85	1491	100	1525	119	1559	187
1458	89	1492	83	1526	126	1560	153
1459	91	1493	97	1527	110	1561	220
1460	84	1494	101	1528	121	1562	150
1461	99	1495	101	1529	102	1563	172
1462	102	1496	99	1530	87	1564	160
1463	152	1497	101	1531	116	1565	219
1464	118	1498	95	1532	131	1566	—
1465	115	1499	91	1533	146	1567	273
1466	118	1500	92	1534	136	1568	231
1467	116	1501	90	1535	121	1569	233
1468	100	1502	87	1536	150	1570	184
1469	89	1503	97	1537	117	1571	234
1470	97	1504	98	1538	108	1572	197
1471	104	1505	83	1539	112	1573	219
1472	109	1506	81	1540	190	1574	226
1473	109	1507	91	1541	155	1575	229
1474	99	1508	101	1542	—	1576	251
1475	97	1509	107	1543	150	1577	254
1476	99	1510	109	1544	141	1578	262
1477	92	1511	103	1545	180	1579	280
1478	99	1512	109	1546	126	1580	257
1479	84	1513	107	1547	120	1581	234
1480	88	1514	119	1548	—	1582	265
1481	107	1515	135	1549	168	1583	234
1482	122	1516	129	1550	281	1584	211
1483	128	1517	141	1551	268	1585	214

Year	Index Number	Year	Index Number	Year	Index Number	Year	Index Number
1586	179	1601	318	1616	420	1631	405
1587	187	1602	370	1617	400	1632	405
1588	217	1603	412	1618	428	1633	401
1589	250	1604	371	1619	403	1634	425
1590	311	1605	362	1620	338	1635	428
1591	322	1606	356	1621	316	1636	424
1592	334	1607	364	1622	267	1637	419
1593	344	1608	334	1623	316	1638	403
1594	346	1609	297	1624	326	1639	371
1595	325	1610	271	1625	378	1640–49	396
1596	324	1611	300	1626	377	1650–59	323
1597	279	1612	286	1627	417	1660–69	332
1598	289	1613	310	1628	407	1670–79	301
1599	276	1614	344	1629	—	1680–89	247
1600	296	1615	371	1630	393	1690–99	335

SOURCES: P. J. Bowden, 'Movements in Wool Prices, 1490–1610', *Yorkshire Bulletin of Economic and Social Research*, iv (1952), 109–24; Rogers, op. cit.; Beveridge Collection of Price Material at the Institute of Historical Research; *Durham Parish Books: Churchwarden's Accounts of Pittington and other Parishes in the Diocese of Durham from A.D. 1580 to 1700* (Surtees Soc., lxxxiv, Durham, 1888), passim; Allison, *thesis*, pp. lxxii–lxxvii; Finch, op. cit., p. 19; Henry E. Huntington Library, ST. 48; L.A.O. HEN. 3/2; L.A.O. H. 97/22/12; L.A.O. MM. VI/5; L.A.O. M.7/12; Oxfordshire Archives Office, DIL. III/b/2; Lancashire Record Office, Derby MS. 1553/48–51; Lumley MS. 2305.

SELECT BIBLIOGRAPHY

I. MANUSCRIPT SOURCES

Public Record Office

C.1.   Early Chancery Proceedings.
C.3.   Chancery Proceedings, Series II.
C.66.   Patent Rolls.
D.L.1.   Duchy of Lancaster Pleadings.
E.36.   Exchequer, Treasury of the Receipt, Miscellaneous Books.
E.133.   Exchequer, King's Remembrancer, Barons' Depositions.
E.134.   Exchequer, King's Remembrancer, Depositions taken by Commission.
E.159.   Exchequer, King's Remembrancer, Memoranda Rolls.
P.C.2.   Privy Council Registers.
Req.2.   Requests Proceedings.
S.P.1.   State Papers, Domestic and Foreign, Henry VIII, General Series.
S.P.10.   State Papers, Domestic, Edward VI.
S.P.12.   State Papers, Domestic, Elizabeth I.
S.P.14.   State Papers, Domestic, James I.
S.P.15.   State Papers, Domestic, Addenda, Edward VI to James I.
S.P.16.   State Papers, Domestic, Charles I.
S.P.18.   State Papers, Domestic, Interregnum.
S.P.29.   State Papers, Domestic, Charles II.
S.P.38.   State Papers, Domestic, Docquets.
S.P.39.   State Papers, Domestic, Sign Manual.
S.P.40.   State Papers, Domestic, Warrant Books.
Cal. Pat.   Calendar of Patent Rolls.
St.Ch.   Star Chamber Proceedings.
Signet Office Docquets.

British Museum

Additional MSS. and Charters; Cotton MSS. (principally Galba E. I; Titus B. II); Harleian MSS.; Lansdowne MSS.; Stowe MSS.

Local Record Offices and Other Bodies

Advocates' Library, National Library of Scotland, Edinburgh: Correspondence of Sir Edward Hoby (ADV. MSS. 34.2.15).
Essex Record Office: Petre Family Estate Accounts (D/DP).

Henry E. Huntington Library, California, U.S.A.: Sir Thomas Temple's Account Book on Wool Sales, 1592–1623 (ST.48).
Institute of Historical Research: Beveridge Collection of Price Material.
Kent Archives Office: Cranfield Family Estate Accounts (U.269); Account Book of Sir George Curtis of Otterden (U.442/E.4.).
Lancashire Record Office: Bailiff's Accounts, Macclesfield (Derby MS. 1553).
Lincolnshire Archives Office: Andrews Deposit (And.); Holywell MSS. (H.97); Massingberd-Mundy MSS. (MM. VI); Newton Papers (M.7).
National Register of Archives: Sackville MSS.
Newcastle Central Reference Library: Delaval Papers.
Oxfordshire Archives Office: Dillon Collection (DIL).
Society of Antiquaries Library: Prattinton MSS.

Private Collections

Earl of Scarbrough, Sandbeck Park, Yorkshire: Lumley MSS.
Mr. T. Cottrell-Dormer, Rousham Hall, Oxfordshire: Lord Dormer's Papers, 1600–30.
Mrs. E. Dunlop of Funtington, Sussex: Fielder Farm Accounts, 1630–1733.
Mrs. A. Heneage, Hainton Hall, Lincolnshire: Account Book of Sir George Heneage, 1613–42 (L.A.O.HEN.3/2).
Mr. M. Kirkby of York: Account Book of Henry Best, 1617–44.
Miss M. Simpson of Wooler, Northumberland: Spindleston Farm Accounts, 1676–95.

II. PRINTED SOURCES

(The place of publication is London unless otherwise stated)

Acts and Ordinances of the Interregnum (1911), ed. C. H. Firth and R. S. Rait.
Acts of the Privy Council of England, 1542–1628 (1890–1940), ed. J. R. Dasent and others.
ANON. *A Dialogue Between Dick Brazenface the Card-maker and Tim Meanwell the Clothier* (B.M. 816, m. 14/59).
An Account of the Late Design of Buying up the Wool of Ireland in Company (B.M. 712, g.16/11), (1674).
An Enquiry into the Nature and Qualities of English Wools, By a Gentleman Farmer (B.M. 547B), (1788).
A Treatise of Wool and the Manufacture of it (B.M. 712, g.16/17), (1685).
British Museum Pamphlets, 712, g.16/3 (title page missing).

England's Glory, by the Benefit of Wool Manufactured therein (B.M. 712, g.16/4), (1669).

Reasons for a Limited Exportation of Wool (B.M. 712, g.16/12), (1677).

Reasons for preserving the Publick Market of Blackwel Hal, and restraining the Factors from dealing in Wool: Humbly offer'd to the Parliament (B.M. 816, m. 14/70).

Reasons for Restraining the Factors of Blackwell Hal from dealing in Spanish and English Wooll (B.M. 816, m. 14/71).

Reasons Presented to the Parliament for a More Strict Prohibition of the Transportation of Wool, on Behalf of the Traders and Manufacturers in Wool (B.M. 816, m. 14/99).

The Blackwell Hall Factors Case (B.M. 816, m. 14/67).

The Clothiers Complaint, or reasons for passing the Bill against the Blackwell Hall Factors (B.M. 711, f. 28).

The Languishing State of our Woollen Manufacture, Humbly Represented to the Parliament (B.M. 816, m. 14/80).

The Present Case of our English Wool and the Manufacture of it (B.M. 816, m. 14/82).

BARNETT, G. E. (ed.). *Two Tracts by Gregory King* (Baltimore: John Hopkins, 1936).

BATESON, MARY (ed.). *Records of the Borough of Leicester, 1509–1603* (Cambridge, 1905).

BOHUN, W. *Privilegia Londini* (1702).

Calendar of Letters and Papers, Foreign and Domestic, of the reign of Henry VIII (1864–1932).

Calendar of State Papers, Domestic, 1547–1640 and *Addenda* (1856–97).

Calendar of Patent Rolls, 1547–63 (1924–48).

CAMDEN, W. *Britannia* (edn. 1789).

CAMPBELL, R. *The London Tradesman* (1747).

CARTER, W. *The Proverb Crossed* (B.M. 712, g.16/14), (1677).

CUNNINGTON, B. H. (ed.). *Some Annals of the Borough of Devizes* (Devizes, 1925).

DEFOE, D. *The Complete English Tradesman* (edn. 1738).

Tour Through Great Britain (edn. 1927).

Durham Parish Books: Churchwardens' Accounts of Pittington and other Parishes in the Diocese of Durham from A.D. 1580 to 1700 (Surtees Soc., lxxxiv, Durham, 1888).

FITZHERBERT, *The Book of Husbandry, 1534* (ed. W. W. Skeat, 1882).

FULLER, T., *The History of the Worthies of England* (edn. 1840).

FUSSELL, G. E. (ed.). *Robert Loder's Farm Accounts, 1610–1620* (Camden Soc., 3rd ser. liii, 1936).

HAYNES, J. *A View of the Present State of the Clothing Trade in England* (B.M. 1229, a. 33), (1706).

Great Britain's Glory (B.M. 1029, a. 6), (1715).

HEATON, H. (ed.). *The Letter Books of Joseph Holroyd and Sam Hill* (1914).

Historical Manuscripts Commission: *Reports; Buccleuch MSS.; Buckinghamshire MSS.; Downshire MSS.; Egmont MSS.; Exeter MSS.; House of Lords MSS.; Ormonde MSS.; Portland MSS.; Salisbury MSS.; Townshend MSS.; Various MSS.*

HOUGHTON, J. *A Collection for the Improvement of Husbandry and Trade* (edn. 1728).

House of Commons Journals.

House of Lords Journals.

LEADAM, I. S. (ed.). *The Domesday of Inclosures, 1517–18* (Royal Hist. Soc., 1897).

L'ESTRANGE, R. *A Treatise of Wool and Cattel* (B.M. 712, g. 16/15), (1677).

LEWIS, E. A. (ed.). *Welsh Port Books, 1550–1603* (Cymmrod. Rec. Ser., xii, 1927).

MANLEY, T. *A Discourse, shewing that the Exportation of Wooll is destructive to this kingdom* (B.M. 712, g. 16/11), (1677).

MARKHAM, G. *Cheap and Good Husbandry* (edn. 1676).

MASCALL, L. *The Countreyman's Jewel: Or the Governmente of Cattell* (1587).

MAY, J. *A Declaration of the Estate of Clothing now used within this Realme of England* (1613).

MISSELDEN, E. *The Circle of Commerce* (1623).

Norden's Description of Essex (Camden Soc., 1st ser. ix, 1840).

NOTESTEIN, W., RELF, F. H., and SIMPSON, H. (eds.). *Commons Debates, 1621* (New Haven, 1935).

PLOT, R. *The Natural History of Oxfordshire* (1677).

RAINE, A. (ed.). *York Civic Records*, Vol. 3 (Yorkshire Archaeological Soc. Rec. Ser., cvi, Wakefield, 1942).

ROBINSON, C. B. (ed.). *Rural Economy in Yorkshire in 1641, being the Farming and Account Books of Henry Best of Elmswell, in the East Riding of the County of York* (Surtees Soc., xxxiii, Durham, 1857).

Rotuli Parliamentorum.

ROZER, E. *Reasons showing the desires of the Clothiers and Woollen Manu-facturers of England . . . Against Ingrossing and Transporting of Wooll and Fullers Earth* (B.M. 816, m. 14/98), (1648).

RYMER, T. (ed.). *Foedera* (1708).

SMITH, JOHN, *Chronicon Rusticum-Commerciale or Memoirs of Wool* (1747).

Statutes of the Realm (1810).

STEELE, R. (ed.). *Tudor and Stuart Proclamations, 1485–1714* (Oxford, 1910).

STOCKS, HELEN (ed.). *Records of the Borough of Leicester, 1603–1688* (Cambridge, 1923).

STOW, J. *A Survey of London in 1603*, ed. C. L. Kingsford (1908).

TAWNEY, R. H., and POWER, EILEEN (eds.). *Tudor Economic Documents* (1924).

WESTCOTE, T. *A View of Devonshire in 1630* (edn. 1845).

WILLSON, D. H. (ed.). *The Parliamentary Diary of Robert Bowyer, 1606–1607* (Univ. of Minn. 1931).

YOUNG, A. *Tour through the East* (edn. 1771).

III. SECONDARY AUTHORITIES

(A) *Books*

BERESFORD, M. W. *The Lost Villages of England* (1954).

BEVERIDGE, SIR WILLIAM, et al. *Prices and Wages in England from the Twelfth to the Nineteenth Century*, i (1939).

CAMPBELL, MILDRED, *The English Yeoman under Elizabeth and the Early Stuarts* (Yale, 1942).

CROSS, F. W. *History of Walloon and Huguenot Church, Canterbury* (Huguenot Soc., xv, 1885).

Dictionary of National Biography, xxvii (1891), ed. Sidney Lee.

FRIIS, A. *Alderman Cockayne's Project and the Cloth Trade* (Copenhagen and London, 1927).

FINCH, MARY, *The Wealth of Five Northamptonshire Families, 1540–1640* (Northamptonshire Rec. Soc., xix, Oxford, 1956).

GLOVER, S. *History of Derbyshire* (1829).

GONNER, E. C. K. *Common Land and Inclosure* (1912).

GRANT, I. F. *The Economic History of Scotland* (1934).

HAIGH, H. and NEWTON, B. A. *The Wools of Britain* (1952).

HAMILTON, E. J. *American Treasure and the Price Revolution in Spain, 1501–1650* (Cambridge, Mass., 1934) (Harvard Economic Studies xliii).

HAZLITT, W. C. *The Livery Companies of the City of London* (1892).

HEATON, H. *Yorkshire Woollen and Worsted Industries* (Oxford, 1920).

HECKSCHER, E. F. *Mercantilism* (edn. 1934).

HOSKINS, W. G. *Essays in Leicestershire History* (Liverpool, 1950).

Industry, Trade and People in Exeter, 1688–1800 (1935).

The Midland Peasant. The Economic and Social History of a Leicestershire Village (1957).

KLEIN, J. *The Mesta, A Study in Spanish Economic History, 1273–1836* (Cambridge, Mass., 1920) (Harvard Economic Studies xxi).

LIPSON, E. *The Economic History of England*, Vols. ii & iii (edn. 1947).

The History of the English Woollen and Worsted Industries (1921).

POLLARD, A. F. *England under Protector Somerset* (1900).

POWER, EILEEN, *The Wool Trade in English Medieval History* (Oxford, 1941).

and POSTAN, M. M. (eds.). *Studies in English Trade in the Fifteenth Century* (1933) (London School of Economics and Political Science: Studies in Economic and Social History, 5).

PROTHERO, R. E. (LORD ERNLE). *English Farming Past and Present* (1912).

RAMSAY, G. D. *The Wiltshire Woollen Industry in the Sixteenth and Seventeenth Centuries* (Oxford, 1943).

RICH, E. E. Introduction to *The Ordinance Book of the Merchants of the Staple* (Cambridge, 1937).

ROGERS, J. E. T. *A History of Agriculture and Prices in England* (Oxford, 1866–1900).

ROWSE, A. L. *The England of Elizabeth* (1951).

Royal Commission on Common Land, 1955–1958, Report. Cmd. 462 (1958).

SCOTT, W. R. *The Constitution and Finances of English, Scottish and Irish Joint-Stock Companies to 1720* (Cambridge, 1910).

STEPHENS, W. B. *Seventeenth-Century Exeter. A Study of Industrial and Commercial Development, 1625–1688* (Exeter, 1958).

SUPPLE, B. E. *Commercial Crisis and Change in England, 1600–1642* (Cambridge, 1959).

TAWNEY, R. H. *The Agrarian Problem in the Sixteenth Century* (1912). Introduction to Thomas Wilson's *A Discourse upon Usury* (1925).

THIRSK, JOAN, *English Peasant Farming. The Agrarian History of Lincolnshire from Tudor to Recent Times* (1957).

Tudor Enclosures (Historical Association Pamphlet, General Series: G. 41) (1959).

TROW-SMITH, R. *A History of British Livestock Husbandry to 1700* (1957).

UNWIN, G. *Industrial Organization in the Sixteenth and Seventeenth Centuries* (Oxford, 1904).

Studies in Economic History ed. R. H. Tawney (1927).

Victoria History of the Counties of England:
Berkshire, Buckinghamshire, Cambridgeshire, Derbyshire, Dorsetshire, Essex, Gloucestershire, Hampshire, Herefordshire, Kent, Lancashire, Lincolnshire, Northamptonshire, Nottinghamshire, Oxfordshire, Rutland, Somersetshire, Surrey, Sussex, Warwickshire, Worcestershire, Yorkshire.

WATERS, S. H. *Wakefield in the Seventeenth Century, a Social History of the Town and Neighbourhood* (Wakefield, 1933).

WESTERFIELD, R. B. *Middlemen in English Business* (New Haven, 1915).

WILLAN, T. S. *River Navigation in England, 1600–1750* (Manchester, 1936).

The English Coasting Trade, 1600–1750 (Manchester, 1938).

WINCHESTER, BARBARA, *Tudor Family Portrait* (1955).

YOUATT, W. *Sheep, Their Breeds, Management and Diseases* (edn. 1890).
YOUNG, A. *The Question of Wool Truly Stated* (1788).

In Typescript:

ALLISON, K. J. *The Wool Supply and the Worsted Cloth Industry in Norfolk in the Sixteenth and Seventeenth Centuries* (University of Leeds Ph.D. thesis, 1955).

(B) *Articles*

ALLISON, K. J. 'Flock Management in the Sixteenth and Seventeenth Centuries', *Economic History Review*, 2nd ser. xi (1958).
'The Sheep-Corn Husbandry of Norfolk in the Sixteenth and Seventeenth Centuries', *Agricultural History Review*, v (1957).

BERESFORD, M. W. 'The Common Informer, the Penal Statutes and Economic Regulation', *Economic History Review*, 2nd ser. x (1957).
'The Poll Tax and Census of Sheep, 1549', *Agricultural History Review*, i (1953), ii (1954).

BOWDEN, P. J. 'Movements in Wool Prices, 1490–1610', *Yorkshire Bulletin of Economic and Social Research*, iv (1952).
'The Home Market in Wool, 1500–1700', *Yorkshire Bulletin of Economic and Social Research*, viii (1956).
'The Regulation of the English Internal Wool Trade, 1552–1624', *Wool Knowledge*, iv (1957–8).
'Wool Supply and the Woollen Industry', *Economic History Review*, 2nd ser. ix (1956).

CLAY, C. T. 'Notes on the Importation of English Wool into Ireland as Affected by the Union', *Thoresby Society*, xxvi (1924).

DEANE, PHYLLIS. 'The Output of the British Woolen Industry in the Eighteenth Century', *Journal of Economic History*, xvii (1957).

FISHER, F. J. 'Commercial Trends and Policy in Sixteenth-Century England', *Economic History Review*, x (1940).
'London's Export Trade in the Early Seventeenth Century', *Economic History Review*, 2nd ser. iii (1950).
'The Development of the London Food Market, 1540–1640', *Economic History Review*, v (1935).

FUSSELL, G. E. 'Farming Methods in the Early Stuart Period', *Journal of Modern History*, vii (1935).

GAY, E. F. 'The Temples of Stowe and their Debts', *Huntington Library Quarterly*, ii (1938–9).

LLOYD PRICHARD, M. F. 'The Decline of Norwich', *Economic History Review*, 2nd ser. iii (1951).

O'BRIEN, G. 'The Irish Staple Organisation in the Reign of James I', *Economic History*, i (1926).

PLUMB, J. H. 'Sir Robert Walpole and Norfolk Husbandry', *Economic History Review*, 2nd ser. v (1952).

PRIESTLEY, M. 'Anglo-French Trade and the Unfavourable Balance Controversy, 1660–1685', *Economic History Review*, 2nd ser. iv (1951).

RYDER, M. L. 'Follicle Remains in Some British Parchments', *Nature*, vol. 187, no. 4732 (1960).

SIMPSON, A. 'The East Anglian Foldcourse: Some Queries', *Agricultural History Review*, vi (1958).

STONE, L. 'Elizabethan Overseas Trade', *Economic History Review*, 2nd ser. ii (1949).
    'State Control in Sixteenth Century England', *Economic History Review*, xvii (1947).

TAWNEY, A. J. and R. H. 'An Occupational Census of the Seventeenth Century', *Economic History Review*, v (1934).

TREVOR-ROPER, H. R. 'The Elizabethan Aristocracy: An Anatomy Anatomized', *Economic History Review*, 2nd ser. iii (1951).

WILLIAMS, N. J. 'Two Documents concerning the New Draperies', *Economic History Review*, 2nd ser. iv (1952).

WILSON, C. 'Cloth Production and International Competition in the Seventeenth Century', *Economic History Review*, 2nd ser. xiii (1960).

INDEX

PRINTED IN GREAT BRITAIN BY ROBERT MACLEHOSE AND CO. LTD
THE UNIVERSITY PRESS, GLASGOW